On the Waves of Empire

THE WORKING CLASS IN AMERICAN HISTORY

Editorial Advisors

A list of books in the series appears at the end of this book.

On the Waves of Empire

U.S. Imperialism and Merchant Sailors, 1872–1924

WILLIAM D. RIDDELL

UNIVERSITY OF ILLINOIS PRESS
Urbana, Chicago, and Springfield

1 2 3 4 5 C P 5 4 3 2 1
∞ This book is printed on acid-free paper.

Library of Congress Cataloging-in-Publication Data
Names: Riddell, William D., 1983– author.
Title: On the waves of empire : U.S. imperialism and merchant sailors, 1872–1924 / William D. Riddell.
Other titles: U.S. imperialism and merchant sailors, 1872–1924
Description: Urbana : University of Illinois Press, [2023] | Series: The working class in American history | Includes bibliographical references and index.
Identifiers: LCCN 2022059020 (print) | LCCN 2022059021 (ebook) | ISBN 9780252045165 (cloth) | ISBN 9780252087301 (paperback) | ISBN 9780252054532 (ebook)
Subjects: LCSH: Merchant mariners—Labor unions—United States—History. | Merchant mariners—United States—Legal status, laws, etc.—History. | Labor unions—20th century—History. | Imperialism—United States—History—19th century. | Imperialism—United States—History—20th century.
Classification: LCC HD8039.S42U637 .R53 2023 (print) | LCC HD8039.S42U637 (ebook) | DDC 387.5092—dc23/eng/20230215
LC record available at https://lccn.loc.gov/2022059020
LC ebook record available at https://lccn.loc.gov/2022059021

For Victoria

Contents

Acknowledgments

Scholarship is a collaborative process. While this book may have my name on it, countless people, including my advisors, mentors, colleagues, friends, and family, helped contribute to its completion.

This book began at the University of Toronto's history department. I owe a huge debt of gratitude to the department's support staff, who helped make it run as seamlessly as possible. I also want to thank the support staff at the University of Toronto, Scarborough's Department of Historical and Cultural Studies, especially Urooj Kahn and Kamal Hassan. Additionally, I am grateful to the librarians and archivists at the U.S. National Archives, The Bancroft Library, The Huntington Library, the California State Archives, and the Labor Archives at San Francisco State University, who made the research process a delightfully enjoyable experience. I am also grateful to the librarians and staff at the Inter-Library Loan office at the University of Toronto's Robarts Library. To Professors Russell Kazal, Donna Gabaccia, and Michael Wayne: though you were not involved directly with the production of this book, whether through lectures, seminars, or conversations, your influence and advice were invaluable.

I want to thank Carol Chin and Neda Maghbouleh for their incisive and encouraging critique. Jo Sharma, you taught me how to view this project in a broader context. I am also grateful to the anonymous reviewers for their thoughtful and constructive comments. This is a better book because of your insights, though any remaining flaws are mine and mine alone. I owe a considerable debt to the many scholars whose work influenced my thinking over the years: Kornel Chang, Tony Ballantyne, Peter Cole, Leon Fink, Moon-Ho Jung, Thomas Lahusan, Jana Lipman, and David Roediger. I was also lucky to have a great group of peers and colleagues in and beyond the University of Toronto: Nathan Cardon, Adrian De Leon, Edward Dunsworth, Holly Karibo, Catherine Koonar, Paul Lawrie, Ruth Percy, Kyle Pruitt, Christine Berkowitz, and Lisa Todd. I especially want to thank my friends and colleagues Matthieu Vallières and Ian Rocksborough-Smith.

Over the years, I tested many of my initial ideas for this book at numerous gatherings and conferences. I want to thank the following individuals and intuitions: the re:work center at the Humboldt University of Berlin and the Association of Indian Labour Historians for organizing an invaluable Summer Academy in Global Labor History in New Delhi, particularly Andreas Eckert and Prabhu Mohapatra; John Beck and the history department at Michigan State University for inviting me to speak at their Our Daily Work/Our Daily Lives Brown Bag Speaker Series; the Society for Historians of American Foreign Relations annual conference provided an excellent sounding board to test out the ideas that would become this book, especially Paul Kramer, Justin Jackson, Andrew Urban, and Joseph Fronczak. I also want to thank LAWCHA and the 2020 Gutman prize jury for providing much needed encouragement as I began turning this into a book.

At the University of Illinois Press, James Engelhardt, Alison Syring Bassford, and Tad Ringo helped make the publication process as smooth as possible. I could not ask for better editors. The Working Class in American History series editors who supported this project, William P. Jones, Thavolia Glymph, James R. Barrett, but particularly Nelson Lichtenstein, provided much need encouragement and constructive criticism of the manuscript. I especially want to thank Julie Greene, whose work has been an inspiration to me since I began my career in graduate school and believed in this project early on.

To my supervisors, friends, and mentors, Rick Halpern and Daniel Bender, where to begin? You created an ideal and open intellectual environment for young scholars to flourish. Most importantly, you both embody everything that good mentors should be. I can only hope to emulate your example.

My friends and family provided me with much needed respite and perspective along the way. I want to thank the Deboran and Kuketz families, especially Ann-Marie Deboran, Flora Deboran, and Peter Kuketz. Your love and support have meant a lot. I also want to thank the extended Riddell and Marshall families for putting up with my long-winded rants and lectures about history over the years. My friends Fraser, Peter, Dan, and Emma, you also suffered through my historical rants and ravings and have no doubt learned to look for the nearest exits every time you hear me say: "well, actually, that's an interesting question."

For my parents, Stephan and Susan Riddell: you have always given one hundred percent of your support no matter what. To my grandfather: you inspired my curiosity, love of process, and reverence of "struggle." To my father: you taught me the value of hard work and the idea that you either commit fully to a task or not at all. To my sister Jenn: the first six years of life weren't nearly as exciting without you around. To my brother-in-law: thank you for being such a steady and loyal presence. To my grandmother: you inspired my love for the past. You were my first history teacher. And to my mother: you taught me about justice and to never accept things as they are.

And to my wife, Victoria: I met you when I was deciding to go to grad school. Your sharp mind and profound intellect have been the perfect sounding boards over the years. Your well of positivity and love of life is as infectious as your beautifully kind heart. You inspire everyone around you to be better. It would be an understatement to say I could not have finished this without your love, support, and, especially, your infinite patience.

On the Waves of Empire

Introduction

The Seams of Empire

Four Sailors Walk Off a Ship

In May 1895, in the port of Knappen, Washington, Robert Robertson, H. H. Olsen, John Bradley, and Morris Hanson participated in a simple and time-honored tactic of maritime labor resistance: unhappy with their treatment and conditions, the four men deserted their posts on the barkentine *Arago* and set out for Astoria, Oregon.[1] The captain of the *Arago* then reported the four men to local and state authorities. When the deserters arrived in Astoria, they were arrested and jailed until the *Arago* was ready to sail sixteen days later. Once the *Arago* was ready to depart, the authorities forcibly returned all four men to the vessel. Upon their return, the captain ordered them to "turn to," which in maritime parlance essentially means "get to work." They refused. The captain then had them placed "in irons" and confined below deck. A few days later, when the *Arago* reached San Francisco, they were subsequently arrested and jailed for desertion. For nine months, Robertson and his compatriots sat in jail while they awaited trial, where they were eventually found guilty of desertion. Under the leadership of Andrew Furuseth, the recently formed Sailor's Union of the Pacific (SUP) and their national organization the International Seaman's Union of America (ISU), challenged the verdict and financed an appeal all the way to the U.S. Supreme Court: they argued that the arrest of Robertson and company was a violation of the Thirteenth Amendment, which banned slavery and involuntary servitude.[2]

In January 1897, the Supreme Court ruled against the four sailors and upheld their desertion convictions. The Court based its decision on the grounds that historically, sailors had been, and in its opinion, still were an "exceptional" class of labor.[3] Writing for the majority, justice Henry Billings Brown demonstrated the general exceptionality of maritime labor by pointing to a long line of precedents stretching all the way back to the "Rhodian Sea Laws" of the seventh century.[4] As to the sailor's specific constitutional challenge, Brown stated that the Thirteenth Amendment did not apply to sailors because their servitude was "voluntary," rather than involuntary as the Constitution states—they had freely signed their employment contracts before a U.S. shipping commissioner in San Francisco harbor. To add insult to injury, Brown further found that the exceptional status of a maritime laborer involved "the surrender of his personal liberty during the life of the contract."[5] In the Court's opinion, this surrender of personal liberty meant that a seaman could not break his contract or desert his ship, pointing out that the "ancient characterization of seamen as 'wards of the admiralty'" still applied.[6] As to the state's role in tracking down the deserting sailors, Brown cited the Maritime Law of 1790—which the SUP called the Fugitive Slave Law of the Sea—and the Shipping Commissioners Act of 1872, which "authorizes the apprehension of deserting sailors, with or without the assistance of the local public officers or constables without warrant."[7] The seemingly endless evidence of statutory precedent cited by the Court raises the question: how could the SUP leadership possibly be so naive in thinking they could win, especially considering Congress passed the 1872 Shipping Commissioners Act after the Thirteenth Amendment?

The SUP's confidence stemmed from the recently passed Maguire Act, which Congress enacted in February 1895, a few months before Robertson and company walked off the *Arago*. Among other things, the Maguire Act abolished imprisonment for desertion in the coastwise or domestic trade (that is, maritime trade between U.S. ports). Indeed, Robertson, Olsen, Bradley, and Hansen deserted the *Arago* believing their actions were lawful under the provisions of the Maguire Act. After all, they signed on to the *Arago* at a U.S. port in San Francisco and deserted in another American port in Oregon. Why, then, were the men arrested and imprisoned if the Maguire Act abolished imprisonment for desertion in the domestic trade? The answer to this question lay in the fact that the American ports of call were only the first leg of the *Arago*'s journey under Robertson and companies' contract. After sailing north to Oregon and Washington, the *Arago* was then on its way to Valparaiso, Chile, and a few other foreign ports. As a result, the courts defined the *Arago* and its laborers as operating in the *foreign* rather than the *domestic* trade.

The *Arago* incident is significant because it raises larger questions about the process through which the lines between foreign and domestic are established and foreshadows how important this question became in the years immediately following the Court's infamous verdict. Even though the sailors in question deserted in an American port, having departed from an American port, because their contract was for a voyage where the ultimate destination was foreign, the Court considered them outside the domestic trade. The Court had created an absurd legal fiction, defining an American citizen standing on American soil as laboring outside the United States. Moreover, as the *Arago* case demonstrates, these boundaries mattered a great deal. Though political boundaries may be abstract concepts, how, why, and where empires draw them has material consequences in the lives of real people. For Robertson and his compatriots, the difference between foreign and domestic was profoundly important. Laboring on the wrong side of the domestic/foreign divide determined whether or not they had the fundamental freedom to quit their jobs. This fact led the SUP to hereafter refer to the *Arago* case as the second Dred Scott decision.[8] In 1895 and 1897, this question concerned a small group of workers in a peripheral part of a peripheral industry in a peripheral region of the country. A year later, geopolitical events conspired to bring the question of the foreign and domestic to the forefront of American politics.

After 1898, when the United States acquired a transoceanic colonial empire, the question of where the domestic ended and the foreign began was elevated into the national consciousness. Americans began to wrestle with something they had previously never considered. After a century of manifest destiny and seemingly endless westward expansion, Americans began to seriously consider placing limitations on this expansion. They were also divided over what form that expansion should take. Since the beginning of the nineteenth century, the process by which the United States acquired new territory and incorporated it into the nation's pre-existing political architecture was largely consistent. There may have been vicious and violent confrontations over which labor system, slave or free, would ultimately prevail in the newly acquired territory. However, whether the United States built that new territory upon slave or free labor, the process of incorporation remained the same: Congress first organized it as a territorial government that would eventually apply for statehood. This happened with the land immediately west of the Appalachians following the Revolution, the Louisiana territory, and the post-1848 trans-Mississippi territorial acquisitions. The idea that new territory would eventually become part of the United States was manifest.[9]

After 1898 this assumption became . . . *complicated*. The former Spanish colonies that the United States acquired during the Spanish-American War could not be integrated so easily, if at all.[10] If this new territory could not become integrated in the same way as before, what kind of relationship would the Philippines, Hawai'i, Cuba, and Puerto Rico have with their new imperial rulers? What status would the people that lived in these territories have within the emergent American imperial system? How would a nation founded upon white supremacy absorb a territory full of people who in the popular imagination fell outside the bounds of whiteness? Were they citizens or subjects? Were they free to move about the imperial system? Or would their movement be controlled? After 1898 the questions were not just how, why, and where the United States should draw lines between the foreign and domestic, but also, how, why, and where it should draw lines between nation and empire.

Labor leaders and the organizations they represented—especially those acting for merchant sailors—were both central to and on the front lines of this process. They were the individuals most affected by these boundaries. Sailors who labored in the foreign trade crossed these invisible boundaries every time they went to work. Indeed, scholars have long held the so-called insular cases as the ultimate arbiter in determining whether the Constitution followed the flag.[11] To be sure, the insular cases were essential in establishing the relationship between nation and empire or metropole and colony. It is important to note, however, that these cases mainly focused on trade, tariffs, and commodities, mostly between the United States mainland and the colonies in the Caribbean. For working people, this was a very different story. Here, the question was about who rather than what could cross these lines, what that meant, and why it mattered. It was less about the trade relationship between nation and empire but about the collision and potential integration of different labor systems and labor markets. In short, the relationship between nation and empire and foreign and domestic was also a labor question.

With that in mind, this book will reveal the vital role played by domestic class conflict in the process by which the boundaries, both internally and externally, of the emerging U.S. imperial system were shaped and reshaped. This was a fluid process, perpetually in motion; the boundaries were rarely, if ever, fixed. This is why merchant sailors are the ideal group of workers to bring this process into sharper focus. They were constantly in motion. As will become apparent over the course of this book, the boundaries ebbed and flowed with them, sometimes to their advantage and sometimes to their detriment. Maritime labor leaders, more than any other segment of the American labor movement, contested and shaped these boundaries. Their attempts to define these boundaries, however, were vigorously resisted by the representatives of shipping capital, who had their own ideas about where these boundaries should be drawn, if at all.

Shipping capital and maritime labor represented the dual threads that stitched together, ripped apart, and restitched the seams of empire. By focusing on their story, we can begin to understand how the class dimensions of this process actually worked.

The boundaries between nation and empire as well as foreign and domestic emerged through domestic or metropolitan class struggle—ebbing and flowing with the changing power dynamics between capital and labor. There has been recent scholarly attention focused on the effect "empire" had on class struggle and formation, whether within the nation or the empire.[12] I will build upon this work by demonstrating the two-way nature of this relationship, as imperial expansion affected domestic class conflict and domestic class conflict affected imperial expansion. By examining the connection between domestic class conflict and U.S. imperial expansion, this book will also reveal the vital role that labor leaders and the organizations they represented played in this process, and will also challenge organized labor's apparent anti-imperial orientation. When all is said and done, although labor leaders and the white working people they claimed to speak for were far from the principal beneficiaries of U.S. imperial expansion, they were nonetheless important and complicit players in its execution.

Organized Labor and U.S. Imperial Expansion

Labor leaders' and their organizations' relationships and attitudes toward emerging, post-1898 U.S. imperial formations reflected a deeper anxiety, both real and imagined, over where the white working classes fit into the "new empire." What did this mean for them? Would they benefit from U.S. imperial expansion? What would the negative effects of this emerging era of overseas expansion be for organized labor and the white working classes? How would the nation manage the integration of more than eight million people who suddenly became subjects of a U.S colonial-imperial system? Though the substance of labor's response connected to a long genealogy of racism, nativism, and xenophobia that stretched well back into the antebellum era, the circumstances of 1898 help place that legacy in a broader imperial context. What had always looked like, and was framed as, anti-immigrant nativism takes on a different meaning when viewed in the context of an emerging imperial system. If the United States were to be an "empire," albeit a much smaller one, that looked and acted like the canonically imperial British Empire, what role would the white working classes play in this system? America's labor leaders opposed annexation, or even initially the idea of a colonial empire, but they made peace with it. And they made it rather quickly. Organized labor accepted it so long as their members were protected. Indeed, the AFL-led craft union movement was already based explicitly on preserving a privileged and protected position within a national labor hierarchy.[13] Similarly, by demanding protection from certain parts of the emerging imperial system, they were implicitly endorsing the concept of colonial imperialism by insisting on a privileged and protected position within an emerging *imperial* hierarchy. With that in mind, labor leaders and the organizations they represented were central members in the dramatis personae of institutional players that defined and redefined the shifting borders of the U.S. imperial system.

Scholars have traditionally looked to the so-called insular cases to understand how the United States worked out its relationship with its newly acquired colonies.[14] Indeed, the Supreme Court's reasoning, particularly Justice White's concurrent opinion in *Downes vs. Bidwell,* which established the idea that the new territory was "unincorporated," remains vitally important.[15] The doctrine of "unincorporation" essentially meant that the Constitution did not necessarily follow the flag. These cases are important in that regard. They provided a legal framework for how the emerging imperial system would function under the United States' pre-existing political and constitutional architecture.

However, as this book will demonstrate, the cases and the issues surrounding them were merely one part of the process through which the boundaries of the imperial system were defined and contested. The disputes at the heart of these cases largely—though not entirely—involved the importation of goods from colony to nation, helping to define what was and was not the United States. Unsurprisingly, tariff policy lay at the heart of these disputes.

Yet what inflamed and informed the discourse surrounding America's new empire concerned the people who lived in the colonies, rather than the goods they produced. From the perspective of American labor leaders such as Andrew Furuseth or AFL president Samuel Gompers and the white working classes they claimed to represent, regulating the movement of people throughout the emerging imperial system was far more important than the movement of goods. To understand the role of organized labor and class conflict more broadly in the emergence of America's imperial boundaries, we must examine labor's efforts to control the movement of people within the imperial system.

Answering this question requires an understanding of empire or imperialism from a laboring perspective and labor from an imperial perspective. Empire is defined as much by its labor systems as it is by its territorial and geographic boundaries.[16] Indeed, the last few years has seen an explosion of scholarship on labor and empire in U.S. historiography. Approaching the study of U.S.

imperialism through its labor and class dimensions has opened up exciting new research possibilities.[17] However, most of the recent historiography tends to focus on the labor history of specific sites of U.S. empire or the imperial dimensions of specific labor projects or sites. There has been less attention paid to the conceptual and systemic relationship between labor and empire: how did the question of labor fit into and inform U.S. imperial expansion? How did imperial expansion fit into the labor history of the United States? Here, historian Julie Greene points the way forward. In her essay entitled, "The Wages of Empire: Class, Expansionism, and Working-Class Formation," she argues that "U.S. imperial projects always and everywhere involved the recruitment, managing, and disciplining of labor."[18] These "processes shaped metropolitan workers as well as working men and women on the various sites of empire."[19] Empire, therefore, "constituted a force that articulated and shaped class experience and formation as much as did, say, race or gender."[20] I agree. But I would go further and turn Greene's argument around and argue that class conflict, formation, and experience shaped U.S. imperial formation as much as the quest for markets. Moreover, labor and markets are not separate things, but two sides of the same interconnected process—an empire rooted in the expansionary forces of capitalism requires simultaneous access to both labor and markets for the system to operate. Before we can fully understand how class conflict and the institutions of the white working class shaped the emerging U.S. imperial system, we must first come to terms with the meaning of empire or the imperial.

I define empire or the imperial as both an analytic concept and a "thing" to identify. It is a system of power where inequities of political status and action, "methods of exceptionalizing" difference, and systems of spatial control and ordering create and reinforce hierarchical relationships between (but not limited to) peoples, territories, and labor regimes.[21] In other words, the imperial is a relational process as well as a "thing."[22] This conceptual understanding of the imperial moves the field into more fertile scholarly ground. It reminds us that empire is more than just space or territory on a map but rather "bundles" of interconnected relationships.[23] These relationships are not static but dynamic, constantly being made and remade as the people who make up the U.S. empire move through or are uprooted by the imperial system. Since the relationships that make an empire possible are being made and remade, empire itself is being made and remade. It is a continuous and ongoing process.

As a result, static concepts such as "empire" or even "colony" can sometimes obscure what is ultimately a process in motion. A more apt articulation of this book's conceptual understanding of terms like empire or colony is "imperial formations." While an empire might be a "thing," imperial formations are a dynamic and dependent process that is constantly being formed and reformed. They are not fixed states and are not limited to easily identifiable or direct imperial and colonial relationships. Imperial formations are states of flux, large scale, and fluid political and economic structures and relationships that are contingent upon mobile classifications and populations.[24] A merchant ship in the foreign trade may not, strictly speaking, qualify as a colony, but it does qualify as an imperial formation. This is not to say the terms empire or colony will not appear in this book. Indeed, they already have and will continue to appear in the following pages and chapters. But they should be understood as reflective of a moving process of formation and re-formation.

A dynamic and fluid understanding of empire as imperial formations as well as a methodological approach to the study of the "imperial" as an analytic concept helps bring organized labor's role in, and attitude toward, U.S. imperial expansion into sharper focus. Just over ten years ago, the late great labor historian David Montgomery argued, "[a]round 1900, the AFL was highly critical of the expansionist policies of the U.S. government. Fewer than twenty years later it had come not only to support those policies, but also even to participate actively in their execution."[25] However, the deeds and actions of the AFL-led labor movement in the wake of annexation tell a different, more nuanced story. Montgomery is correct that the AFL and its affiliates opposed annexation in 1898. Yet the AFL and the broader craft union movement's complicity and support of those policies happened almost immediately, rather than twenty years later. Labor leaders and the institutions they represented were not directly responsible for administering colonial possessions or formulating U.S. imperial policy generally. However, they were among the primary drivers that advocated for repertoires of imperial rule steeped with uneven scales of political action and systems of spatial control and ordering that produced hierarchies of people, territory, and systems of labor within the emerging U.S. imperial system. All of which were being made and remade. Opposition to U.S. expansionist policies of 1898 is not the same thing as anti-imperialism, nor did it necessarily reflect wholesale enmity toward U.S. expansionism and imperialism. As this book will demonstrate, labor leaders (especially the sailors' unions) were against a particular type of U.S. expansionism. This is reflected in the repertoire of imperial rule they insisted upon in the aftermath of annexation.[26]

In short, organized labor took the seemingly paradoxical position of resisting empire by aligning with it. More precisely, organized labor resisted colonial-imperial expansion by advocating policies that affirmed their commitment to white settler colonialism. Because, when the leaders of America's dominant labor organizations looked at their nation's newly acquired colonial possessions, they did not see a new frontier of opportunity and possibility that imperialists in the vein of Theodore Roosevelt or Alfred Beveridge did. Rather, what they saw was the end of U.S. white settler colonialism and the rise of a different form of imperial expansion in its place—a form that did not provide white working people with any tangible and foreseeable benefits. Instead, they saw millions of potential low-wage workers that would increase the labor supply and drive down wages. As a result, in an effort to insulate its members from job competition, the AFL and the SUP/ISU led the charge to enact legislation that would place limitations on the movement of America's newly acquired colonial subjects. These limitations took the form of racially motivated, exclusionary immigration policies designed to prevent U.S. colonial subjects from migrating to the North American mainland. The most notable of these policies was the 1902 Chinese Exclusion Act, which prevented people of Chinese descent from entering U.S. colonial possessions and stopped Chinese residents of the Philippines and Hawai'i from migrating to the mainland.[27] These efforts were not limited to the exclusion of Chinese individuals, as labor organizations attempted to exclude all Asians, especially people of Japanese descent.

I argue that efforts to extend exclusion both through and around the nascent U.S. imperial system lay at the heart of the process in which the boundaries of that system were being made and remade—making immigration restriction organized labor's primary repertoire of imperial power. Meanwhile, the public and all three branches of government fiercely debated the now-famous question of whether the Constitution followed the flag. However, the question most pertinent to America's labor leaders and the white working class they claimed to speak for was rather: does exclusion follow the flag? This question reflected labor leaders' anxiety over the position of white working-class Americans within this imperial system. What did this new empire offer them? In many ways, organized labor's apparent anti-imperialism reflected not opposition to imperialism or an American empire but an alternative vision of U.S. expansion, different from the Roosevelts, Tafts, and Beveridges of the world, rooted in white settler colonialism.

Labor leaders' alternative vision of U.S. expansion evinces the deeper, dueling domestic class struggle over the structure, organization, and repertoires of imperial rule. Indeed, the longer and broader pattern of U.S. imperial expansion is a duality between the desire to create strictly policed borders and to transcend those borders in the interests of unrestricted expansion.[28] These dueling impulses do not necessarily follow a linear order. As this book will show, sometimes the impulse to erect boundaries is in response to unfettered expansion as much as the impulse to transcend pre-existing borders or barriers to expansion.

The non-linearity of this impetus, I argue, is underpinned by the dynamics of domestic class struggle. A struggle between unfettered expansion on the one hand and the impetus to erect boundaries and police movement across them on the other—though not always perfectly or precisely—corresponds to the clashing interests of capital and labor; for organized labor, expansion was fine so long as it was fettered. In contrast, the imperatives of capitalist expansion could not abide the limitations insisted upon by labor leaders.[29] It is a process that had its roots in U.S. continental expansion, whereby an ideology of white settler colonialism placed racial fetters on who was permitted to migrate to the American West.[30] This was the beginning of what Beth Lew-Williams called "the enduring conflict between the dreams of West Coast workers hoping to build a white republic and cosmopolitan imperialists with their sights set on China."[31]

After formal U.S. sovereignty reached the Pacific Coast in the wake of the Mexican-American War in 1848, the expansionary forces of American capitalism blazed a bridge across the Pacific. This began a process that linked the labor markets of China and East Asia with the emerging extractive industries of the western United States by importing Chinese laborers across the world's largest ocean.[32] However, California's almost instantaneous incorporation into the metropolitan architecture of the U.S. political system complicated matters. As white settlers began streaming into the state after the completion of the transcontinental railroad in 1869, the dueling forces of U.S. imperial expansion were on a collision course. The abstract expansionary forces of American capitalism confronted the concrete reality of U.S. white settler colonialism.

The uneven process by which California was quickly shifting from a colonial imperial outpost to an incorporated white settler colony and state disrupted the prevailing relations between capital and labor in the region. Not only did white settler colonialism have no place for the Chinese laborers that initially had supplied the expansionary forces of American capital with its labor requirements. White settler colonialism meant that colonists from the East who came with a sovereign status conferred upon them by their citizenship (or eventual citizenship) were supplanting a labor force of subjects. This contrasted with Chinese workers who the United States incorporated into its production process but not its citizenry.[33] The emerging citizen labor force, however, could contest the power of capital through the ballot box. This contestation first manifested through the emergence of a xenophobic anti-Chinese movement that culminated in the Chinese Exclusion Act of 1882.

Post-1898 imperial expansion and the subsequent fetters and limitations placed upon that expansion was the continuation of this process.[34] Moreover, as Lew-Williams also notes, "[b]y the turn of the twentieth century, Chinese exclusion and U.S. imperialism had become synergistic projects drawing parallel lines to divide citizens from aliens at home and Western Civilization from eastern barbarism abroad."[35] Labor leaders and the institutions they represented were seeking to both exclude Chinese subjects of the new U.S. empire from the emerging metropole while simultaneously seeking to defend the expanding Pacific empire from "eastern barbarism" and the labor systems that came with it by insisting that exclusion follow the flag of conquest and commerce.

However, to fully understand and appreciate how this process played itself out on the ground, we must shift our focus from the broader craft labor movement and the most visible heights of U.S. imperial expansion to more opaque processes of imperial expansion and the laborers who were central to it: white merchant sailors. Because for the vast majority of the AFL membership, the threat from America's new subjects was largely an abstract, potential threat. For the members of the International Seaman's Union of America it was not only very real but predated the 1898 expansionist thrust. For sailors were the few white American workers, apart from soldiers, who actually ventured out into what was being reconstituted as the U.S. "empire."

The SUP, ISU, and the U.S. Imperial System

Merchant sailors and the merchant marine were as central to the construction of modern globe-spanning empires as soldiers and the military. They helped facilitate the rise of the Spanish and Portuguese maritime empires of the sixteenth century to the Dutch, British, and French empires of the seventeenth, eighteenth, and nineteenth centuries, as well as the emerging U.S. and Japanese empires of the twentieth century.[36] Indeed, merchant sailors did not directly dispossess anyone of their lands, nor did they explicitly deny peoples' freedom and take lives. However, merchant sailors made possible the overseas deployment of military resources, including soldiers, to subjugate colonial populations, dispossess indigenous peoples of their land, and transport slaves across the middle passage. They helped mobilize the fruits of empire by carrying the resources from plundered lands back to the imperial metropole. They circulated the goods produced by colonial subjects, whether as free laborers, indentured servants, or slaves. The merchant ship was an indispensable institution of modern, globe-spanning empires. In short, soldiers made empire possible, but sailors made empire work.

Merchant sailors, therefore, were key voices in figuring out what empire meant to white working-class Americans. The SUP and the ISU leadership's relationship and attitudes toward emerging, post-1898 U.S. imperial formations reflected the broader imperial anxieties, both real and imagined, of America's labor leaders and the white working class they claimed to represent. They were the front lines in the struggle to define and defend the boundaries of the U.S. imperial system. They lived and worked in the space that was part of an expanding American imperium. U.S. imperial and economic expansion beyond the continental United States held immediate and tangible consequences for merchant sailors, especially those based on the Pacific Coast. As a result, their representatives in the SUP and the ISU, particularly SUP secretary and ISU president Andrew Furuseth, as well as *Coast Seamen's Journal* editors Walter Macarthur and Paul Scharrenberg, helped lead the AFL's efforts in Washington in the aftermath of annexation to ensure white American workers remained protected from the peoples and practices of U.S. imperial formations. The SUP and ISU leadership understood all too well how links between uneven labor markets disrupted and subverted potential wage increases. It was the SUP and the ISU leadership that took the strategy of resisting the effects of empire by aligning with it far beyond the efforts of the AFL, especially Furuseth. The ISU leadership sought to not only align with empire but also use U.S. imperial expansion to their advantage in an effort to reimagine white American merchant sailors as agents of empire.

The 1880s was a pivotal decade in the history of U.S. capitalist expansion. When Congress passed the Chinese Exclusion Act in 1882, it marked the first time since the 1808 ban on the importation of African slaves that the United States placed restrictions on U.S. capital's ability to source labor beyond its shores. However, the 1880s was also when the United States changed its navigation laws to provide U.S. shipping firms in the foreign trade (trade between U.S. and foreign countries) access to a global labor market for maritime labor.[37] By accessing a global labor market, U.S. shipping firms could replace their white American crews with cheaper foreign workers. Additionally, the technological evolution from sail to steam allowed U.S. shipping firms to better exploit the global labor market because shipping company executives were convinced that steam power rendered skilled seamanship obsolete. In the view of shipping company executives, anyone could crew a merchant ship in the age of steam.

The combination of steam power and the internationalization of the maritime labor market both brought down the wages of the U.S. merchant marine and significantly reduced the number of American citizens employed in the trade.[38] It was on the West Coast where sailors most felt the effects of the internationalization of maritime labor given its proximity to the labor markets of East Asia. Shipping firms such as the Dollar Steamship Line and the Pacific Mail Steamship Company were keen to take advantage of Asian labor markets to combat the high wage status of West Coast ports. In the same decade that a working-class protest movement had closed off U.S. capital's access to the labor markets of China, the state had relinked these markets by internationalizing the maritime labor market in the foreign trade. Workers from China (and anywhere else) were once again drawn into the service of U.S. economic and imperial expansion, disrupting the pre-existing maritime labor market on the West Coast.

The genesis of the SUP and the ISU was rooted in attempts to reform the unfree labor practices of the merchant marine. They fought for the abolition of crimping—a system designed to create what was essentially a form of debt peonage between ship captain and sailor. Moreover, they fought for the fundamental right to quit their jobs without criminal penalty. It was during this burst of activism in the late 1880s and early 1890s that shipping companies began using Chinese crews from the Far East. To preserve the regime as it was, shipping companies shifted to new sources of labor that were subjects of the United States rather than citizens or potential citizens. Indeed, while aboard ships white American sailors had virtually no avenues of labor resistance, but once back home in California they had all the rights that their citizenship conferred, including the right to organize against their industry's labor practices as well as the ability to lobby all branches and levels of government to intervene on their behalf. They lived as citizens but worked as subjects.

In an effort to maintain the unfree orientation of maritime labor relations, shipping capital sought to replace a workforce of citizens and potential citizens with a workforce of subjects who lacked access to the institutions of American democracy—creating an imperial relationship between captain and crew. As a result, Chinese workers laboring aboard American flagged (or owned) merchant vessels became subjects of an emerging U.S. imperial system. The United States never ruled directly over Chinese territory (though it did rule over Chinese people), but as long as workers from China labored onboard American vessels, they fell under the direct influence, control, and subjugation of a key economic institution of U.S. empire. In the case of Chinese workers in Hong Kong, they were subjects of two empires: colonial subjects of the British empire and, when on American vessels, imperial subjects of the United States.[39] Indeed, this would not be the last time the United States turned to another imperial system to satisfy its labor needs. The workers that would later build the Panama Canal were largely British colonial subjects from the West Indies.[40] Yet wherever they came from, the results were the same to white American sailors—competition with foreign sailors that cost a fraction of white American sailors.

Whiteness, therefore, became one of the central organizing principles of the ISU leadership, especially in the northern European–dominated SUP. Whiteness also had the added benefit of expanding their pool of potential members. After all, American citizens were an ever-decreasing percentage of the U.S. merchant marine.[41] Indeed, Andrew Furuseth himself originally hailed from Norway, arriving in San Francisco in 1880 at the age of twenty-six. By insisting upon a merchant marine occupied solely by white Americans or newly arrived white immigrants, the SUP and the ISU were articulating an alternative vision of maritime labor relations in the foreign trade that would shift the maritime labor market from imperial and foreign to domestic and metropolitan—an alternative vision that was rooted in the genealogy of white settler colonialism. I argue that this shift would result in the extension of the United States' domestic labor market and, thus, its national boundaries to the deck of American flagged vessels.[42]

For the ISU, the most essential marker of the domestic U.S. labor market was the protection that the Chinese Exclusion Act offered. In other words, they were seeking to extend the "dream" of a "white republic" into the foreign merchant trade in contrast to "cosmopolitan" shipping company executives "with their sights set on China['s]" vast labor market.[43] In the decade preceding Pacific annexation, SUP and ISU efforts to insulate the maritime labor market in the foreign trade involved using the courts and convincing members of Congress that if American ships, by statute and legal precedent, were considered sovereign American soil, then they should be protected by the Exclusion Act and the Alien Contract Labor law. Congress, the courts, and the executive disagreed. As a result, in the aftermath of Pacific annexation, Andrew Furuseth helped lead the AFL lobbying campaign to update the Exclusion Law for the post-1898 reality. Furuseth and the AFL legislative committee had their allies in Congress propose a new law that prevented Chinese migrants from entering the U.S. empire as well as stopping Chinese residents of the empire (in the Philippines and Hawai'i) from entering the nation. Most important for the SUP and the ISU was a clause that extended the exclusion law to U.S.-flagged vessels in the foreign trade. They were successful in applying exclusion to U.S. colonies and preventing Chinese subjects from entering the nation from the colonies, but unfortunately for sailors, they were not successful in expanding the new law to U.S. merchant ships. They were defeated but not deterred.

After the defeat of maritime exclusion, the SUP and the ISU became a key voice in organized labor's ongoing struggle to control and enforce the boundaries of the U.S. imperial system by resisting attempts to weaken, or find ways around, the 1902 exclusion law. Some efforts to weaken exclusion consisted of schemes to disempower immigration agents from barring Chinese migrants that the law exempted. The sailors' unions also fought attempts by the Roosevelt administration to move the enforcement mechanism of exclusion from water's edge of the nation on the Pacific Coast to the far edges of the U.S. imperial system to American consular offices.

Running parallel with efforts to defend the exclusion law was the emergence of a strong anti-Japanese movement that framed Japanese immigration more as an imperial competition for control of the Pacific Ocean and the West Coast of the United States. Again, the SUP and the ISU were at the center of this movement as founding members of the Asiatic Exclusion League (AEL), which called for an expanded exclusion law to include all Asians. The movement for Japanese exclusion helped force the infamous Gentlemen's Agreement between the United States and Japan. However, the Gentleman's Agreement was not a formal treaty, which meant that it was not subject to congressional approval. This meant that organized labor's congressional allies had far less influence over the substance of the agreement.[44] Additionally, a loophole was left in place whereby Japanese citizens could still enter the United States by way of Hawai'i. For the AEL and the SUP, U.S. imperial formations on the Pacific were subverting the white settler status of the Pacific Coast. Furthermore, by 1908, despite the best efforts of the ISU and the SUP, the use of Chinese crews by American shipping companies was only increasing owing to international competition.

From here, the transnational reality of the shipping industry forced the SUP and the ISU to move beyond simply aligning with empire to using U.S. imperial and economic expansion to their advantage. The central reason for the failure of maritime exclusion in 1902 was the fact that any law passed by Congress only applied to U.S.-flagged ships. American shipping companies, however, could register their vessels in any country they pleased. Indeed, both the Dollar Line and the Pacific Mail Line took advantage of this privilege, to the point where most of their fleet was registered outside the United States.[45] From 1900 onward, 90 percent of the goods coming to and from the United States were shipped on foreign-flagged or foreign-owned vessels.[46] As a result, the biggest effect of maritime exclusion would be to discourage U.S. shipping companies from registering their vessels in the United States.

To get around this problem, the SUP and the ISU lobbied for maritime legislation that would apply to all vessels regardless of national registry. As long as a ship was destined for a U.S. port, it would have to conform to the American standards. These guidelines, under the controversial 1915 La Follette Seamen's Act, used craft union standards and protections and an appeal to increased safety standards (which was under significant public scrutiny after the 1912 sinking of the *Titanic*) to drive Asian sailors from the trade.

To be sure, this was not entirely about excluding Asian sailors, even though racial exclusion was one of the primary motivations. Furuseth and the union leadership had long worried about the decline of skilled seamanship and often lamented the lack of skill and respect for the traditions of the craft among the new generation of young American sailors. Moreover, preventing the downward spiral of skilled workers ensured that the potential size of the maritime labor market remained small. Historically, craft union standards and trade agreements were a means to "insulate labor markets" and maintain the traditions of the trade by "specifying training requirements or recruitment rights and carefully fixing work rules."[47] The idea was to legislate work rules and standards that the ISU leadership believed were impossible for Chinese workers to meet. Chief among those rules and standards was a clause that mandated at least 75 percent of the crew be able to speak the language of the officers. The effect was to both preserve the skill and traditions of the trade *and* insulate the U.S. maritime labor market in the foreign trade from Chinese competition. The law would provide de facto if not de jure exclusion.

This strategy did not come without consequences, however, especially since the ISU had now expanded to the far more ethnically diverse East Coast, where ships resembled the motley crewed vessels of Melvillian legend and whiteness was more complicated.[48] In contrast to the northern European–dominated SUP, the East Coast membership had a high percentage of southern Europeans and Latin Americans, many of whom could not speak English. As a result, the SUP's use of broader and indirect means to exclude Asians, such as the language clause, meant the exclusion of non-Asian sailors who could not meet the standards set by the La Follette Act. Additionally, since East Coast sailors did not face the same level of Asian competition as the SUP, insulating the maritime labor market was less of a priority. This meant that members of the East Coast branch were more likely to view the La Follette Act's skill standards as unnecessary and outdated and looked to the industrial unionism of the recently formed Industrial Workers of the World (IWW), who offered an alternative working-class politics that eschewed hierarchies of skill, race, and nationality.

Beyond simply setting new skill standards, the La Follette Act also created a free labor market for maritime labor in U.S. ports by abolishing the criminal punishment of desertion for both foreign and American sailors, again regardless of the vessel's country of origin. This meant that a British sailor, for example, could desert his ship in an American port and reship on a U.S. vessel with higher wages. The law would then force British shipping companies to raise their wages or risk losing their crew every time they entered a U.S. port. The ISU and the SUP were betting that emerging U.S. economic dominance would force a wage increase of the global shipping industry, while at the same time create what Furuseth called "free soil" for seamen.[49]

The effect of the La Follette Act, I argue, was to incorporate the foreign maritime trade into the U.S. domestic labor market by harnessing the economic dimensions of U.S. imperial expansion. If a ship, foreign or American, was destined for a U.S. port, it had to conform to the La Follette Act regulations. This shifted the national or metropolitan boundaries of the United States from the water's edge of the nation to any ship bound for a U.S. port. As a result, the act would globalize exclusion by stitching together the transnational legal regime of Asian restriction through the abstract forces of U.S. economic expansion. Exclusion went beyond following the flag of conquest (when Congress extended it to the Philippines in 1902), to riding the waves of U.S. imperial expansion by following the long arm of American capitalism. This builds on Leon Fink's examination of the La Follette Act, where he argued that it was a "nationalist solution" to an international problem, which is indeed true. I take Fink's argument further and argue that it was an imperial solution to an international problem.

Yet the ISU's various tactics to insulate the maritime labor market in the foreign trade were particular examples of their larger ambition of amalgamating merchant sailors with the national interest. In the view of Andrew Furuseth and the ISU leadership, the merchant marine, more specifically merchant sailors, were a strategic national resource. Furuseth's philosophies and views of the merchant marine, labor politics, and a sailor's place within a society, nation, and empire were central to the union's outlook, organizing strategies, and philosophy. To understand the ISU is to understand Andrew Furuseth.[50] Indeed, the peculiarity of the trade—where union members were often scattered across the globe—amplified the power of ISU and SUP executives, but especially its president, to set union policy. For the first twenty-five years of the union's existence, the membership rarely challenged Furuseth and the leadership's strategies and tactics. Furuseth's views were rooted in his reading of U.S. naval theorist Captain Alfred Thayer Mahan, particularly his hugely influential 1890 work, *The Influence of Sea Power on History.* Citing Mahan, Furuseth argued that having a supply of well-trained, experienced sailors was a necessary ingredient for a nation to become a great and powerful empire and was just as important as the number of ships a nation had in its navy and merchant fleet.[51] This was something the United States could never hope to accomplish with a merchant marine composed of foreign sailors.

Furuseth and the ISU leadership believed that insulating the maritime labor market from foreign competition was essential in cultivating a skilled and experienced pool of American sailors. The union leadership maintained that without a protected labor market, the U.S. merchant marine would end up training sailors for the navies of other nations, mainly China. The SUP and the ISU justified attempts to insulate the maritime labor market from foreign sailors as part of an imperial competition to control and occupy the world's oceans. Yet any amalgamation with the national interest had to be achieved on their terms, as free and independent workers who set the rules of the labor market. In this respect, Furuseth and the union leadership had reimagined merchant sailors as agents of empire rather than a cheap, commodified, and dependent maritime proletariat.

The First World War temporarily affirmed but ultimately subverted the ISU leadership's ambition to remake U.S. merchant sailors into agents of empire. The war laid bare the inadequacies of the United States' maritime policy that relied largely on foreign carriers and foreign crews, forcing the state and industry into a scramble to build a new American merchant marine. The government and even shipping company executives agreed to shift U.S. maritime policy away from access to cheap labor and over to cultivating a reservoir of skilled and independent American sailors, and even to prioritize union members in the hiring process. Suddenly, everyone saw the need for highly paid and highly skilled native-born white American sailors. Additionally, the war provided the conditions for a massive reorganizing campaign on the East Coast. As a result of the war, the ISU expanded its membership from thirteen thousand members in 1914 to one hundred thousand by war's end.[52]

However, despite the SUP and ISU gains, the war also served to consolidate the U.S. shipping industry on a scale never before seen and entangled the industry within a corporatist state structure that the government could easily turn against the ISU. In short, though the war may have empowered the ISU, it had made the shipping industry even more powerful and profitable. The consolidation and expansion of the U.S. shipping industry during the war placed it in an ideal position to reverse many of the hard-fought gains made by the SUP and the ISU over the last thirty years, namely the La Follette Seamen's Act, which the shipping companies were calling for repeal even before the war ended. Furthermore, the SUP and the ISU saw the institutions created by the Paris Peace Conference, such as the International Labor Organization, as a direct challenge to the unilateralism of the La Follette Act. Moreover, the SUP and the ISU would get little to no help from their European counterparts, who had a different understanding of maritime labor relations. In the end, the shipping industry became more intensely amalgamated and integrated with the national interest, but white American merchant sailors did not. While the First World War may have allowed the SUP and the ISU to be acknowledged as the agents of empire Furuseth always believed they were, it simultaneously planted the seeds of their demise.

Shipping capital and organized labor emerged from the First World War in structurally opposite positions. The origin of this opposition was in the divergent effects that expansion had on shipping capital and the ISU. For shipping companies, expansion had no downside. For the unions, there was a tension between expansion—both geographically and numerically—and their exclusionary craft unionism. Whenever the ISU expanded beyond the Pacific Coast and increased its numbers, the leadership was confronted with challenges to its governing ideology and its legislative program.

Additionally, judicial and regulatory decisions during the war helped lay the groundwork for U.S. shipping companies to gain near unrestricted access to cheap Chinese labor when the war ended, and the need for highly skilled American sailors abated. The effect of these decisions was to reverse the labor market protections established by the La Follette Act, bringing the boundaries of the domestic labor market back to the water's edge of the continental United States. Members of the ISU's recently reorganized Atlantic branch offered a potential solution whereby the ISU would abandon its pursuit of labor market protections and instead incorporate Chinese sailors into the union. However, the ISU could not take this step because its underlying justification for insulating the maritime labor market was to build up U.S. maritime power by ensuring there was a ready supply of American sailors who could be called up to the navy. To the SUP and ISU leadership, especially Andrew Furuseth, Chinese sailors could never be incorporated into the white republic's merchant marine and the labor institutions that came with it. Instead, they were always viewed either as "slaves" or what Elliot Young called "perpetual aliens."[53] As a result, the ISU leadership doubled down on exclusion and tried to use the 1924 Immigration Act to exclude Chinese sailors on ships bound for the United States once and for all. This proved unsuccessful. Much to the leadership's frustration, the Immigration Act of 1924 (also known as the Johnson-Reed Act) reaffirmed the wartime judicial decisions that placed the limits of the domestic labor market at the water's edge of the continental United States.

With the shipping industry and the government recommitted to a maritime policy of cheap labor, the still extant wartime corporatist infrastructure was turned against maritime labor in an effort to break the ISU and impose an open shop on the industry. As a result, a rank-and-file rebellion emerged within the ISU that questioned whether its strict craft union tactics were suited to the postwar labor environment. To counter the much more aggressive actions by the government and the shipping industry, the rank and file urged the ISU and its district unions to form bonds of solidarity with workers beyond the sailing trades. The rank-and-file push culminated in the formation of the Marine Transport Workers Federation of the Pacific, which was an umbrella organization for sailors, longshoremen, and other marine trades. ISU and SUP members, led by J. Vance Thompson, saw this organization as a middle way between the ISU's strict craft unionism and the Industrial Workers of the World's more radical industrial unionism. Again, the ISU doubled down on its craft union ideology and centralized its control over the unions and expelled members that challenged it. The effect of this policy led to a mass exodus from the ISU and the SUP. By 1923 the wartime membership gains had disappeared, and ISU and the SUP were back to prewar levels.

Whether challenged from shipping capital or the rank and file, the effect was the same: the erosion of the labor market protections that the ISU had been building up since the 1890s, all of which the union designed to insulate white American sailors from foreign competition. These protections were the foundation of the union leadership's efforts to elevate the status of white American sailors from objects and instruments to agents of U.S. empire. The combination of a consolidated and empowered shipping industry together with rank-and-file hostility toward exclusionary craft unionism jeopardized white American sailors' tenuous hold on their status as agents of empire and their place within the U.S. imperial hierarchy. In a bitter fit of irony, the ISU's efforts to preserve its place in the U.S. imperial labor hierarchy is what led to their fall from it. Exclusion failed.

1898 and the Racial and Class Dimensions of the U.S. Imperial System

By now, I hope it is evident that this book approaches and conceives of the United States as a highly complex imperial system made up of multiple component parts engaged in an ongoing and fluid process of order and reorder across time and space, rather than merely a nation-state with spatially static boundaries. In fact, the United States nation was but one part of the U.S imperial system composed of its own component parts, whether by region, race, ethnicity, gender, or class. These component parts are ultimately the product of the multidimensional, interconnected, and overlapping webs of relations between individuals and groups of people both spatially and temporally. Moreover, these component parts are often defined and understood based on the people who occupy them and the labor systems under which they work. This book conceptualizes class conflict in the nation within that broader imperial context. In a narrower sense, my focus lay on how class conflict within the nation both informed and reverberated throughout the webs of relations that stitched together the U.S. imperial system. This is not to suggest that domestic class conflict is the only process that shaped the emerging U.S. imperial system. It is not. However, that its influence is nonetheless undeniable is the central argument of this book. Class conflict underpinned the process by which the United States nation emerged out of the expanding imperial system. With that in mind, the lens of class conflict reveals the ultimate significance of "1898" in understanding the longer history of the ever-expanding U.S. imperial system both before and after the Spanish-American War.

Conceptualizing the United States empire as a living, breathing system in motion allows us to understand how a specific component part (such as the nation) emerged and was defined and redefined. Empire is an "inherently relational" system.[54] The inherent relationality of empire means that its component parts manifest and are given form only in relation to each other. That is, we can only understand the part of the imperial system that became the nation by also understanding what the nation was not. As a result, I argue that the United States, as a nation, was made by its imperial projects.[55] Moreover, these component parts were given form by the people who lived and occupied them. This book, therefore, is less about simply delineating these boundaries than it is about understanding the processes by which people attempted, with uneven and varying levels of success, to both create and contest them.[56] Yet by understanding the process of boundary creation and contestation, we cannot help but see them. Furthermore, these boundaries are multidimensional, underpinned by, though far from limited to, racial and class identities. Indeed, the racial and class identity of a person or group of people determined how much access they had to the imperial system as a whole, where they could and could not go, and *how* they went where they went. If white organized labor had a stake in limiting the movement of U.S. colonial and imperial subjects, the state and its partners in private capital had an interest in limiting the movement of working-class whites within the imperial system.

Therefore, I argue that the ability to move freely within the imperial system was contingent upon a particular class status, while racial status often determined the specific parts of the system a person or people could access. Though racial animosity underpinned the impulse for the Chinese Exclusion Act, class status was a way around the barrier.[57] Only Chinese "laborers" were denied access under the Exclusion Acts of 1882, 1892, and 1902. Similarly, middle- and upper-class whites were permitted to move freely throughout the empire, but working-class whites were not. This was true beyond the U.S. imperial context, as Ann Stoler and Frederick Cooper pointed out, "class impinged on the making of empire" by "constraining who came to the colonies."[58] Working-class whites who could access U.S. imperial formations were in highly disciplined and hierarchically rigid institutional environments, such as the military or foreign sailing trade.[59] Working-class imperial mobility was, therefore, contingent upon the surrender of many basic freedoms that the privilege of citizenship bestowed.

From class-contingent imperial mobility emerged a racialized imperial division of labor. If working-class whites in the continental United States sought protection and insulation from the U.S. empire, the imperial state and representatives of private capital looking to profit from U.S. imperial formations sought to keep working-class whites—with their unions and high wage demands—out of the empire, whether in territorial colonies like the Philippines or other imperial formations like the merchant ship. This is what members of the SUP and the ISU were up against. The presence of their members on U.S. merchant ships in the foreign trade threatened an emerging imperial division of labor and thus the merchant ship's status as an imperial formation. If the merchant ship in the foreign trade remained in a foreign or imperial labor context, complete with its physical and financial disciplinary apparatus, whites would no longer find the trade desirable. If SUP and ISU members wanted to stay in the foreign merchant trade, they had no choice but to incorporate it into the national labor market and the protections that came with it. However, shipping capital's ongoing search for ever-cheaper sources of labor meant shipping companies had to ensure the foreign maritime trade remained outside the domestic labor market and its protections.

Out of the interplay of these impulses from both capital and organized labor, the continental United States (and eventually, Hawai'i) was being reconfigured as an imperial metropole. The U.S. metropole, therefore, emerged as a consequence of organized labor's fears over the collision and potential effects that the integration of the low-wage labor markets of the Pacific and the Far East would have on the nation.[60] As a result, the question of the U.S. metropole was fundamentally a labor question. The SUP's and the ISU's central goal between the mid-1890s to 1924 was to extend the emerging metropolitan framework, and therefore the national labor market, from the water's edge of North America to the deck of American-flagged vessels on the high seas. Conversely, shipping company executives spent the same period working to ensure the foreign maritime trade remained outside the U.S. metropole as a foreign and imperial labor market. What is more, understanding the imperial division of labor and its consequences reveals the ultimate significance of 1898 in U.S. imperial historiography.

I recognize the potential pitfalls of making "1898" a key axis point of this book. Indeed, the specter of 1898 has loomed large over the historiography of U.S. empire for nearly a century. Initially, scholars saw the so-called imperial turn as an "aberration" in the history of the United States—a historical accident in which the United States was thrust into the unwanted role of imperial master.[61] This interpretation took a narrow view of empire and overlooked the myriad ways the United States and other empires exercised imperial power by ignoring anything that was not, strictly speaking, a direct colonial relationship. Yet despite significant revision of this interpretation as well as the conceptual expansion of how historians define empire and the imperial, the idea that 1898 represented a complete break from earlier U.S. history has been oddly persistent.[62]

This book takes a more nuanced view of 1898 and argues that it was both a break from, and the logical extension of, more than a century of U.S. territorial expansion. It was continuity and disruption. The United States existed as an imperial system both before and after the Spanish-American War. Post-1898 expansion continued the United States' westward march but did so under markedly different repertoires of imperial rule.

With that in mind, I argue that 1898 rendered the U.S. imperial system visible to most Americans. It was the first time Americans could not help but see it or identify it as a "thing" that existed. Between the 1860s and 1890s, the United States was rapidly expanding its power and influence around the world, but especially in the Western Hemisphere. Indeed, the United States had a myriad of imperial relationships with many nations in Latin America and the Caribbean, as well as Hawai'i before official annexation. The pre-1898 U.S. imperial system was largely an abstraction for most Americans, underpinned by economic coercion and military force, but rarely if ever overt bonds of political domination.[63] There was no map school-aged Americans could look at and see the U.S. empire in the same way all British schoolchildren could. Indeed, all Americans understood westward expansion. However, they did not see or conceive of it as imperial expansion, mainly because it benefited them by providing a frontier of opportunity, both real and imagined.[64] As author Upton Sinclair once wrote, "it is difficult to get a man to understand something, when his salary depends on his not understanding it."[65] Similarly, the dreams and aspirations of white Americans often depended upon them not seeing how their upward mobility was built upon the oppression or erasure of others.[66]

If working-class Americans did stumble upon the pre-1898 U.S. imperial system, it was framed as almost anything but imperialism. The most obvious dimension of the U.S. imperial system working-class Americans could see was the mass mobilization of labor to meet the demands of a rapidly expanding capitalist economy. However, Americans did not view this as evidence of an imperial order. Rather, mass labor mobilization was understood strictly as an immigration issue. Yet as I argued earlier, fear over immigration was the same as the fear of 1898 annexation: the integration of low-wage labor markets with the higher-wage American market, whether from European immigrants arriving in the East, potential northern migration of African American sharecroppers, Asian immigrants in the West, or foreign workers on U.S.-flagged ships.[67]

In 1898 the politics of racialized immigration restriction and imperial expansion flowed into the crucible of the Spanish-American War and its consequences, beginning a process that would eventually forge them together in U.S. political discourse—a process that culminated in the passage of the 1924 Immigration Act.[68] After annexation, white working-class Americans, through their labor institutions, worried about immigration from their new colonies and from places like China where the United States had an imperial relationship. They also worried about Japanese immigrants using U.S. imperial possessions to gain a foothold within the U.S. imperial system before moving to the U.S. metropole in North America. From 1898 onward, Americans, led by labor leaders like Furuseth and Samuel Gompers, fought to insulate the United States from the people and practices of its current and future empire. By 1924 they had finally and fully succeeded when President Coolidge signed the Immigration Act of 1924 into law, both consolidating and expanding every restrictionist law passed since 1882 into one piece of legislation. The era of legal, mass immigration finally ended (at least until 1965). Yet the 1924 Immigration Act was so much more than immigration restriction. It was an act of imperial settlement that defined the parameters of the U.S. imperial system, including the boundaries of the United States nation, as well as providing a road map for metropolitan incorporation or decolonization. More than that, it divided up the world into potential Americans and those unfit to be American.[69] In this way, the 1924

Immigration Act was also a profound statement of the nation's future imperial ambitions—one that conceived of a metropolitan/imperial dichotomy on a planetary level.[70]

This book is organized into five chapters, divided both chronologically and thematically. Chapter 1 examines how the annexation of Hawai'i and the Philippines disrupted the U.S. labor market by subverting the nation's racialized immigration regime—something the Sailors Union of the Pacific referred to as a "leak in the ship of state."[71] It argues that the "leak in the ship of state" was actually the most visible part of a longer, less visible, and more peripheral struggle to define the boundaries of the U.S. labor market rooted in the West Coast shipping industry—a process that began a mere two years after the passage of the 1882 Exclusion Act. In 1898 this process moved from the periphery to the center of American politics and rendered visible an opaque process that had begun fifteen years earlier in the shipping industry. Chapter 2 focuses on how organized labor's efforts to resist the effects of empire by aligning with it disrupted the imperial labor process and led to a domestic class struggle for control over the boundaries of the emerging U.S. empire. It argues that by placing racialized, legal safeguards between nation and empire, a metropolitan imperial framework emerged around the North American white settler territory of the U.S. imperial system.

Chapter 3 examines how the SUP and the ISU dealt with their failure to include U.S.-flagged ships in the 1902 exclusion law by moving from aligning with empire to using U.S. imperial expansion as an alternative means of insulating the maritime labor market from foreign Chinese competition. It argues that the La Follette Seamen's Act of 1915 was the culmination of this alternative route to exclusion. Chapter 4 analyzes the effect the First World War had on the ISU's efforts to amalgamate merchant sailors with the national interest by reimagining them as agents of empire and argues that the war temporarily affirmed but ultimately subverted these ambitions. The war helped the ISU reach the peak of its power while simultaneously laying the seeds for its downfall. Finally, chapter 5 looks at how the consequences of the war played out in the postwar labor environment. It argues that the ISU leadership was caught between a massively expanded and increasingly assertive rank and file that relentlessly questioned the ISU leadership's exclusionary craft union ideology and an empowered shipping industry supported by a still extant wartime corporatist infrastructure. The contradictions that came with aligning with power had consequences.

In many ways, then, this book is a tragic tale. No one person embodies this tragedy more than SUP secretary and ISU president Andrew Furuseth. A man whose biography was titled *Emancipator of the Seamen* spent his entire life fighting for the freedom of the "world's" sailors. For the freedom of men like Robert Robertson, H. H. Olsen, John Bradley, and Morris Hanson. The union, his men, and the craft of sailing were his life. But Furuseth and the union he loved and led, just as passionately and zealously chased what W. E. B. Du Bois called the "psychological wages" of whiteness.[72] Like the forefathers of his adopted nation, Furuseth may have spoken in universals when he pontificated about freeing the world's sailors. But for Furuseth, the privilege of freedom was reserved only for sailors that looked like him. He chose not to see Chinese sailors as brothers and comrades. Instead, he saw them as either enemies to be feared or weapons to be wielded. Like many white labor leaders that came before him, he is guilty of the American labor movement's original sin—the sin of choosing white supremacy over solidarity.

CHAPTER 1

"A Leak in the Ship of State"

Maritime Labor Reform and U.S. Imperial Expansion, 1872–1900

The year 1882 was a watershed moment in the history of the United States. It marked the beginning of what immigration historian Erika Lee argued was the United States' emergence as a gatekeeping nation.[1] After a hysterical, decade-long racist campaign led by the California Workingmen's parties finally put the mantra of the "Chinese must go" into practice, Chinese laborers no longer legally could enter the United States.[2] Yet the 1882 Chinese Exclusion Act did not just limit a group of people from entering the United States.

The exclusion law also placed a key legislative limitation on the expansionary forces of American capitalism. When the United States annexed California after the Mexican-American War of 1848, the development and exploitation of the newly acquired state's resources required labor. The Mexican population living in Alta-California numbered only in the thousands, nowhere near large enough to constitute a viable labor force. Plus, a high percentage of California's Mexican population (made U.S. citizens under the treaty of Guadeloupe-Hidalgo) were already landowners.[3] The indigenous population was significantly larger, with some estimates placing it as high as one hundred thousand.[4] However, the United States' policy toward indigenous peoples rarely saw them as a source of labor, whether slave or free. Rather, official U.S. policy waffled between dispossession of territory and systematic genocide.[5] Between 1848 and the completion of the transcontinental railroad in 1869, the time and resources required for white Americans east of the Mississippi to migrate to the Pacific

Coast ensured a scarcity of labor in California. As a result, highly capitalized, labor-intensive industries such as mining and railroad construction looked west to China's seemingly endless labor markets. For the first two decades of California's history as a state, Chinese labor was essential.[6] After the railroad's completion, when white Americans and recent immigrants began to stream to the Pacific Coast, the anti-Chinese movement dominated California politics in the 1870s, culminating in the 1882 Exclusion Act. The 1882 exclusion law closed off the world's most populous country and largest labor market from the long arm of American capitalism. This marked the first time the U.S. state placed limitations on where American businesses could recruit and import labor since the constitutionally mandated 1808 ban on the importation of slaves. By insulating the region from the labor markets of China, the Chinese Exclusion Act marked a critical victory in the triumph of white settler colonialism on the Pacific Coast.[7]

The U.S. victory in the Spanish-American War in 1898 and the subsequent annexation of Hawai'i and the Philippines disrupted the U.S. labor market by subverting the nation's racialized immigration regime and unleashed the forces of American capitalism on the western Pacific. The nation's labor organizations, led by the American Federation of Labor and the Sailor's Union of the Pacific, opposed the annexation of both territories on the grounds that their populations were incompatible with both U.S. standards of living and citizenship. Moreover, because the discourse surrounding depictions of Asian and Pacific Island laborers almost always described them as slaves and linked their presence with the emergence of slave systems, the SUP argued that annexation brought with it both slave-like people and unfree labor systems under U.S. dominion that might spread and infect the nation. Or, as the *Coast Seamen's Journal* argued, the annexation of Hawai'i and the Philippines constituted a "leak in the ship of state."[8]

However, "the leak in the ship of state" that the Sailor's Union of the Pacific identified in 1898 was actually the most visible part of a longer, less visible, and more peripheral struggle to define the boundaries of the U.S. labor market rooted in the West Coast shipping industry—a process that began a mere two years after the passage of the 1882 Exclusion Act. Shortly after that, Congress relinked the labor markets of China with the expansionary forces of American capitalism by permitting U.S. shipping companies in the foreign trade (trade between the U.S. and foreign ports) unlimited access to labor markets beyond the United States. For the transpacific trade, West Coast shipping companies gradually began shifting their labor force from white American crews and recent immigrants on the Pacific Coast toward much cheaper all-Chinese crews based in Hong Kong or Shanghai. This shift occurred as the United States was in the process of reforming the shipping industry by removing the archaic, unfree labor practices that had long characterized the relationship between sailors and ship's captains. The emergence of the Sailor's Union of the Pacific and its national affiliate, the International Seamen's Union of America, in the late 1880s and early 1890s gave shipping companies an added incentive to turn toward foreign Chinese labor. With the help of their newly elected congressional ally, James Maguire, the SUP began an aggressive and sustained legislative campaign in 1892 aimed at reforming the industry by domesticating the maritime labor process. Because workers recruited in China lacked access to America's political institutions, the move to foreign Chinese labor amplified the asymmetry of power between maritime labor and shipping capital—creating an imperial relationship between officers and crew. This reconstituted American flagged vessels in the transpacific trade as a U.S. imperial formation, pushing the trade decidedly outside the domestic labor market.

In 1898 the struggle over the U.S. labor market moved from the periphery to the center of American politics and rendered visible an opaque process that began fifteen years earlier in the shipping industry. As those previous fifteen years demonstrated, even the Thirteenth Amendment did not necessarily guarantee white American workers protection from unfree labor conditions. Could the Supreme Court's justification of the shipping industry's "exceptional" labor practices in the *Arago* decision provide the legal precedent for the admission of new territories with unfree labor systems? This was the question foremost on the minds of SUP leaders Andrew Furuseth, Walter Macarthur, Paul Scharrenberg, and the AFL leadership when the political winds blew toward annexation.

The Unfree Labor Practices of the Merchant Marine and the Birth of the SUP

When white American sailors signed on to crew an American merchant vessel, they were entering into an unfree relationship with their employer. As the Supreme Court said in 1897, sailors were considered an "exceptional" class of labor and were not covered by the most basic constitutional protection: the Thirteenth Amendment.[9] Indeed, white American sailors were perfect exemplars of David Montgomery's argument that workers ceased to be democratic citizens while on the job.[10] While aboard ship, particularly in the foreign trade, sailors were under the almost complete control and domination of their employer. The disciplinary apparatus in place was a rigid, almost military hierarchy in which questioning an officer's order could put the ship in danger and lead to physical punishment. There were few if any avenues of resistance available to merchant sailors. This system of oppression did not end when a sailor's contract was over and they left their ships in the United States. The contract labor system that underpinned the maritime labor process ensured that the shackles of dependency followed sailors onshore.

Maritime labor reform began under the shadow of Reconstruction. As the United States was attempting to reform the labor regime of the former Confederacy, calls to address the horrendous working conditions of U.S.-flagged merchant vessels grew louder. Improving the working conditions of U.S. merchant ships, however, was more than just creating rules and regulations to ensure a safer working environment. The underlying problem of maritime working conditions resulted from a labor system that produced such dependency in its workers that they were mostly powerless to resist the demands of their employers. With the rise of free labor as the dominant labor system—at least the dominant labor system for white Americans—the labor process of the merchant marine seemed out of step with the prevailing norms of the domestic U.S. labor market. With that in mind, efforts to reform the maritime labor process necessarily meant shifting it from an unfree labor system to the emerging domestic system of free labor. This process took the form of both legislative statutes and worker organization. Between 1872 and 1898, statutory reforms combined with the unionization of white maritime workers, especially on the West Coast, began to break down the pillars of the industry's unfree labor regime.

Merchant shipping was one of the few industries that provided its labor force with access to different, often disparate labor markets. Indeed, the mobile nature of shipping had always been a problem for the industry's labor process. For the workers that labored on board vessels engaged in long-distance trade, such mobility provided them with one of their only means of resistance. Desertion, therefore, was central to a sailor's "strategy for survival."[11] Not only could a sailor desert a ship in search of better working conditions, but he could also seek out better wages. But unlike other workers, sailors' wide-ranging geographic mobility provided them with access to an international labor market where wages varied from port to port. This allowed a sailor who signed on with a vessel in a lower-wage port the potential to desert in a higher-wage port and reship on a different vessel for more money.[12] Indeed, this is how SUP secretary and future ISU president Andrew Furuseth—born and raised in Norway—ended up in the United States in the first place, after having deserted his ship in San Francisco harbor at the age of twenty-six in 1880.[13] More systemically, as Marcus Rediker pointed out, "desertion destabilized the [maritime] labor market and drove wages up."[14] As a result, "[m]erchants, masters, and government officials made resolute efforts to control the autonomous mobility of maritime workers."[15] Failure to control such movement would allow a more competitive labor market to develop that could put shipping capital in a weaker bargaining position, particularly in more isolated ports where labor was scarce. In the United States, efforts to control the movement of maritime workers took the form of both exploitative hiring practices that created and encouraged debt dependency as well as asymmetrical legal prohibitions against breaking employment contracts.

This financial dependency was rooted in what was known as the "crimping system." Crimping was a labor recruitment system that financially shackled sailors to their ships by forcing them into a form of debt peonage. As Andrew Furuseth explained to Congress, a crimp was a labor agent for the maritime industry that was "found in almost every part of the United States, and nearly everywhere in the world."[16] A crimp would get paid by "the head" to find and provide the labor necessary for ship captains to crew their vessels. Like other labor agents or "padrones," crimps were often of disreputable backgrounds with a history of criminal behavior, such as Hendrick Hendrickson, also known as "Hoodlum Harry," whom the SUP described as a "thief, murderer, stool-pigeon, crimp and perjurer."[17] In 1877 authorities charged Hendrickson with murdering a sailor, but he escaped before being prosecuted. Three years later, he was again suspected of murder but evaded trial by breaking out of jail and leaving his accomplice to face prosecution. By the mid-1880s, "Hoodlum Harry" became one of the West Coast's more notorious crimps.[18]

Essential to the crimping system was the way shipping companies paid their crews. Though wage labor has a longer history in the maritime industry than almost any other, the payment method was different.[19] Sailors were not paid biweekly or even monthly. Instead, shipping companies paid their crews at the end of their employment contract, however long it had been. This meant that during the life of their contract, sailors lived practically cashless and could not pay for basic necessities while in port. Under this system, ship captains would advance their wages to crimps that subsequently would provide sailors with clothing, food/drink, and lodging. The crimps then would provide the captain with an accounting of the sailor's expenses, which the captain would pay and then deduct from the sailor's wages when they were paid out at the end of their contract.[20] As a result, the sailors often did not know how much they were actually spending. Moreover, crimps encouraged sailors to spend lavishly on food and drink or women, since they owned saloons and boardinghouses that also employed sex workers.[21] Sailors that refused to spend liberally suddenly would find themselves without a job. On the other hand, the more they spent, the more likely ship captains would hire them.[22] In many instances, however, sailors would spend more money than their contracts were worth under pressure from the crimps so that by the end of the voyage, they ended up owing money to the ship's captain.[23] Even if the sailor did not spend all his wages in the boardinghouses, ship captains would often just lie about how much they owed or say that the value of the haul was less than they thought. Either way, the sailor would have to work off the money owed by reshipping on the same vessel or another owned by the shipping company.

This was the situation two sailors named Victor Greenhorn and Constantine Lindholm found themselves in 1887—a situation the *CSJ* called "extremely hideous, barefaced, unlimited robbery."[24] The two men arrived in San Francisco on the whaling vessel *Hidalgo* expecting a payment of $212 with $60 deducted in advances they had already received, leaving them with $152. Their captain then added further deductions from their slop chest (provisions provided by the shipping company on the journey), which amounted to a further $70. Having far less money than expected, necessity forced Greenhorn and Lindholm to ship out much earlier than anticipated. As a result, the captain of the *Hidalgo* offered to find them work on the barkentine *Ella,* whose captain was having difficulty securing a crew because he refused to pay the $45 per month demanded by the SUP.[25] Once Lindholm and Greenhorn went to the shipping office and signed-on to the *Ella,* the captain of the *Hidalgo* told them that the haul was considerably lower than anticipated and that instead of an $82 payment, they were now in considerable debt to the shipping company. The men became angry and refused to leave until their captain paid them correctly. At this point, they were arrested on a complaint from the shipping commissioner and thrown in jail (likely to prevent them from deserting their new ship) and released just in time to sail on the *Ella*. These incidents happened all too often on the Pacific Coast. According to the *CSJ,* the same thing happened to the *Reindeer* and *Seabreeze* crews just a week earlier.

As Greenhorn and Lindholm learned, the payment system not only shackled sailors to specific ships or captains, but it also shackled them to the industry itself. If a sailor managed to finish the contract without "spending" *all* his money along the way, the maritime payment system still encouraged debt dependency. When ships' captains discharged their crews, sailors often had to wait up to ten days to receive their wages—and that was only if the value of the wages were not in dispute.[26] If they were, it could take up to a year to receive payment, if at all.[27] This meant that sailors were discharged in their homeport in the United States without any money. Furuseth again explained the problems with this system to Congress, stating, "[k]eeping a man on shore after his discharge from a vessel without the payment of his wages . . . forces him into the boarding houses, where he can get board and lodging on credit."[28] Even if a sailor decided that the horrendous working conditions of a merchant ship were too much to bear, the crimping system made it difficult for them to explore other avenues of employment, and the cycle of dependency continued.

The payment system dovetailed with the industry's infamous legal shackles to create a labor process that left sailors with such little autonomy that even the simple act of quitting their job was often not an option since desertion was a criminal offense in the United States and many other nations.[29] When a sailor deserted his ship, under the maritime law of 1790 and the Shipping Commissioners Act of 1872, shipping companies could request assistance from state, local, or federal officials in tracking down the sailor. In which case, the sailor was either returned to his vessel and forced to complete the contract or jailed for up to six months.[30] Even if the sailor managed to elude law enforcement, he would still lose all of his earned wages because they were paid only at the end of their contract. If a sailor chose to exercise the one method of resistance available, he was surrendering his unpaid wages back to the shipping company.

Indeed, the fact that many maritime workers chose this speaks to the brutal conditions and violent treatment visited upon sailors at the hands of officers, especially in the foreign trade. The brutality that sailors too often endured consisted of everything from deliberate malnourishment to outright murder. In April 1890, the steamship *Reuce* arrived in San Francisco with all but three of its crew of twenty sick with severe cases of scurvy from malnourishment. Additionally, the crew reported that the officers routinely beat and brutalized the crew throughout the long journey from New York to the Pacific Coast.[31] A few months later, a sailor named Frank Lawler accused the *Louisiana*'s first mate of striking the crew with a belaying pin.[32] In one particularly brutal incident, Lawler said the first mate used the belaying pin to beat a sailor unconscious and then had him placed in irons until he woke up. The first mate also forced Lawler to work a long shift after stepping on a rusty nail at great pain.[33] In May 1892, Louis Beauveer told the *Coast Seamen's Journal* that his officers treated sailors "worse than brutes."[34] Beauveer said the officers routinely whipped the crew and that one of the mates "knocked [him] senseless," again with a belaying pin. The mate then proceeded to drag Beauveer to his cabin and kicked him until he became too tired to go on kicking.[35] A few years earlier, in March 1890, the *CSJ* reported that James Macdonald, first mate of the steamer *Al-Ki,* was so brutal that one sailor jumped to his death trying to avoid Macdonald's wrath. The union later found out that Macdonald was actually the assumed name of a notorious first mate, known only as Watts, who served four years in San Quentin prison for brutalizing the crew of the *Gatherer.* This was after a jury acquitted Watts of murdering a crew member on a technicality.[36]

Legislative efforts to reform the brutalization and exploitation of sailors began in the early 1870s as Congress attempted to end the crimping system. The 1872 Shipping Commissioners Act created the Office of the Shipping Commissioner, which was to oversee the hiring and discharge of seamen and settle disputes between sailor and master.[37] The idea was that all sailors would sign employment contracts in the presence of a government official to certify that they were not coerced into the service of shipping companies and were of sound mind.[38] This hopefully ensured that captains did not have sailors dragged aboard their ships from the boardinghouses in a drunken stupor—a practice known as "shanghaiing."[39] Twelve years later, the Dingley Act of 1884 banned the allotment of wages to anyone except the sailor and his wife or close relative to cut crimps and labor agents out of the hiring process.[40]

Despite these reform efforts, the financial and legal shackles proved persistent. The Dingley Act reforms were too much as far as the shipping companies were concerned. It took only two years for the shipping industry to neutralize the act's attempted reformation of the crimping system. In 1886 Congress passed an amendment to the Dingley Act that allowed for the allotment of wages to "original creditors."[41] This change ensured that crimps would continue to be a mainstay within the industry for some time since they qualified as "original creditors." Moreover, while the Commissioner's Act provided state supervision over the hiring process, it affirmed the criminalization of desertion by specifying a three- month prison sentence.[42]

Ironically, this measure led to the temporary abolition of imprisonment for desertion in the coastwise trade (trade between U.S. ports). In 1874 shipping companies complained to Congress that the provisions of the 1872 Act were too burdensome in the coasting trade since a voyage might be as short as ten miles.[43] This led Congress to amend the act by exempting the coastwise trade from the law altogether, including imprisonment for desertion. However, this, too, would prove short-lived. By 1890 the shipping companies forced a bill through Congress that explicitly applied the desertion penalties of the Shipping Commissioners Act to the coastwise trade.[44] After almost two decades of legislative reform, both the crimping system and the criminal penalty for desertion in the foreign and coastwise trade remained firmly in place.

However, efforts to domesticate the merchant marine were given a significant boost by the late 1880s and early 1890s when the recently formed Sailor's Union of the Pacific and its national arm, the International Seamen's Union of America, began a comprehensive legislative lobbying effort under the leadership of SUP secretary and ISU president Andrew Furuseth. The SUP was initially founded in 1885 as the Coast Seamen's Union by a group of socialists led by an eccentric lawyer named Burnette G. Haskell. However, Haskell's control over the SUP did not last long, especially after he led an unsuccessful strike in 1886 and participated in a failed scheme to create a socialist utopian community partially financed by union funds. These failures allowed Furuseth and Walter Macarthur to take over the organization in 1887. Once in control, Furuseth and his allies affiliated the CSU with the American Federation of Labor and its craft union philosophy, with Macarthur eventually taking charge of the *Coast Seaman's Journal.*

Like Furuseth, Macarthur was a recent immigrant to the United States, arriving in San Francisco from Scotland in the mid-1880s. Born in 1862, he first went to sea in 1876 at the age of fourteen, eventually reaching the rank of able seamen in 1881. By the late 1880s, Macarthur permanently settled in San Francisco and became an active member in the nascent SUP. He was elected business manager of the *CSJ* in 1891 and then editor in 1895, a position he held until 1911 when he became the harbor commissioner for San Francisco. Macarthur easily transitioned to his new role as a "white shirt" sailor, and his position as journal editor allowed him to lean into his more literary sensibility. In his long career, Macarthur would author several books on sailing and maritime law. He was a kind of Melvillian poet sailor. Indeed, his protégée and successor at the *CSJ,* Paul Scharrenberg, described Macarthur as a "high class [*sic*] gentleman . . . in all respects."[45]

Though not present during the formative years of the SUP and the ISU like Furuseth and Macarthur, Paul Scharrenberg became not only a major force within the sailors' unions but also in both California and national labor politics. On paper, he seemed to be the most career-oriented SUP leader. Born into a middle-class family in Hamburg, Germany, in 1877, Scharrenberg's fortunes took a turn when his father died just before the young Paul's twelfth birthday. As a result, Scharrenberg left school for the working world. Having grown up on the tales and adventures of his seafaring grandfather, he signed onto a ship and began his life at sea as a young teenager. Scharrenberg soon found his way to New York, taking jobs up and down the Atlantic from South America to Canada. By March 1898, at the age of twenty-one, he arrived in San Francisco after having survived a shipwreck near Halfmoon Bay, just south of the city. He soon joined the SUP, and after taking classes at the local YMCA to improve his English, Scharrenberg started working with Macarthur as business manager of the *CSJ* in 1901.[46] He would go on to become editor in 1911 when Macarthur was appointed harbor commissioner. A year before, Scharrenberg was first elected secretary of the California Federation of Labor, a position he would hold until 1937 when he became the AFL's legislative representative in Washington. In 1943 California Governor Earl Warren enlisted Scharrenberg to serve as director of the State's department of industrial relations until his retirement in 1955.[47]

Yet no one loomed larger over both the SUP and the ISU than Andrew Furuseth, or "Andy" as his friends and comrades called him. From the early 1890s to the late 1910s, it was his union. In Furuseth's heyday, the membership not only revered him, but he was also a major voice in the AFL-led craft union movement. His knowledge of maritime affairs and maritime law was unmatched, impressing congressmen, maritime lawyers, and even shipping company executives.

In his long tenure as president of the ISU and secretary of the SUP, Furuseth would become an almost mythical figure in the annals of U.S. maritime history. He was less polished than Macarthur. But if Macarthur was like a Melville, Furuseth was more like a character created by Melville. Much like Ahab, Furuseth spent his entire career with a single-minded, near-obsessive focus on sailors' freedom—freedom from the industry's arcane legal shackles and from competition with racial others.[48] Born in Norway in 1854, he grew up dreaming of becoming a military officer. When the admissions board of Norway's officer training school (its West Point equivalent) shattered those dreams by rejecting his application, Furuseth turned to a life at sea, hoping to find adventure, learn new languages, and see the world. He was a stoic man with a flair for the dramatic, often blurting out, "I will stake my reputation of twenty years for veracity and truth," when debating maritime law or policy.[49] He looked the part of the sailor. Furuseth had a weathered face (even when young) and a steely disposition. He lived a solitary life, and despite his reverence among sailors, he never let anyone get too close to him. His friends and comrades rarely saw him in the company of women. Such life choices were often the subject of rumors and gossip concerning his sexuality, though rarely did these stories ever spill out into the open. However, Paul Scharrenberg saw Furuseth's lack of attachments as strategic. He was more like a "catholic priest," Scharrenberg would later state, explaining that Furuseth's "one theory in life" was "that anybody who has anything or wants something can't be independent."[50] Indeed, journalist George P. West would later describe the ISU president as a "Jeffersonian democrat" who "fear[ed] the state" and "oppos[ed] government ownership." Furuseth saw "in unionism the voluntary coming together of men 'who know principles,' and "know what they are fighting for."[51] Despite Furuseth's shortcomings, for better or worse, he dedicated his life to "emancipating" his fellow sailors. Indeed, his biography, published in 1959 by Hyman Weintraub, is titled *Andrew Furuseth: Emancipator of the Seamen.*

Even after his death, the mythology of Andrew Furuseth continued. On what would have been his ninety-second birthday in 1946, former SUP secretary Carl Lynch told the (likely apocryphal) story of Furuseth's organizational awakening in a speech to the Furuseth Club of New York. When he was eighteen or nineteen years old, while sailing in the Indian Ocean, Furuseth was struck with a severe fever and asked one of the officers if he could be relieved. Instead, the officer forced him to work until he could barely stand. After the young sailor finally made his way to his bunk, Furuseth resolved to kill the officer. However, when he regained his strength, he became ashamed to have even contemplated such a thing. More than that, he realized that killing the officer would accomplish nothing other than to get himself hanged. Instead, he asked himself why sailors did not band together and fight such wretched treatment? At this point he supposedly decided to dedicate his life to the cause of sailors by organizing them. In fact, Lynch said that "Andy" later told him that he resolved to head for the United States—the only place Furuseth believed it was possible to fight for the freedom of the world's seamen.[52]

Perhaps some of this story could have been true. He likely was forced to work while ill; that kind of treatment was all too common in the late nineteenth century. In all likelihood, he came to these realizations gradually. Furuseth was eighteen or nineteen in 1873–74, but it would take him another six years to make it to the United States when he arrived in San Francisco harbor in 1880. Or maybe, looking back on that moment later in life, Furuseth saw it as the beginning of his awakening. In any event, it is an origin story that befits the reputation that Andrew Furuseth would build among his sailors—a reputation that would eventually start to fray after the First World War. Until then, Furuseth was a giant of the U.S. and global maritime labor movement who faced few, if any, challenges to his leadership.[53] With Furuseth's tenacity and skill as a lobbyist and organizer, his unparalleled knowledge of maritime affairs and law, combined with his and Scharrenberg's important positions within the AFL, the SUP, and the ISU became an important voice in the early twentieth century labor movement.

The SUP and the ISU leadership were remarkable in their hierarchical rigidity, giving the SUP and ISU leadership, especially Furuseth, unprecedented power over its membership. Even within the SUP, the leadership's San Francisco headquarters held far more authority over other SUP branches on the Pacific Coast. In contrast to the "territorial separation of shore trades," wrote former Seattle branch leader Peter Gill, "the union remained a single coastal unit, retaining authority at headquarters [in San Francisco] and establishing branches in each port as the need for them arose."[54] As a result, there was one membership book that served the whole coast with "no separate designation of branches [that] in any way segregated the members of each locality."[55] The intensely top-down approach to organizing reflected the practical challenges of representing an itinerant membership that not only traversed the Pacific Coast but could often end up on the far corners of the globe. It was not unusual for members to be absent for months at a time. These absences concentrated more power in the hands of the leadership. Indeed, there was little to no internal dissent within the SUP until after the First World War. However, even if there was, the leadership could schedule policy changes subject to a membership vote when dissenters were at sea, a practice Furuseth and the leadership often used.

The SUP leadership was also the preeminent force within the national organization and firmly in control of the *Coast Seamen's Journal,* which was edited and published in San Francisco until 1920. The SUP was the "backbone" of the ISU.[56] Moreover, the *CSJ* was widely influential even beyond the ISU and its branches and became one of the most important labor weeklies west of Chicago.[57] Such influence allowed the SUP to drive the agenda of the ISU. Indeed, the priorities of the ISU in the early years reflected the desires of the SUP leadership more so than any other branch. It was not until the early 1910s that the SUP faced any problems or challenges from its branches beyond the Pacific Coast. But as chapter 3 will demonstrate, Furuseth and the SUP leadership were able to crush the rebellion, though not without consequences—consequences that would become evident after the war. But until then, the ISU was Andrew Furuseth's union. He was highly respected and trusted by the membership. They revered him. And even when he faced serious challenges in the early 1920s, it was more that the old man had lost touch with a new maritime reality. As a result, Furuseth's organization was cohesive and highly disciplined.

More than simply a passionate advocate, Andrew Furuseth was a savvy lobbyist and effective union strategist. Initially Furuseth did not believe unions should get involved in "politics," preferring instead to rely on industrial conflict rather than legislative reform. However, he began to change his tune in the early 1890s when he realized just how effective shipping companies were at marshaling the power of Congress. In 1886–87 Furuseth successfully exploited the loophole that Congress created in 1874 when it amended the 1872 Commissioners Act to exempt the coastwise trade from the burdens of the original act, and with it, sailors from imprisonment for desertion. In the aftermath of Burnette Haskell's failed 1886 strike, shipping companies dropped their wages and introduced a gradebook system to keep track of agitators, something sailors had long resisted. However, Furuseth convinced the membership to accept the gradebook system and go aboard their ships without protest, but at the last minute, before the ship was about to sail, he told them to throw all their belongings overboard and jump ship.[58] This forced the captain to delay the voyage until he could secure another crew. Each replacement crew would repeat this action over and over again, delaying the ship for days and even weeks. Because these sailors could no longer be arrested for desertion and brought back to the ship, wages started to go up, and the shipping companies eventually abolished the gradebooks.[59] Furuseth's strategy provided the union with a powerful bargaining chip against shipping companies' abuses. But once shipping companies convinced Congress to reinstate the penalties for desertion in 1890, the SUP lost its leverage. When this happened, Furuseth threw his support behind a legislative strategy.

In January 1892, the SUP elected a legislative committee to recommend a sweeping series of reforms to end the industry's unfree labor practices. These reforms covered almost everything from safety standards, food rations, living space, and shore leave. Most importantly, the reforms focused on ending the financial and legal shackles that proved so persistent.[60] That same year, the union put its resources behind electing key ally and local attorney James G. Maguire to California's fourth congressional district (Sacramento). So aggressive was Furuseth in championing Maguire that his critics accused him of being a "member of the Democratic Party's waterfront organization, the Neptune Club."[61] Furuseth would have argued that supporting a legislative program to lobby Congress for reform did not mean that he or the union was getting involved in politics. Instead, Furuseth believed that he and the SUP were working to reform an unjust industry. Lobbying Congress and working to elect Maguire was simply the means of accomplishing this goal.

James Maguire would prove an effective and invaluable congressional ally for Furuseth and the SUP. Originally born in Boston to Irish parents in 1854, a year before the family moved to California, where they settled in Santa Cruz County, Maguire began his career in politics at the state level when he was elected to the California State Assembly in 1875, serving only one term. He was admitted to the California bar in 1878 and worked in private practice for a few years, eventually becoming a Superior Court judge in San Francisco County from 1882 to 1888 before returning to private practice. After four years of private practice, Maguire reentered politics when Andrew Furuseth and the SUP backed him in his run for Congress. Maguire was heavily influenced by the ideas of famous social reformer Henry George, particularly his belief that the economic rent of land and resources should be shared collectively through the taxation of land values. Supporters of this policy, known as single-tax men, believed that such a tax would help redistribute economic resources and discourage land speculation. For his efforts, Henry George and other prominent single taxers held a dinner and reception for Maguire in 1889.[62] Maguire's support of the single tax reflected his opposition to corporate control over strategic resources, such as mining and shipping. Like Furuseth, he understood the merchant marine and its workers as a strategic national resource.

Maguire's election to Congress, combined with the SUP's lobbying efforts, proved decisive. By 1894 Maguire convened a series of hearings before the House Committee on Merchant Marine and Fisheries to consider the reforms recommended by the SUP's legislative committee.[63] Andrew Furuseth was front and center at these hearings, providing Congress with firsthand accounts of the industry from the sailor's perspective as well as championing the SUP's legislative recommendations from the 1892 appeal to Congress. According to his biographer, he had an uncanny ability to "appeal to the hearts of legislators."[64] He positioned himself as a humanitarian who abhorred cruelty toward sailors. Moreover, he knew how to discredit his opponents by focusing on the worst abuses that shipping companies inflicted upon sailors and argued that shipping firms cared more about profits than lives. The legislative recommendations of Furuseth and the union leadership were broken up into eight separate bills for consideration before the committee. By the beginning of 1895, the efforts of Furuseth, Maguire, and the legislative committee finally had some measure of success, at least as far as the coastwise trade was concerned.

With the passage of the Maguire Act in February 1895, the SUP and the ISU had established, at least in theory, the domestication of the coastwise trade under a labor process that increasingly relied on a free labor market. Or as Maguire himself said, "[t]he purpose of the seamen's bill introduced by me in Congress is to conserve to your important branch of American industry all of the rights guaranteed by the Constitution of the country," and that "inalienable rights shall appertain wherever the American flag floats, whether it be on sea or on land."[65] The law successfully pushed back against the 1890 law that foisted the disciplinary apparatus of the foreign trade's labor process onto the coastwise trade. The Maguire Act abolished the criminal imprisonment for desertion and banned the allotment of wages as a means of ending the crimping system in the coastwise trade.[66] In the words of the *CSJ*, "[i]t means that the coastwise seamen shall be granted the same rights as a workman ashore to quit his employment."[67] I say "in theory" because the law did not create or empower any workable enforcing mechanism. As the *CSJ* also remarked, "[t]he enforcement of these provisions rests with the seamen themselves through their unions."[68] This statement would prove prophetic.

Though as the SUP and the ISU would soon learn, the problem went beyond simple enforcement and questioned where the domestic labor market ended and the foreign began. It was only three months later that Robert Robertson and company deserted from their vessel in Oregon, leading to the infamous *Arago* decision. Following through on their promise to ensure the law's enforcement, the SUP and the ISU financed Robertson's appeal against his desertion conviction to the nation's highest court. The Supreme Court's 1897 affirmation of Robertson's conviction was because the voyage that Robertson and his compatriots signed on with ended up going as far as Chile, even though the act of desertion took place in an American port. As a result, the court defined Robertson's contract as part of the foreign and not the coastwise trade (which was outside the jurisdiction of the Maguire Act) since it only abolished imprisonment for desertion in the coastwise trade. The *Arago* precedent created a situation whereby the labor process of the foreign trade was leaking into the coastwise or domestic trade. As long as there was a foreign port of destination at some point in the voyage, the court viewed the route as operating outside the domestic or coastwise trade and allowed shipping companies to skirt the protections afforded by the coasting trade under the Maguire Act.

The SUP and the ISU could not abide a porous border between the domestic and the foreign trade. After a year of lobbying from Andrew Furuseth and representative Maguire, the SUP succeeded in stopping the labor process of the foreign trade from leaking into the domestic. In December 1898, the White Act unequivocally ended imprisonment for desertion in the domestic trade. It neutralized the *Arago* precedent by banning the criminal punishment for desertion in American ports, whether part of a foreign voyage or not, though only for American sailors. Moreover, the act also expanded slightly the boundaries of the domestic trade to nearby foreign ports in "Canada, Newfoundland, the West Indies, and Mexico."[69] Additionally, in a blow against the crimping industry, the act allowed sailors in both foreign and domestic trades the right to demand one-half of the wages they were due in any port, though again only for American sailors in American ports. Despite this, the bill still permitted allotment to "original creditors" (crimps) in the foreign trade, and affirmed imprisonment for desertion of U.S sailors in foreign ports and foreign-flagged vessels in U.S. ports. Even with these limitations, the White Act had established a firmer line between domestic and foreign, ensuring that shipping companies could not skirt domestic protections while in U.S. ports. Despite significant progress in reforming the domestic trade, Congress also provided shipping companies with the means to undermine the SUP's attempts to reform the foreign trade and potentially break the union movement itself.

The Maritime Labor Process and the Internationalization of the Maritime Labor Market in the Foreign Trade

Parallel to the postbellum maritime reform efforts aimed at protecting sailors were two key developments that would forever change the industry and undermine attempts to extend the domestication of the maritime labor process into the foreign maritime trade: the rise of steam technology and the internationalization of the maritime labor market. These changes provided U.S. shipping companies with a means of bypassing the new regulations put in place between 1872 and 1898. Access to an international labor market created a reserve source of labor on hand to help fight the creeping threat of maritime labor organization, especially on the West Coast. If the SUP and the ISU became too bold in their agitation, shipping companies could simply replace their members. These developments dramatically expanded the scope of their labor pool. Not only did they have access to a global labor market, but steam technology meant that the pool of potential sailors expanded since skill was less important because shipping company executives now believed anyone could do this job.[70] As a result, shipping companies on the West Coast began turning to the labor markets of China as a means of undermining maritime reform efforts and unionization. This would become *the* challenge for the SUP and the ISU over the next thirty years. These developments ensured that shipping capital could maintain the unfree orientation of the industry. Steam technology and the internationalization of maritime labor transformed the dynamic between captain and crew into an imperial relationship since shipping companies would no longer rely on a workforce of citizens or recent white immigrants protected under the U.S. Constitution.

The mid-1880s saw a significant shift in U.S. maritime policy. Under section twenty of the 1884 Dingley Act, U.S. shipping companies were permitted to sign up foreign crews in foreign ports without having to reship them in the United States.[71] With the Dingley Act, American shipping companies had gained access to a global labor market, which at worst allowed them to replace the much more expensive American sailors with cheaper foreign workers, or at the very least, serve as a disciplinary tool to bring down the wages of U.S. ports. At the same time, the rise of steam technology on merchant vessels convinced shipping company executives that skilled seamanship was no longer necessary.[72] The emergence of steam power combined with the effects of the Dingley Act allowed shipping companies to source non-unionized, less-skilled workers in lower-wage labor markets.[73] This was a boon to the U.S. shipping industry that had long struggled with the United States' status as a high-wage labor market for seaman. Indeed, as Andrew Furuseth explained to Congress, the Dingley Act "was enacted specifically for the purposes of equalizing the wages of American and foreign vessels in the foreign carrying trade."[74] While it affected U.S. ports all over the country, it was most pronounced on the West Coast.

What set West Coast sailors' experience apart was the greater wage disparity between the labor markets of American ports and those in Asia, as well as the racial dimensions of that disparity. On the East Coast, foreign sailors began making significant inroads, but the vast majority of those foreign sailors were European. Even though the wages of American sailors were higher on average than their British and European counterparts, the difference was less pronounced than that between white American and Chinese seamen. The Dingley Act had effectively linked the Pacific Coast maritime labor market in the foreign trade with the labor markets of Hong Kong and Shanghai. A working-class protest movement may have closed off U.S. capital's access to the labor markets of China in 1882, but it took only two years for a small tear to appear in the fabric of exclusion. The Dingley Act pulled workers from the Far East into the service of U.S. economic and imperial expansion, disrupting pre-existing maritime labor markets on the West Coast.[75] However, Pacific Coast shipping companies were initially slow in embracing the promise of cheaper all-Chinese crews. It was not until the early 1890s, almost ten years after the passage of the Dingley Act, that they began signing up Chinese crews in Hong Kong and Shanghai. Part of this likely had to do with the fact that steam technology was not quite as widespread yet, and shipping companies still viewed skilled seamen as necessary. More importantly, the early 1890s was also when the SUP began to influence U.S. maritime policy. In 1892 the SUP issued its appeal to Congress announcing the union's legislative agenda, one year after the first reported incident of a Chinese crew on U.S. ships in San Francisco. The use of Chinese crews would continue with greater ubiquity thereafter.[76]

U.S. shipping companies began testing the union's resolve by pushing the limits of both the Dingley Act and the Chinese Exclusion Act. In the summer of 1892, the steamship *City of Peking* of the Pacific Mail Steamship Company entered San Francisco Harbor with seventy-six Chinese crewmembers sourced in Hong Kong. This was perfectly legal under the Dingley Act. What the SUP took issue with was the Pacific Mail Company's attempt to transfer the crew from the *City of Peking* to another ship, the *Peru,* in San Francisco harbor. As the *Coast Seamen's Journal* argued, "[u]nder the Dingley Act a ship may sign her crew in China and take them back there, but there is no provision in that or any other act for a transfer from one vessel to another."[77] By transferring the crew to another ship, the SUP argued that they were essentially being reshipped.

For a crew or an individual sailor to be legally reshipped in the United States, the crew must sign on in the "presence of a Commissioner and a copy of the articles containing the name, age and personal description of each member, together with the signature, must be lodged before the collector of Customs" as specified by the 1872 Shipping Commissioner's Act.[78] Yet if the crew were to sign before the shipping commissioner, the SUP maintained that they would be in "violation of the Chinese Exclusion Act in spirit, if not actually in letter, for the process of signing before the Commissioner implies a landing."[79] The SUP appealed to Treasury Secretary Charles W. Foster, who ruled that the Pacific Mail Company did violate the Shipping Commissioners Act and thus the Chinese Exclusion Act, and ordered the seventy-five Chinese crewmembers returned to Hong Kong at the company's expense.[80]

Despite the SUP's successful appeal to the Treasury Department, in many ways, this was a hollow victory since it demonstrated how to cut white American sailors out of the foreign trade. The ruling established exactly how a shipping company could sign on a crew in China without violating either the Exclusion Act or the Shipping Commissioners Act. So long as shipping companies kept the crew on the same ship that they signed on to in Hong Kong or Shanghai, they would not have to sign new articles in front of a shipping commissioner in the United States. As a result, they would not violate the Exclusion Act since the crew would never officially "land" in the United States.

What is more, the use of Chinese sailors would allow shipping companies a legal way around the decriminalization of desertion. Indeed, the combination of the Maguire and White Acts ended the criminalization of desertion in U.S. ports (whether as part of a domestic or foreign voyage) for U.S.-flagged vessels. However, as Andrew Furuseth explained, the White Act "does no good to the Chinese signed in any foreign territory—the exclusion law holds them on board."[81] Since the idea behind the criminalization of desertion was to neutralize a sailor's autonomous movement with the threat of prison time, exclusion served a similar disciplinary function. Chinese sailors technically would have the right to desert, but they would not be able to legally enter the United States because it would violate the Exclusion Act.[82] This provided further incentive for U.S. shipping companies to employ all-Chinese crews in place of white Americans or recent white immigrants on the Pacific Coast.

The shift to foreign sailors, especially those of Chinese descent, undermined the SUP's efforts to reform the maritime labor process in the foreign trade and created an imperial relationship between shipping capital and its labor. Though white West Coast sailors may have ceased to be democratic citizens while aboard ship, back in San Francisco, they regained all the rights conferred upon them as citizens or residents of the country under the U.S. Constitution. For instance, they could organize a labor journal, they could get allies like James Maguire elected to Congress to help enact their labor reform program, and they had access to the courts to enforce maritime reform legislation.

Few of these avenues were available to foreign, but especially Chinese sailors. People of Chinese descent were deemed racially ineligible for U.S. citizenship. Their ability to testify in court initially was called into question since they could not swear on the Bible. Between 1854 and 1873, Chinese individuals could not legally testify in court in the state of California.[83] Additionally, U.S. shipping companies sourced these workers from colonized space in Hong Kong or imperial space in Shanghai, where the United States and other European empires were economically dominant and enjoyed the privilege of extraterritorial legal protection. Americans and Europeans were not subject to Chinese law, only the law of their home countries.[84] This situation would make it difficult for Chinese sailors to report any abuse on the part of white American officers because Chinese sailors' access to American courts was hardly secure. Furthermore, given the Treasury Department's ruling that the reshipment of Chinese sailors in American ports constituted "landing," and therefore admission to the United States, shipping companies had every incentive to keep Chinese sailors onboard their vessels and far away from U.S. authorities—else they risked violating the Exclusion Act.

The use of Chinese sailors increased as the United States more formally extended its imperial reach to the doorstep of China during the Spanish-American War and its aftermath. Ships owned by the Pacific Mail Steamship Company and contracted by the War Department to ferry troops to the Philippines increasingly turned to Chinese-crewed vessels. In the summer of 1898, the *Coast Seamen's Journal* reported three separate incidents. One incident occurred in June when the steamship *China* left San Francisco with an all-Chinese manned deck and engine room crew.[85] A month later, the steamer *Peru* shipped an all-Chinese crew with white officers.[86] In response, the SUP lodged an official protest with the War Department and "several members of congress [*sic*]" in the case of the *Peru*.[87] The SUP's congressional representatives told the union leadership that they "had nothing to do with the case."[88] As the *CSJ* explained, "nobody seems to have authority to stop the shipment of Chinese."[89] Unfortunately for the SUP, the journal's assessment was accurate. Since these incidents did not involve the transferring of Chinese sailors in San Francisco harbor from one ship to another, neither the Pacific Mail Company nor the War Department violated both the Exclusion Law and the Shipping Commissioners Act. In fact, the United States government had been financing Chinese-crewed vessels for quite some time by offering mail contracts and subsidies to the Pacific Mail Company.[90] Despite these setbacks, the SUP had more luck with a third vessel, the *Arizona,* which was planning on shipping an all-Chinese crew.

Remembering the Treasury Department's ruling from the 1892 incident involving the *City of Peking,* the SUP argued that since the United States government purchased the *Arizona* and its crew from a British firm, the use of Chinese crews *did* violate the exclusion law and the Shipping Commissioners Act. Though the government did not physically transfer the crew of the *Arizona* from one ship to another, they were transferred from one flag to another. The SUP argued "the transference of the Arizona's Chinese crew from the British to the American flag, along with the vessel herself" was tantamount to bringing "the Chinese legally into the country, as much as though they had been first landed from the British or other foreign vessel[s] and then shipped on board an American vessel."[91] After failing to make any headway with local military officials, the SUP in cooperation with the San Francisco Labor Council (which the SUP were founding members of) began aggressively protesting against the use of Chinese sailors on the *Arizona,* even appealing directly to President McKinley in a letter dated August 5th, 1898.[92] This lobbying campaign paid off. Two weeks later, a reply from Assistant Secretary of War G. D. Meiklejohn (on behalf of President McKinley) informed the SUP that the Chinese sailors on the *Arizona* would be discharged and replaced by a white American crew.[93] Yet like in the case of the *City of Peking,* this victory was specific to the circumstances unique to the *Arizona.* The two previous incidents involving the steamers *China* and the *Peru* still managed to ship a Chinese crew despite protests from the SUP and the San Francisco Labor Council, and there was nothing, legally speaking, the SUP could do about it.

The emerging internationalization of the maritime labor force, particularly on the West Coast, provided U.S. shipping companies with a way around legislation that was chipping away at the unfree practices of the foreign merchant trade. Moreover, the use of Chinese sailors who were ineligible for U.S. citizenship and lacked access to the privileges that came with it only amplified the asymmetry of power between U.S. shipping capital and its labor. This also provided shipping companies with the means to help bring down the maritime wages in San Francisco, which were comparatively high because of the West Coast's relative isolation from the larger labor markets of the East Coast (a fact true of San Francisco labor generally). The Dingley Act ended this isolation by linking the maritime labor markets of San Francisco with the Far East, creating a much more competitive labor market for white West Coast sailors. Shipping companies could completely cut white American sailors out of the trade or force them to accept lower and lower wages until the job became even less attractive, and they left on their own. Unfortunately for SUP members, the disruption caused by the internationalization of the maritime labor market was only in its beginning stages. American capital's potential access to the labor markets of the Far East was about to increase dramatically with the annexation of Hawai'i and the Philippines.

"A Leak in the Ship of State": Pacific Annexation and the Domestic Labor Market

To the SUP and the AFL, the annexation of the Philippines and Hawai'i was ultimately a question of labor, not a stepping-stone to a vast imaginary market teeming with potential consumers.[94] Instead, it was a stepping-stone to a vast source of cheap labor teeming with potential "coolies," that had the potential to destabilize or disrupt the domestic U.S. labor market—much like how the internationalization of the maritime labor process was beginning to destabilize the West Coast maritime labor market. The absorption of a vast, racialized Pacific proletariat with the annexation of Hawai'i and the Philippines scaled up this process to the national level. What was once a problem for a group of peripheral workers in a peripheral industry in a peripheral part of the country now had the potential to affect all workers, and the SUP knew it. Pacific imperial expansion ripped a hole straight through the Chinese Exclusion Act. With the annexation of the Philippines came an entrenched Chinese community dating back to the Ming Dynasty of the sixteenth century.[95] With Hawai'i, the United States acquired a plantation economy worked primarily by imported Chinese contract laborers.[96]

An act meant to insulate the U.S. labor market by stopping Chinese immigration could potentially collapse under the weight of an advancing imperial state that brought over 150 thousand Chinese individuals under U.S. dominion.[97] Of course, Pacific annexation also came with eight million Filipinos/as. But it was the Chinese that most concerned the country's labor leaders. Moreover, the SUP and the AFL argued that the annexation of Hawai'i and the Philippines was fundamentally different from previous U.S. territorial expansion because neither territory could "abide" American settlement. In other words, white settler colonialism was not possible in either Pacific territory. Furthermore, the United States was not just absorbing space, but laborers and labor systems. Would the United States also annex the labor systems under which Hawaiian plantation workers toiled? Pacific annexation, therefore, not only would destabilize the domestic U.S. labor market but also potentially challenge the ascendency of free labor within the nation. The SUP's recent legal dilemma concerning the *Arago* decision convinced them that the peoples and practices of the annexed territories could seep into the nation.

The SUP's position that the annexation of Pacific territories was fundamentally a question of labor was based on the leadership's view that the admission of Hawai'i would bring with it a system of labor that was at odds with the United States' domestic free-labor market. In November 1897, as sugar interests in both the United States and Hawai'i were again raising the issue of annexation, the *CSJ* told its readers that "it is well known that the labor of the Islands is practically slave labor."[98] A few weeks later, the SUP argued, "If [Hawai'i is] maintained as a territory it will be under a slave system."[99] Similarly, AFL Secretary P. J. McGuire stated that the principal objection to the annexation of Hawai'i was that "it would be tantamount to the admission of a slave state."[100] How exactly the SUP defined "slavery" varied. At times, they based their definition upon a more specific understanding of Hawai'i's labor laws. In this sense, they were mainly referring to the fact that under the territory's contract labor laws, plantation owners could have their workers criminally prosecuted for breaking their contracts, not unlike in the maritime industry. Yet more often than not, the union leadership's thinking was underpinned by a virulent racist discourse that essentialized Asians as inherently servile. Indeed, the legacy of this thinking stretches back to the first wave of anti-Chinese hysteria in the 1870s and the current practice of U.S. shipping companies employing Chinese-crewed steamships. In the same article of November 3, the *CSJ* maintained, "if there is one fact of history that stands out more clearly than any other, it is that the Mongols are essentially a servile race."[101] The assumption that Asians were necessarily a "slave race" colored all aspects of the SUP and the AFL's attitude toward Pacific annexation.[102]

As a result, the SUP and AFL's attitudes toward Philippine annexation were informed largely by the leadership's belief in the inherent servility of Asian workers rather than any specific knowledge about the country's labor system. Like most of the American public, the union leadership did not know very much about the Philippines. Indeed, the famous (though likely apocryphal) story that aids had to show President McKinley the location of the Philippines on a map after the American victory is demonstrative of the broader American public's paucity of knowledge about the archipelago. In many ways, the Philippines was more of an afterthought, with Hawai'i taking most of the SUP's focus. This likely had to do with the union's greater understanding of Hawai'i's specific labor systems, its closer proximity to the West Coast, and the fact that it relied on imported Asian workers under American plantation interests. For instance, in November 1898, the *Coast Seamen's Journal* stated that they "opposed Hawaiian annexation for reasons sufficient to have condemned the scheme. . . . We are now opposed to Philippine annexation for the same reasons, and with hope of a different result."[103] What is more, though there was little if any mention of the labor systems that existed in the Philippines, the focus was on the Filipinos and Chinese that lived there rather than the colony's specific labor practices. As the *CSJ* added, "[i]t is not conceivable that the country will ever give voluntary consent to the plan of annexing a multitude of Asiatic slaves and savages."[104] Again the assumption is that Filipinos were slaves by their very nature. Samuel Gompers made a similar argument against Philippine annexation in a speech he delivered at Saratoga Springs, New York, in the summer of 1898. The AFL president argued that preventing the annexation of the Philippines would save "American labor from the evil influence of close and open competition of millions of semi-barbaric laborers in the Philippine[s]."[105] Whether these new territories operated under what the SUP and the AFL hyperbolically referred to as a slave system or were populated by "servile," "slave-like" people, labor was fundamental to the SUP and the broader AFL-led labor movement's objection to the annexation of both Hawai'i and the Philippines.[106] Moreover, the SUP quickly dismissed the possibility of reforming or altering Hawai'i's labor system to make annexation more palatable.

Reforming the labor regime of Hawai'i was impossible because the SUP and the AFL did not believe the territory could ever support free labor given its tropical location. In November 1897, the SUP observed that "nowhere within the tropic zone, nor within a few degrees either side of it, has free labor maintained itself on the soil of any country."[107] Similarly, Samuel Gompers argued that "the climate of the Philippines forbids forever manual labor by Americans, as it does the planting there of [*sic*] American families."[108]Additionally, the SUP pointed out that "the islands lie within the zone [of the earth] that has, up to the present time, been worked by slave labor."[109] The implications of Hawai'i's tropicality immediately disqualified the islands for annexation or incorporation into the United States. Indeed, behind the SUP and the AFL leadership's understanding of the latitudinal distribution of the world's labor systems was a racialized thinking that linked climate and racial origins.

The main reason why the earth's tropical zone could not support a free labor regime was that it could not support a white population. As the SUP saw it, another key objection to annexation was "the unfitness of the Hawaiian islands [*sic*] as an abiding place for the American people"—and by American, they meant white.[110] The inability of Hawai'i to abide an American or white population was neither because of distance nor the fact that it was separated by half an ocean. After all, the Pacific Coast is just as far from the eastern seaboard as Hawai'i is from San Francisco, and Americans did not historically view overseas travel as an obstacle to migration. In fact, before the completion of the transcontinental railroad, the majority of Americans that made it to California came by ship via the Isthmus of Panama, especially since the mid-1850s.[111]

Drawing on the era's emerging "scientific" literature that entangled ideas about race, labor, and climate, the SUP argued that whites or "Anglo-Saxons" could not live in such a tropical environment, observing that, "looking over the world we fail to find Anglo-Saxons as a worker on the land anywhere within the tropical zone."[112] In July 1898, as the debate over annexation was reaching a fever pitch, the *Coast Seamen's Journal* reiterated this belief, stating that "tropical lands are unfitted [*sic*] for American labor."[113] Without a white working population, the SUP argued that the islands could not support a free labor system since all "Anglo-Saxons" had ever been able to do in the tropical zone is little more "than take possessions of the people in tropical countries, leaving them to cultivate the soil."[114]

Gompers echoed these sentiments and added that even if the Philippines had a temperate climate, the islands were still unsuitable for American settlement. To contextualize his thinking, the AFL president explained that the only other time the United States had "ruled savages against their will" was "in the process of our uprooting of the Indian tribes."[115] Still, Gompers added, we did this only because it was "reasonably certain their [indigenous peoples'] places would soon be taken by a settled white population," much larger in numbers.[116] However, Gompers argued: "In the Philippines, with its 7,000,000 or 8,000,000 [people] in an area the size of the State of Texas, no such change can ever take place."[117] The president of the country's largest labor organization was essentially arguing that the real problem of Philippine annexation was that it would be too difficult for the United States to dispossess its indigenous inhabitants from their land and replace them with white American settlers.

The inability of "Anglo-Saxons" to work in the Hawaiian Islands solidified the SUP and AFL leadership's conclusion that free labor could never take root—a view they believed the recent history of imperial expansion supported. Specifically, they linked what they called "colonization" with the emergence of free labor in Canada, Australia, and New Zealand—three white settler colonies that were "peopled by the mother stock," mostly working-class individuals from Great Britain.[118] Conversely, colonies acquired by "conquest" and "domination," such as the British possessions in the East and West Indies, which are "owned by the mother country but peopled by foreign races," led to unfree labor systems.[119] In the case of the settler societies, the colonizer worked the land but the conqueror, according to the SUP, "does not really own the land, but the people who work it."[120] To further drive home the point about the connection between different repertoires of imperial expansion and the emergence of free and "unfree" labor, the SUP added that, "[w]e see the difference between colonization and conquest in . . . our own southern and northern states."[121] The comparison with the American South is telling because it distills the central fear the SUP and the AFL had with Hawaiian or Philippine annexation, a fear similar to the one white northern workers had over southern slavery, especially its potential expansion.

For the SUP and the AFL, Hawai'i and the broader Pacific region were places where incompatible people and labor practices came from rather than a new frontier of promise and opportunity for white Americans to settle. In this sense, the SUP and the AFL were part of a long and ongoing tradition that sought to define the Pacific to suit their ends. Indeed, Pacific historian Arif Dirlik posited that "the idea of the Pacific . . . is not so much a well-defined idea as it is a discourse that seeks to construct what is pretended to be its point of departure."[122] The Pacific, therefore, was necessarily constructed as a place of unfreedom (set against a free U.S. West Coast) that would infect the United States with slavery once again. This is why the SUP argued that all the United States would gain from Hawaiian annexation was "50,000 coolies, and a leper settlement of 2,500 living corpses."[123]

This viewpoint was part of a broader transnational discourse endemic to Anglo white settler societies that viewed Asian or Chinese laborers as nothing more than harbingers of "slavery" that would destroy the free, white settler society. This was not about the plight of the imported Hawaiian contract workers. The SUP and the AFL were less interested in how "slavery" affected those living under it. Indeed, this is consistent with Mae Ngai's recent work, who argued that "slavery remained the central organizing concept of a global discourse against Chinese immigration. Americans . . . opposed the slavery of the Chinese but did not support their freedom."[124] The SUP and the AFL were no different. They could never stand up for Chinese or Asian freedom because they believed slavery and servitude was their natural laboring condition. The SUP could only ever see Chinese laborers as either slaves or "perpetual aliens."[125] Indeed, this also connects to a specific vein of antebellum anti-slavery discourse. In antebellum America, many abolitionists or "free soilers" felt similarly about slavery in that opposition to slavery was also about opposition to the presence of "Africans" within the United States.[126] White Americans who opposed slavery were afraid of its potential to spread westward. Or, even more alarmingly, after the infamous Dred Scott decision, there was widespread fear that slavery could spread into the free labor northern states.[127] This was the basis for Lincoln's famous prescription on the eve of the Civil War that the nation could not live "half slave and half free."[128] The *Coast Seamen's Journal* made a similar statement regarding Hawai'i. Paraphrasing Lincoln, the journal stated: "no country can exist part slave and part free."[129] One system would eventually prevail over the other. This thinking convinced the SUP and the AFL that Hawai'i's labor system would eventually find its way into the nation, and they explained exactly how this could happen.

Both the SUP and the AFL believed that there were insufficient legal barriers to prevent Hawai'i's labor system from "leaking" into the nation and argued that the *Arago* case might even provide legal precedent to encourage such unfree labor encroachment. This is part of the reason why the sailors often referred to the case as the "Second Dred Scott decision."[130] The SUP argued that the key to the legal continuation of Hawaii's contract labor system lay in the Supreme Court's willingness to tolerate exceptions to the Thirteenth Amendment based on "exceptional" labor arrangements. Specifically, they were referring to the Supreme Court's logic behind the *Arago* decision. To justify the penal enforcement of maritime labor contracts, the Court argued, "[f]rom the earliest historical period the contract of the sailor has been treated as an *exceptional one*, [emphasis added] and involving, to a certain extent, the surrender of his personal liberty during the life of the contract."[131] The SUP was worried that the *Arago* precedent could give legal sanction to Hawai'i's contract labor laws, should the Court find the labor regime on the islands "exceptional." The AFL's legislative committee came to the same conclusion, pointing out that even if the Organic Act (the law that created the territorial government) incorporated Hawai'i into the laws and Constitution of the United States, the *Arago* precedent ensured "there would be no legal barrier to the continuation of the slavery there existing."[132] Additionally, the SUP felt that Hawaii might be only the beginning of such exceptions, stating in November 1898 "that the law of involuntary servitude now applying to seamen may be applied to other classes whenever deemed necessary."[133] Justice John Marshal Harlan's dissent in the case made the same point. Harlan argued, "those who seek support for extraordinary remedies that encroach upon the liberty of freemen will" refer to the *Arago* case.[134] While the country would eventually begin a debate over whether the Constitution followed the flag, America's West Coast sailors implied as early as late 1898 that it did not matter. The Constitution could follow the flag and tolerate apparent "unconstitutional" labor systems so long as the Supreme Court deemed those labor systems "exceptional." By February 1899, the SUP called attention to the fact that Hawaiian Supreme Court Justice and member of the Hawaiian Commission (the colonial government) Walter F. Frear "publicly declare[d] that the decision in the *Arago* case removes all doubt as to the legality of the contract labor of the islands."[135] But would these exceptions be tolerated *only* outside the nation, whether on ships or in conquered territory?

The SUP and the AFL feared that the *Arago* precedent could go beyond exceptional "*classes* of labor" and make exceptions for whole swaths of territory. "If the United States has the power to impose slave laws upon one part of its territory," the SUP argued, then "it has the power to do the same everywhere throughout it's [*sic*] domination."[136] Planter interests in the American South, who were arguing exactly that, exacerbated the SUP's fears. The *Coast Seamen's Journal* quoted a speech by Senator Benjamin "Pitchfork" Tillman, given on the floor of the Senate during debate over annexation: "We will have equality on the question of contract laborers. If you [northern imperialists] are going to have them when you annex the Hawaiian Islands, we will have them in our states, too!"[137] Aspects of this tension have been explored before. C. Vann Woodward first noted the South's use of the "imperial" moment to convince northern liberals to turn a blind eye to the emerging system of segregation.[138] The Mississippi plan became the American plan, as Woodward argued. However, the sailors took Tillman literally. They felt he and his allies wanted to use Hawai'i as a means to reintroduce "slavery" into the nation rather than simply justify segregation, as Woodward contended. For example, the *Coast Seamen's Journal* argued that Tillman was making "no idle threat; it is a plain declaration of purposes that has all the force and consistency of American constitutional law behind it."[139]

Tillman, whether serious or not, seemed to confirm everything that the SUP feared could happen. The *Arago* precedent led the SUP and the AFL to conclude that there was nothing the government could do to prevent southern plantation owners from "making good on the intention to extend slavery from the Islands to the South. When that is done what is to prevent the extension of the same system to 'we of the north.' "[140] The existence of Hawai'i's "slave system" was a threat to free labor everywhere under American dominion: "This country must either be all slave or all free," the SUP argued.[141] If the United States eventually admitted Hawai'i to statehood with their "plantation owners in Congress," the SUP reasoned, "the influence of the 'peculiar conditions' will be felt in the degradation and repression of American labor."[142] The annexation of contract labor interests in Hawai'i could strengthen the hand of similar interests within the nation, such as West Coast shipping companies. Given the SUP's fight to abolish maritime labor contracts, the incorporation of interests devoted to contract labor into the nation would be another setback.

While it might be tempting to dismiss the SUP's fears as a convenient justification against annexation, it is important to remember that from the SUP leadership's perspective, the idea that unfree labor practices could leak into the nation was very real. After all, they had seen it before in their industry. The 1890 amendment to the Shipping Commissioners Act applied the provisions of the Commissioners Act to the coasting trade, including the criminal punishment for desertion.[143] Moreover, when the SUP thought they had plugged the leak with the 1895 Maguire Act, the Supreme Court's *Arago* opinion found a way to justify, albeit in more limited circumstances, the criminalization of desertion for Americans in American ports.[144] Even though the White Act had finally and permanently abolished the criminal punishment for desertion in the coasting trade by December 1898, the United States had already annexed Hawai'i and the Philippines. The moment the SUP succeeded in securing the coasting trade from the most restrictive practices of the foreign trade, the United States had a much larger leak that went well beyond the shipping industry.

This also helps explain the SUP's skepticism over the "incorporation" of Hawai'i into the Constitution and laws of the United States under the Organic Act of 1900. While the SUP celebrated the end of the islands' contract labor laws, they felt this was mostly symbolic since the island's labor force was still overwhelmingly Asian. Such a demographic make-up would continue to discourage American colonization of Hawai'i because whites would not be able to compete with Asian workers, even if they could brave the colony's tropical climate.[145] Furthermore, the SUP doubted the constitutionality of section 101 of the act, which prohibited Chinese residents of the islands from entering the continental United States.[146] Even though the Organic Act seemingly plugged the Hawaiian aspect of the "leak in the ship of state," given the SUP's recent experience in the maritime industry, they remained skeptical over the permanency of the section. They assumed that some intrepid businessman in cooperation with the state could find a way around it. As a result, the SUP would be center stage in the AFL-led struggle to plug the "leak in the ship of state" created by Pacific annexation.

CHAPTER 2

Does Exclusion Follow the Flag?

Imperial Labor Mobilization, Domestic Organized Labor, and the Emergence of a U.S. Metropole, 1902–1908

With the United States in possession of an expansive transoceanic empire, the emerging U.S. imperial state and its potential partners in private capital faced the challenge of how to make the empire work.[1] After a century of continental, land-based expansion, the United States had to set up far more distant territorial/colonial governments and organize and invest the necessary capital to exploit the resources of the new colonies. Each of these ventures required labor, and lots of it. While the new colonies—but especially the Philippines—had the population necessary to potentially fill the labor needs of the empire, they did not necessarily have the specific kind of labor that U.S. investors desired. Sourcing labor for imperial development was more than mere numbers; they needed the right kind of laborer, and U.S. investors did not think Filipino labor was up to the job.

The Philippines might have eight million potential laborers, but indigenous laborers can be difficult to mobilize and discipline. The early Chesapeake society quickly learned that Native American labor was almost impossible to discipline, even when enslaved, and shortly after that turned to imported indentured servants from Europe and then slaves from West Africa. After the Mexican-American War and the acquisition of the trans-Mississippi West from Mexico in 1848, the development of that region was contingent upon the importation of Chinese contract labor across the world's largest ocean, rather than the hundreds of thousands of Native Americans already living there. The American planters who developed Hawai'i in the nineteenth century also made use of imported Chinese labor rather than indigenous Hawaiians. Finally, West Coast shipping companies were attempting to transition from white Americans on the Pacific Coast to foreign, mostly Chinese labor sourced in Asia.

Imported mobilized labor might allow Americans looking to invest in the Philippines a level of control over their labor far beyond what was possible with indigenous labor. First, imported workers were more isolated and dependent on their employers, with transportation, food, and living arrangements usually provided by the employer. Additionally, imported workers lacked local community and kinship networks beyond their immediate workplace environment. Second, imported workers could serve as a disciplinary tool to keep indigenous labor in-line with a potential supply of foreign labor waiting in the wings. With that in mind, the newly created Philippine Commission (the colonial government) and its partners in private capital dismissed Filipino labor and laborers as inadequate. Additionally, the recently passed Organic Act halted the endless supply of cheap Chinese labor to Hawai'i by incorporating the territory under the blanket of the Constitution and laws of the United States, which included the Chinese Exclusion Act. As a result, both colonies would have to mobilize and import alternative sources of labor to make the empire work. In the Philippines, imperialists looked toward China to solve their labor problem, and in Hawai'i, the plantation aristocracy looked to Japan. Finally, West Coast shipping companies continued their shift from white sailors to foreign sailors sourced in the Far East.

Meanwhile, the Sailor's Union of the Pacific (SUP) and its national affiliate, the International Seamen's Union of America (ISU), worked with the American Federation of Labor (AFL) to protect their members from the peoples and practices of the Pacific empire. If the administration and American industrialists were grappling with how to make the empire work, the SUP and the AFL were struggling with how to prevent the empire from working against their interests. For organized labor, the emerging U.S. Pacific empire was potentially disruptive to the U.S. domestic labor market by absorbing millions in nonwhite labor competition. This was the crux of why organized labor opposed Pacific annexation in 1898. The AFL and the SUP sought to insulate the free labor domestic market from what they saw as the unfree imperial labor space emerging on the Pacific.

To that end, AFL and SUP leaders took the seemingly paradoxical position of resisting empire by aligning with it. More precisely, organized labor resisted colonial-imperial expansion by advocating legislative policies that affirmed their commitment to white settler colonialism. Nevertheless, by demanding protection from certain parts of the emerging imperial system, labor leaders were implicitly endorsing the concept of colonial imperialism by insisting on a privileged and protected position within an emerging imperial hierarchy. This alignment with empire disrupted the imperial labor process and led to a domestic class struggle for control over the boundaries of the U.S. imperial system. For the AFL- and SUP-led faction of organized labor, controlling the border meant policing the movement of the newly acquired subjects of the American empire, as well as placing limitations on who could enter U.S. imperial formations.[2] For the imperial state and its investors, controlling the borders meant ensuring that organized labor could not influence the repertoire of rule necessary to make the empire work. By restricting the movement of U.S. imperial subjects, organized labor was challenging the imperial state and private capital's desired repertoire of rule by placing limitations on the mobilization of imperial labor.

To police the movement of U.S. imperial subjects, organized labor called for the extension of the Chinese Exclusion Act into the Pacific empire. Extending exclusion into the empire reoriented immigration restriction as an alternative repertoire of imperial rule that sought to limit U.S. colonial subjects' ability to move throughout the imperial system. This alternative challenged the imperial state and its partners in private capital's ability to mobilize the Pacific proletariat. Additionally, the SUP's call to extend exclusion to the deck of U.S. flagged ships went even further by seeking a legislative challenge to an emerging, racially inflected, imperial division of labor.

After organized labor succeeded in extending exclusion to the Philippines, the imperial state and private capital sought to reassert their control over the borders of the U.S. imperial system by modifying exclusion in both nation and empire. To that end, the Roosevelt administration tried to weaken the law by transferring its enforcement mechanism outside the nation and into U.S. imperial formations. Organized labor responded by calling for a more rigid exclusion law that excluded all Chinese individuals by abolishing the notion of the exempted classes. This new rigidity on the part of organized labor further reoriented exclusion by reimagining it as a legal garrison that protected not just American workers but American civilization. The SUP viewed any attempt to water down the act's enforcement or placate the Chinese imperial government's objections to it as a surrender of U.S. imperial sovereignty to China.

The SUP applied this same thinking to restrict Japanese migrants who began replacing Chinese labor in Hawai'i and on the West Coast. Organized labor on the West Coast, led by the Asiatic Exclusion League and the SUP, responded by reframing Japanese immigrants as agents of Japanese imperialism. This allowed organized labor to depict the struggle for Japanese restriction as an imperial contest between the United States and Japan for control of the Pacific and the U.S. West Coast. However, it seemed that the Roosevelt administration had learned from its failure to prevent the 1902 exclusion law and ensured that any policy of Japanese restriction remained solely in the hands of the executive, outside the influence of organized labor's allies in Congress. By placing legal safeguards between nation and empire, as well as restricting the movement of certain subjects within the empire, the class struggle over the boundaries of the U.S. imperial system allowed a metropolitan imperial framework to emerge around the North American white settler territory of the U.S. imperial system.

Imperial Borders and the Labor Mobilization

In the winter of 1901–1902, after the successful annexation of the Philippines and Hawai'i, the SUP, ISU, and American Federation of Labor sought to insulate their membership from the peoples and practices of the new empire by extending the legal architecture of the Chinese Exclusion Act into the imperial space of the Pacific. By restricting the movement of Chinese subjects within the empire, the SUP and the AFL challenged the imperial state and its private investors' ability to mobilize the labor they thought necessary to make the empire work. For organized labor generally, this meant applying the Exclusion Act to the entire U.S. imperial system on the Pacific.[3] This ensured that Chinese nationals could neither enter the empire nor move from the empire to the U.S. mainland. However, since exclusion disrupted the mobilization of imperial labor sources (and potentially undermined the U.S./China relationship), the U.S. imperial state and its partners in private capital, as well as those with business interests in China, opposed to imperial exclusion, vigorously lobbied against it, and succeeded in significantly watering down the bill. Despite the law's shortcomings, the effects of imperial exclusion transformed immigration restriction into a repertoire of imperial power or rule.[4] Additionally, the SUP's call to extend exclusion to the deck of U.S.-flagged ships went even further and constituted a larger, systemic challenge to the imperial state and its partners in private capital's efforts to make the empire work. Extending exclusion to U.S.-flagged vessels did not just disrupt the maritime labor process. Instead, it represented the expansion of the domestic U.S. labor market by extending a crucial domestic protection beyond the nation. This directly challenged an emerging imperial division of labor that shipping companies were keen to exploit.

The AFL and the SUP saw keeping the Chinese out of the Philippines as essential to defending the U.S. mainland from the peoples and practices of the new empire. AFL president Samuel Gompers testified before the Senate Committee on Immigration that it was the position of the American Federation of Labor that "the Chinese shall be excluded from the Philippines, and that they too, shall be excluded from coming from one insular possession of the United States to another."[5] Indeed, the SUP had been adamant since the acquisition of the islands in 1898 that Chinese individuals must be prevented from both entering U.S. imperial possessions and migrating from U.S. colonies to the mainland United States. To that end, the SUP helped organize the California Exclusion Commission to lead the fight in Washington for a more geographically expansive exclusion law, with ISU president Andrew Furuseth as a key member.

The emerging domestic class struggle over the United States' imperial boundaries held profound consequences for the subjects of America's empire. If the SUP, AFL, and the California Exclusion Commission were successful, extending exclusion to U.S. imperial formations would alter the United States' repertoire of rule by placing limitations on the movement of Chinese residents within the empire. Additionally, this also would disrupt a crucial migratory and trade route between China and the Philippines that had existed for centuries. China's imperial commissioner, Prince Ch'ing, pointed this out in a protest against the law with the U.S. State Department, stating that Chinese subjects had been migrating to the Philippines since "the time of the Ming Dynasty."[6]

The SUP and AFL's insistence on excluding Chinese laborers from the Philippines altered the United States' repertoire of rule in the Philippines. First, it would override the authority of the Philippine Commission to control immigration into the colony. Second, it would disrupt the ability of investors and industrialists to mobilize a source of labor they deemed essential to develop the islands. This represented two competing visions of colonial rule that corresponded to specific class interests. Organized labor's need to insulate its members from the peoples and practices of the empire was the driving force behind its desired repertoire of rule. On the other hand, representatives from private industry unsurprisingly favored modes of colonial governance that would allow them to better profit off the empire.

We can see these alternative visions of rule in the three incarnations of the exclusion bill between December 1901 and its eventual passage in May 1902. The first two incarnations of the bill, written as if Pacific annexation never happened, were manifestations of the administration, the colonial government in the Philippines, and U.S. corporations and individuals looking to invest in the new territory.[7] This meant neither bill would prevent Chinese immigration to the Philippines nor curtail their freedom of movement within the empire or to the U.S. mainland.[8] Almost immediately the AFL, the SUP, and the California Exclusion Commission condemned the bills as unsatisfactory.[9] The second version of the bill was particularly troubling to the SUP and the AFL because of the possibility that the law could be voided when the Gresham-Yang Treaty—in which the Chinese gave a ten-year blessing of the 1892 Exclusion Law—with

China expired in 1904.[10] If China and the United States failed to renew the treaty or renegotiated it under terms more favorable to the Chinese government, the SUP and the AFL feared that exclusion could permanently end or be weakened by 1904.

The idea of simply renewing the current law until the Gresham-Yang Treaty expired reflected Congress' attempts to assuage the fears of American industrialists with business interests in China. Indeed, for many U.S. industrialists a key benefit from Philippine annexation was that it provided a stepping-stone for greater access to the China market.[11] A new exclusion law potentially threatened this access. Americans with interests in the China trade mobilized under the American Asiatic Society and American Association of China.[12] John Foord, representing both organizations, told Congress the people he represented felt strongly that "no substantive legislation shall be had while the present treaty [the Gresham-Yang Treaty] is in force."[13] Instead, he advocated for merely extending the "present law . . . so that the expiration of the law and the treaty may coincide."[14] Foord argued that "the great trade" with China could be "seriously endangered" with a new, more expansive exclusion law "by driving" the Chinese "Government [*sic*] to some measure of retaliation or by compelling them to adopt an attitude of resentment and opposition of the United States."[15] Such resentment, he reminded Congress, could undermine the United States' "most favored-nation" status with the Chinese government and, therefore, affect U.S. business access to the China market.[16] Moreover, in a February 1902 *New York Times* opinion piece (that subsequently was read into the Senate committee testimony), Foord argued that an open market in China was essential to important sectors of American industry. Citing one example, he pointed out that "the prosperity of the cotton textile industry of the United States is absolutely dependent on the maintenance of an open market in China."[17]

Dissatisfied with both versions of the bill, the AFL, in cooperation with the California Exclusion Commission's lobbying committee, drafted a version that reflected the interests of organized labor. The federation bill, as it became known, sought to extend the Exclusion Act to the Philippines, prevent Chinese residents of the colony from moving between island territories, and, most importantly, prohibit the migration of Chinese residents of the island empire to the United States mainland.

For the SUP, the most important feature of the federation bill was a clause that extended the Exclusion Act to the deck of American flagged ships. If the bill were successful, American sailors finally would have the same protection against Chinese competition as workers within the nation. Without such protection, the SUP and the ISU feared that white Americans would be driven from the Pacific maritime trade altogether. Or, as Furuseth himself told Congress, the Chinese "simply absorb the trade and drive us out."[18] This prompted *Coast Seamen's Journal* editor Walter Macarthur to state, "[t]he time has come when the people of the United States must decide whether or not the American people are going to be predominant on . . . the Pacific Ocean."[19] Though the AFL and the Exclusion Commission were able to introduce a bill that reflected labor's interests, getting a fully formed version of the bill passed was another matter. From the perspective of U.S. capital interests looking to invest in the Philippines, the new exclusion law was bigger than immigration restriction or repertoires of colonial governance. The law evinced the ability of labor leaders to place limitations on capital outside the nation, in this case, U.S. capital's access to its desired pool of labor.

Shipping companies, in particular, could not abide labor leaders forcing legislative limitations on their behavior beyond the nation, which would disrupt the imperial labor process. After all, the allure of empire was based partly on the notion that U.S. business could operate with the support of the state but beyond the reach and agitation of domestic organized labor. For instance, Pacific Mail Steamship Company director Maxwell Evarts implied that U.S. labor organizations had no right to interfere with the development of the Philippines. "What interest, gentlemen, what earthly interest, has the Federation of Labor [referring to the AFL] in the Philippines," an exasperated Evarts roared before the Senate committee.[20] "Capitalists" such as Evarts could live with an exclusion law that prevented Chinese subjects in the empire from migrating to the continental United States because it did not affect their ability to recruit and mobilize labor in U.S. imperial formations. However, extending the law to the Philippines would restrict the colonial government's ability to meet any potential labor shortages.

For organized labor generally, the committee added two key amendments that the AFL argued were devastating because they gave anti-exclusionists significant loopholes. First, Senator Thomas Platt of New York—also a shareholder in the China American Development Company—offered a substitute into the bill (known as the Platt Substitute) that added the language: "not inconsistent with treaty obligations."[21] This potentially voided the legislation if China and the United States failed to renew the Gresham-Yang Treaty in 1904. More than that, the AFL argued the Platt Substitute could open the floodgates of Chinese migration from British Hong Kong since the current treaty between the United States and Great Britain permitted open immigration from that colony.[22] Finally, maritime exclusion was stricken from the bill entirely in what would prove to be a devastating setback for the SUP and the ISU.

Maritime exclusion had consequences beyond the shipping industry because it presented a larger, systemic challenge that disrupted an emerging imperial division of labor that had no place for white working-class Americans in U.S. imperial formations—whereas exclusion that simply protected the nation from the peoples and practices of the empire did not challenge this division of labor. In fact, it actually affirmed it by creating and differentiating two distinct labor spaces, one imperial and in various levels of unfreedom, the other domestic and mostly free.[23] Former senator John M. Thurston—who testified on behalf of, in his words, "certain capitalists"—explained this division of labor during his Senate testimony, though he attributed its existence to climate, arguing that in the Philippines, "[t]he Caucasian can become the merchant, he can become the railroad manager, he can become banker, the lawyer, the doctor, but he can not labor in that climate."[24] Though extending exclusion to the Philippines disrupted the colonial state's ability to mobilize and import labor, it did not necessarily disrupt the emerging racialized imperial division labor. The alternative to Chinese labor in the Philippines was Filipino labor, not white labor from North America. Pacific Mail Steamship Company director Maxwell Evarts alluded to this racialized division by arguing that there would never be American laborers in U.S. imperial formations, stating, "[t]he Americans who go to the Philippine Islands will be the leaders, the captains of labor, the men with money, the men who have the sinews of war, and the power to make others do the work."[25] Though he does not state it explicitly, Evarts's characterization of the type of American who "works" in the empire could also apply to the direction he was taking the Pacific Mail Steamship Company, where white Americans command, manage, or administer, and nonwhite foreign labor does the "work." Andrew Furuseth pointed this out as well, stating, "[t]he only white men they [the Pacific Mail Steamship Company] carry are the captain, the first mate, the second mate, and third mate."[26] By attempting to move toward an all-Chinese crew commanded by white officers, Evarts (and the rest of the West Coast shipping lines) actively had been seeking to create the same division of labor that was emerging in other U.S. imperial formations.

The ISU and the SUP's push for maritime exclusion would subvert the emerging division of labor and incorporate the foreign maritime trade into an emerging U.S. national/metropolitan space by integrating it within the U.S. domestic labor market. Since maritime exclusion offered white American sailors a key privilege and protection enjoyed by workers within the nation, it was the first step in moving the foreign trade from an imperial labor formation to a domestic or national labor formation. Maritime exclusion would create a space for white working-class Americans to labor in the empire by neutralizing the racial competition that would come with it. Shipping companies and any form of capital with interests in U.S. imperial formations could not allow this because of its financial consequences.

For instance, the House Committee on Foreign Affairs did not consider American ships to be part of the country or nation and aimed to keep it that way. The emerging U.S. imperial system would be more expensive to operate if Congress forced American shipping companies to hire only white sailors. Indeed, forcing U.S. business operations in the Philippines to hire Filipinos instead of imported Chinese contract labor was not ideal. The importation of Chinese contract labor was not about reducing costs but the apparent absence of surplus labor, particularly skilled labor, among the working population of the Philippines. As Governor Taft himself stated, without Chinese labor, "I do not think there will be a sufficient supply of skilled labor" to develop the territory's manufacturing sector.[27] This was not ideal for American firms looking to invest in the Philippines, but it would not necessarily affect their bottom line to the extent that shipping companies claimed white sailors would. According to Captain William Brownell Seabury of the Pacific Mail Company, white sailors cost $35 per month, whereas Chinese crews cost $15 or less.[28] If shipping companies employed only white sailors, the costs of shipping goods from the Philippines to the United States (or anywhere else) would significantly increase.[29] The imperial system would be more expensive to operate on a systemic level with an exclusively white merchant marine laboring in a domestic labor context. Maxwell Evarts called any law that forced U.S. shipping lines to hire white crews on routes between the West Coast and the Far East tantamount to a "tax on American commerce."[30] As a result, the House committee rejected the domestication of the foreign trade, and thus the maritime exclusion clause, stating, "[w]e regard this provision as foreign to the purpose of the bill, which, is to prevent the entry of Chinese into this country."[31] This implied that U.S.-flagged ships in the foreign trade were not part of the country.

More than that, the Foreign Affairs Committee concluded that maritime exclusion would be detrimental to efforts aimed at reviving the U.S. merchant marine. The committee report argued that applying Chinese exclusion to U.S. ships would "compel steamships that now float the American flag to take British registry," arguing that "this is not the way to build up our merchant marine, for which there is so great a demand."[32] Even if maritime exclusion were successful, U.S. shipping companies could adapt to the disruption by moving their ships beyond the jurisdiction of Congress and into British registry. Though Pacific expansion took the form of U.S. imperial formations, the imperatives of capitalism were often the driving force behind that expansion rather than some kind of national imperial destiny.[33] American shipping firms would, therefore, move their operations into an imperial system—in this case, the British—that would allow them the flexibility to crew their ships with whomever they wanted. The failure of maritime exclusion meant that U.S shipping companies on the Pacific continued their shift to foreign Chinese sailors. By 1905 less than 50 percent of sailors in the foreign trade were U.S. citizens, though this was an improvement over the 1890s when about one-third of all sailors were American citizens.[34] The slight rise in U.S. citizens after 1900 likely owed to greater recruitment drives by the unions combined with the naturalization process. Furthermore, the uptick of American citizens in the trade after 1900 had little to no effect on the China trade (trade between the United States and China as well as other southeast Asian nations).

However, this did not mean that 50 percent of all foreign sailors were Chinese; in fact, the majority were actually European. All-Chinese crews were dominant only in the east Asia trade. On transpacific routes to the British white settler colonies of Australia and New Zealand, shipping companies opted for all-white crews. This was because the sailors' unions of Australia and New Zealand had, much to the annoyance of the imperial government in London, successfully agitated to extend Asian exclusion into their respective merchant marines.[35] In addition, the 50 percent also included foreign sailors or recent immigrants on the far more ethnically diverse East Coast, the majority of whom came from Europe (especially southern Europe), Canada, or Latin America. It is also not entirely clear how the SUP and the U.S. government defined foreign sailors. For instance, many SUP members and the broader ISU membership might have lived in the United States but lacked U.S. citizenship. Indeed, Furuseth, Macarthur, and Scharrenberg were all recent immigrants, arriving between 1880 and 1898.

This is why whiteness was such an important and central organizing principle for the sailors' unions, especially Pacific branches.[36] If the SUP or the ISU organized only sailors with American citizenship, it would severely limit their pool of potential members. Indeed, this is likely why the national union was called the *International* Seamen's Union of America rather than the *National* Seamen's Union. While exact statistics for a given year are difficult to determine, we do know that the ethnic and racial make-up of the SUP was largely northern European, specifically Scandinavian and German. Some were American born, though the largest percentage were recent arrivals who came to San Francisco and the broader West Coast after deserting their ships. This is how Furuseth (Norwegian), Macarthur (Scottish), and Scharrenberg (German) all ended up in the city by the bay. In the early years of the SUP, according to the union's Seattle branch agent Peter Gill, even in the coastwise trade, 40 percent of its members were Scandinavian, 11 percent were Finish, and 10 percent were German. American-born members made up just 8 percent of its total membership.[37] When SUP officials spoke of Asians driving "American" sailors from the trade, it was just another way of saying they were driving out white sailors (emphasis on northern European), "American" or otherwise. Northern European immigrants like Furuseth were seen as potential Americans, whether they held formal citizenship or not. The SUP leadership, like much of the American public and federal naturalization law, viewed people of Chinese descent as incompatible with (and ineligible for) American citizenship.

Despite the SUP and the AFL's insistence, the shortcomings of the 1902 exclusion bill never materialized into the catastrophic consequences they imagined. The final bill extended the law to the Philippines and prevented America's Chinese subjects from migrating to the U.S. mainland. Platt's amendment did not open the floodgates for Chinese migrants from Hong Kong, nor did the expiration of the Gresham-Yang Treaty in 1904 lead to open immigration by voiding existing exclusion legislation. The act remained in force. Though the SUP and the ISU were still fighting for a white, free labor merchant marine, new challenges emerged for West Coast workers. Organized labor's 1902 victory proved short-lived as forces within the Roosevelt administration and its allies in private business began working on ways to subvert the spirit of the 1902 exclusion law. Additionally, Japanese immigration was steadily rising since the late 1890s and dramatically increased by 1905 on the West Coast, but even more so in Hawai'i. Yet before the SUP- and the broader AFL-led labor movement could marshal their forces to push for Japanese exclusion, their top priority was ensuring that the U.S. government properly enforced the new Chinese exclusion.

Enforcing Imperial Boundaries

After organized labor succeeded in extending exclusion to the Philippines, the imperial state and private capital sought to reassert their control over the boundaries of the U.S. imperial system by modifying exclusion in both nation and empire. To that end, the Roosevelt administration tried to weaken the law by transferring its enforcement mechanism outside the nation and into U.S. imperial formations. Organized labor responded by calling for a more rigid exclusion law that excluded all Chinese individuals by abolishing the notion of the exempted classes. This new rigidity on the part of organized labor further reoriented exclusion by reimagining it as a legal garrison that protected not just U.S. workers but American civilization. The SUP viewed any attempt to water down the act's enforcement or placate the Chinese imperial government's objections to it as a surrender of U.S. imperial sovereignty to China for the sake of mercantile interests.

In the fall of 1902, a report commissioned by the War Department reflected an emerging strategy on the part of anti-exclusionist interests to subvert the spirit of the law. Written by Professor Jeremiah Jenks, an economist at Cornell University, the report echoed critiques by Governor Taft, arguing that the development of the Philippines was contingent upon the importation of at least some Chinese "coolie" labor.[38] To this end, the report agreed with Taft's testimony earlier in the year that recommended empowering the Philippine Commission to legislate the admission of Chinese laborers to the territory.[39] The report stopped short of opening the floodgates and set specific guidelines for the importation of Chinese "coolies," limiting them to employers of "not less than 25 laborers," and limiting the contracts to a "period of not over three years."[40] Despite the restrictions placed on the importation of Chinese "coolies," the report's recommendations subverted the intentions of the new exclusion law. By recommending the Philippine Commission as the arbiter of Chinese immigration to the Philippines, Jenks's proposal effectively would move the law's enforcement mechanism outside the nation and the legislative branch and beyond the reach of organized labor's scrutiny. Such an arrangement would allow the Philippine Commission to directly respond to the labor needs of U.S. firms working on colonial development contracts. Jenks's proposed changes to the Exclusion Act's enforcement would prove prescient because—over the next five years—the Roosevelt administration's efforts to modify the exclusion law more often than not involved placing vital elements of the law's enforcement mechanisms outside the nation.

The AFL and the SUP rejected the veracity of Jenks's report. Indeed, Gompers agued that Jenks's assumption that there was insufficient labor in the Philippines was false and that the better way forward in developing the archipelago was the "gradual training and elevation of the Filipino laborers."[41] The AFL president added that "with Chinese labor in the Philippines it will be almost impossible to prevent its coming into competition with American labor at home."[42] The SUP echoed Gompers, stating that "to permit the immigration of Chinese labor to the Philippines or Hawaii [*sic*] would be unjust and dangerous to the Filipino, Hawaiian, and American."[43]

Whether the AFL and the SUP truly cared about the plight of Hawaiians and Filipinos is difficult to determine, especially given how both organizations described Filipino workers as an inherently servile race of "semi-barbaric" "savages."[44] Instead, the AFL and the SUP were likely projecting their specific views and fears of Chinese immigration onto Filipino workers. Historian Clark L. Alejandrino pointed out that for Filipinos, their issue was not with Chinese laborers but Chinese merchants, who were still permitted entry to the Philippines under the 1902 law.[45] Like the previous exclusion laws of 1882 and 1892, the 1902 law restricted only the entry of Chinese "laborers." Nevertheless, making common cause with Filipino workers, if only abstractly, made sense because it helped insulate labor leaders from charges of racism and xenophobia toward the Chinese. This was about protecting Filipinos whose livelihoods potentially were threatened by the same capitalists that recently gushed to Congress over the role Chinese labor played in developing the U.S. West Coast. Indeed, American capitalists looking to invest in development projects in the Philippines spent most of their congressional testimony complaining about Filipinos' work ethic; the Jenks report had come to the same conclusion.[46] It was the same argument shipping capital used to justify their move toward Chinese crews; white labor was too scarce and often unreliable. Whether for or against Chinese labor in the Philippines, Filipinos were a rhetorical pawn in the United States' domestic class struggle to control U.S. imperial borders.

After the controversy surrounding the Jenks report subsided, anti-exclusionists saw an opportunity to permanently weaken the entire legal apparatus of restriction after the Gresham-Yang treaty expired in 1904. Officially, the law did not prevent diplomats, students, merchants, and tourists from entering the United States. However, as Paul Kramer recently pointed out, "since 1897, U.S. officials had, more and more, refused to mark this distinction, tightening their enforcement of restriction and harassing and deporting Chinese migrants with certified exemptions, including many merchants and students."[47] The more stringent enforcement mechanism resulted from former Knights of Labor head and prominent exclusionist Terence Powderly's appointment as commissioner of immigration by President McKinley that same year.[48] Additionally, anti-exclusionists were alarmed by the 1905 boycott of U.S. products by the Chinese diaspora to protest U.S. immigration officials' refusal to recognize exempted class certificates.[49]

The 1905 boycott of American products caused great concern among U.S. business interests in China. For instance, in 1907, the Commerce Department's annual report to Congress noted that though the boycott could have been much worse, "the degree to which American commercial interests in China are menaced, is not to be overlooked."[50] The report also noted that U.S. exports to China fell from fifty-three million in 1905 to forty-four million in 1906 and twenty-six million in 1907.[51] Indeed, the report carefully stated that this was not wholly to do with the boycott, especially since 1905 was a particularly good year for U.S./China trade. Yet the report ultimately concluded that "[s]o large a decline, however, as a drop in our exports to that country of from 53 to 26 millions (50 per cent) in two years is sufficiently startling to challenge the attention of legislators and statesmen."[52] The 1907 report reflected growing concerns among U.S. businesses with an interest in the China trade that the exclusion law's enforcement mechanism was damaging trade between the two countries. All the while, the Roosevelt administration was facing mounting pressure to deal with the overly harsh enforcement measures directed at exempted class Chinese nationals trying to enter the United States.[53] Initially, the White House responded by "modifying" the enforcement of the exclusion law to ensure that exempted-class Chinese were not subject to humiliating treatment.[54]

The SUP interpreted Roosevelt's Modification Order as an attempt by the administration to wrest control of exclusion from organized labor's influence. Though organized labor did not get everything it wanted with the 1902 restriction law, its successful enactment demonstrated to anti-exclusionists the influence labor could mobilize in Congress, especially in the House of Representatives. The key problem that the SUP and the AFL had with Roosevelt's modifications was that it was issued as an executive order through the Department of Commerce and Labor, "without any real regard to the views of congress [*sic*]."[55] Additionally, the SUP took issue with the part of the order that required immigration officials in the United States to "accept the certificates of diplomatic or consular agents as prima facie proof of the right of Chinese to the admission of the United States."[56] The SUP argued that this change constituted a "surrender of the whole act to the mercantile interest in China, since it is well known that these agents are practically the representatives of the commercial class in their respective localities."[57] This would transfer the entire enforcement mechanism of exclusion outside the nation to American consuls in China.

Whether organized labor had allies such as Powderly running the Commission of Immigration or not, the Modification Order transformed the office into little more than a rubber stamp on decisions made by U.S. consular officials abroad. With the Modification Order, the Roosevelt administration did an end-run around organized labor's influence by issuing it as an executive order rather than a formal legislative change through Congress. Moreover, Roosevelt instructed immigration officials in the United States that harsh enforcement of the law no longer would be tolerated.[58] The SUP argued that the modifications meant that any "discourtesy" shown toward Chinese persons "will be cause for immediate dismissal."[59] Such language appalled the SUP, asserting that the administration cared more about mercantile interests and the sensitivities of exempted Chinese than it did about protecting the American workingman. By September 1905, organized labor's outrage became so acute that Roosevelt met with AFL president Gompers and offered his assurances that the modifications were meant only to protect the exempted classes.[60] Gompers said he understood the administration's concerns, but explained to Congress a year later that he told the president the problem was that "there were very few [Chinese nationals] who come here who are really bona fide merchants and students."[61] Roosevelt's reassurance did not assuage the SUP's concerns.[62] By manipulating the enforcement mechanism of restriction, the SUP argued that the administration's actions constituted a "virtual repeal of the Exclusion Act."[63]

The SUP responded to the Modification Order by assuming a more rigid position on restriction that went beyond the idea that Chinese laborers were merely a threat to the domestic labor market to a more totalizing racialization that portrayed their continued presence in the nation (whether they were laborers or not) as a threat to American civilization. This change makes sense given that the exempted classes were now viewed as a back door for mass Chinese immigration to the United States, whether from China or U.S. Pacific imperial formations. Before the Modification Order, the SUP's argument—though always racialized—against Chinese immigration emphasized the unfair labor competition Chinese immigrants brought upon white American laborers. The SUP and other labor organizations, such as the AFL, argued that the admission of Chinese immigrants created a race to the bottom for wages. For white labor to compete, they would have to accept lower and lower wages until they were barely subsisting or left the trade or industry altogether. The SUP had been making this same argument to Congress since the late 1890s when U.S. shipping companies began using Chinese crewed merchant vessels, maintaining that the continued hiring of Chinese crews would bring sailors' wages to the point where white sailors would simply leave the trade on their own.[64] Indeed, race was an essential component of this argument. For example, the SUP opined that because the Chinese could subsist on rice alone, they were better able to tolerate such low wages.[65] Nevertheless, the emphasis was on economic competition. The AFL made a similar argument in a pamphlet published by the U.S. Senate in 1902 entitled "Meat versus Rice."[66]

To maintain their control over the boundaries of the U.S. imperial system, organized labor, led by the SUP, called for a far stricter exclusion law. By seeing the exempted class modifications as the new threat, the SUP shifted its thinking to emphasize racial inferiority far more than economic competition, calling for the total exclusion of Chinese immigrants to the United States by abolishing the notion of exempted classes altogether. In the eyes of the SUP, the Modification Order transformed the exempted classes into another leak in the ship of state. In June 1905, the SUP argued, "there is no visible difference between any two classes of Chinese."[67] Before the Modification Order, the SUP and organized labor never liked the idea of exempted classes, but they never saw them as a significant threat, especially since immigration commissioner Terence Powderly tended to ignore them between 1897 and 1905.[68] Focusing on race rather than economic competition had the added benefit of portraying Chinese immigration as a threat to every American, rather than just laborers.[69] Publicly, this was no longer just about protecting American jobs, but about "preserving this continent to the American people."[70] In 1907, Andrew Furuseth, in his new capacity as vice president of the Asiatic Exclusion League, told Congress that "if Mongolians are permitted to come . . . there is no escape from the fact that they will drive the Caucasian back over the Rockies."[71]

Even when the SUP did foreground Chinese economic competition, they began shifting their emphasis to immutable racial inferiority more so than incompatible living standards. Their desirability as laborers, especially in the maritime trade, now owed to their racial character rather than their tolerance for low wages and a smaller food ration. The SUP argued that Chinese laborers were racially ideal for industrial production because "he actually constitutes a machine in himself."[72] Yet this racial characterization was precisely why they were incompatible with American civilization, "because his racial character unfits him to share the responsibilities of popular suffrage."[73] This was no longer just about their jobs, but about the survival of American democracy.

A year later, when exclusion opponents made a more ambitious attempt to move the enforcement mechanism even further beyond the influence of organized labor, the SUP argued it constituted a U.S. surrender to China. The SUP was reacting to a new exclusion bill, known as the Foster bill, introduced by Congressman David Foster in January 1906. If the Modification Order was a "virtual repeal" of the Exclusion Act, the SUP argued that the Foster bill was a "total repeal," with "American sovereignty surrendered to China."[74] The key clause to which the SUP referred was section eight of the proposed bill.

Section eight contained two changes to the exclusion act that the SUP saw as potentially voiding the entire concept of exclusion while also transferring much of that enforcement mechanism to the government of China. First, the bill sought to change the language of exemption to sound more expansive. Instead of excluding all Chinese except the exempted classes of students, diplomats, merchants, and travelers, the Foster bill reversed this policy by admitting "all Chinese persons other than laborers."[75] This reflected an effort by the Roosevelt administration to give legislative authority to the Commerce Department's Modification Order. In his State of the Union message of December 1905, Roosevelt told Congress that, "[o]ur laws and treaties should be framed not so as to put these people in exempted classes, but to state that we will admit all Chinese, except Chinese of the coolie class."[76] While the difference may seem subtle, the new language shifted the emphasis to be less about whom to *exclude* and more about whom to *include,* moving the burden of proof from Chinese individuals entering to U.S. immigration officials. As Gompers testified during the Foster bill hearings, if the "[F]oster bill should pass . . . the burden of proof to show that a Chinaman had no right to come to the United States, would devolve to our Government."[77] Moreover, Gompers pointed out that this would be next to impossible for government officials since they were unlikely to go to China and investigate.[78]

The other key problem with the Foster bill was that it both transferred the policing of U.S. imperial boundaries outside the nation (beyond the influence of organized labor) and gave the Chinese government a critical role in enforcing U.S. immigration law. This rolled back a twenty-year precedent Congress set in 1888 when it passed an expanded version of the 1882 Exclusion Act unilaterally, without the approval of the Chinese government.[79] The Foster bill compelled U.S. immigration officials to admit Chinese immigrants based on passports "issued by the officer duly authorized . . . by the Government of China."[80] The SUP argued that this clause grants "to China the absolute right and final authority to say who shall and who shall not enter the United States."[81] This, the SUP and the recently formed Asiatic Exclusion League opined, was a "plain relinquishment to China of the sovereignty of the United States."[82] If the bill passed, the consequences could be devastating to the American hold on western North America, the SUP argued. Exclusion, the SUP posited, made it possible for the "white race to remain in California; without the act, the glorious golden state, by nature the richest and most beautiful state in the Union, would today be a colony of China."[83] This thinking reframed the Exclusion Act as a legal garrison, protecting not just white American workers, but the continued presence of American civilization on the North American continent and the Pacific. Luckily for the SUP, the Foster bill came to nothing in the end. The Roosevelt administration and anti-exclusionist business interests may have been able to modify the legislation through executive action, but getting a new bill through Congress was a tall order given organized labor's greater influence within the legislative branch.

Whether or not Roosevelt's modifications affected the rate of Chinese immigration into the United States is almost beside the point. At bottom, this was a class struggle over who controlled and policed the emerging borders of the U.S. imperial system. The legislative route meant that organized labor could have a significant amount of influence and control of the United States' borders. Whereas the administration, big business, and other anti-exclusionists learned that whatever organized labor managed to get through Congress, executive orders could significantly weaken any laws concerning U.S border control championed by America's labor leaders. In fact, proponents of exclusion viewed executive modifications as a "virtual repeal." In the future, anti-exclusionists either had to keep Congress out of the equation or simply modify the legislation in their favor by manipulating its enforcement through executive action. Any new restriction policies would have to be kept out of Congress as much as possible. For the SUP, and to a lesser extent the AFL, the struggle to maintain the 1902 exclusion law against executive modifications reinforced organized labor's belief that the executive branch could not be trusted to enforce the boundaries of the American imperial system no matter what Congress did or said. Moving forward, they would double down on their call for total exclusion and expand it to include all other peoples from East Asia, particularly Japanese immigrants.

Japanese Immigration and U.S. Imperial Sovereignty

While labor, the administration, and anti-exclusionist business interests battled over the enforcement of the Chinese Exclusion Act, Japanese immigration was steadily increasing and emerged as an alternative labor source for Hawaiian plantation owners who could no longer import Chinese contract workers. Since there was no law preventing Japanese immigrants from entering the Pacific empire or the mainland, the SUP and a cross-section of West Coast labor organizations helped found the Asiatic Exclusion League in 1905 to lobby for the exclusion of all persons of Asian descent, but especially the Japanese. The SUP and the AEL responded to the Japanese threat by making a case for U.S. imperial sovereignty on the Pacific by reframing Japanese immigrants as more than mere "coolies," but agents of Japanese imperialism. Japan's crushing defeat of Russia in the 1905 Russo-Japanese War bolstered this characterization by creating fear of a potential Japanese invasion of the Pacific island territory, and ultimately the West Coast. However, the Roosevelt administration had learned from its mistakes with Chinese exclusion and was determined to keep any form of Japanese restriction out of Congress and purely between governments. Though Japan's growing imperial power was an ally in labor's quest to paint Japanese immigrants as agents of empire, that same imperial power gave the Japanese government more leverage and respect in negotiations with their American counterparts. In the end, the SUP and the AEL were unsuccessful. Roosevelt was able to keep organized labor's voice out of the process and ensure the entire enforcement mechanism was out of U.S. hands entirely. This prompted the SUP to declare the Gentleman's Agreement as a surrender of U.S. sovereignty to imperial Japan.

For American sugar planters in Hawai'i, Japanese migrants were an attractive, alternative source of potential cheap labor that current restrictionist legislation did not regulate in either the nation or the Pacific empire. With the passage of the Organic Act in 1900, Congress incorporated Hawai'i into the

U.S. constitutional framework. This meant that the Chinese Exclusion Act now applied to the paradise in the Pacific, bringing Hawai'i's era of unrestricted Chinese contract labor to an abrupt halt. By extending the "constitution and laws of the United States to the territory of Hawai'i," the Organic Act disrupted Hawaiian plantation owners' ability to mobilize their own sources of labor. Yet as the representatives of U.S. labor organizations were campaigning for the 1902 Chinese Exclusion Law, Japanese immigration was steadily increasing on the West Coast and surging in Hawai'i.[84] By 1902 the Japanese population in Hawai'i was quickly supplanting Chinese laborers as plantation owners' preferred source of labor. The Organic Act may have stopped Chinese immigration to Hawai'i, but neither it nor the 1902 law said anything about Japanese migrants. What is more, there was nothing to stop Japanese laborers from entering the U.S. West Coast, whether from Hawai'i or the Japanese home islands. Instead of attempting to subvert the act like their counterparts in the Philippines, Hawai'i's plantation aristocracy adapted to exclusion by simply switching their sources of labor from China to Japan.

Though primarily focused on Chinese exclusion, the SUP and their allies had been monitoring the increasing threat of Japanese immigration since the late 1890s, but by 1905, with a Japanese victory in the Russo-Japanese War looking more and more likely, calls for Japanese restriction were reaching a critical mass. Two weeks before the Japanese Imperial Navy inflicted the final, decisive blow against their Russian adversaries at the now famous battle of Tsushima, the SUP helped found the Asiatic Exclusion League in San Francisco in May 1905.[85] The league was officially a joint effort by two of San Francisco's most powerful labor organizations: the Building Trades Council and the SUP-affiliated San Francisco Labor Council. Indeed, the SUP was one of the most vocal and powerful factions of both the SFLC and the AEL and liked to boast that the "fight for Japanese exclusion [was] inaugurated by the Sailors Union of the Pacific and endorsed by the San Francisco Labor Council (SFLC) and the American Federation of Labor at its recent convention."[86] Both of the SFLC's delegates to the founding meeting of the Asiatic Exclusion League were SUP members: ISU president and SUP secretary Andrew Furuseth and *Coast Seamen's Journal* editor Walter Macarthur. Moreover, the SUP and Macarthur were responsible for organizing the first "large scale protest against the Japanese in California" in May 1900.[87] Additionally, Andrew Furuseth and Walter Macarthur became active and effective members of the league's lecture bureau—a group of orators that the league could deploy to give lectures on the urgency of Asian exclusion, with emphasis on the Japanese threat.[88] In many ways, the decisive Japanese victory in the Russo-Japanese War was the best thing that could have happened to the push for Japanese exclusion. The SUP and their exclusionist allies would be effective at exploiting the war for their own agenda, allowing them to create a much more menacing image of Japanese immigrants that went beyond labor competition.

In light of Japan's growing imperial power, the SUP and the AEL reframed Japanese immigrants as agents of Japanese imperialism rather than mere "coolies." Labor leaders saw Japanese migrants as an advanced guard that could lay the groundwork for a Japanese invasion of America's Pacific dependencies and, perhaps, the West Coast. This sentiment was not as far outside the political mainstream as it might appear. After all, fear that Japan could take over Hawai'i was one of the key reasons the McKinley administration pushed for annexation.[89] Between 1905 and the Gentleman's Agreement of 1907, Hawai'i was central to the SUP and AEL's characterization of Japanese immigrants as agents of Japanese imperialism. In many ways, this line of thinking was a continuation of the SUP's critique of the administration's efforts to relax the enforcement of Chinese exclusion. The SUP referred to such efforts as surrendering the sovereignty of the United States to the Chinese government. However, the SUP never extended this line of thinking to the Chinese migrants themselves. Rarely did they see Chinese immigrants as agents of anything.

Japan's stunning success in the war against Russia bolstered the SUP and their allies' characterization of Japanese immigrants as agents of imperialism, allowing them to frame future Japanese immigration as a militarized, imperial contest. Even before the Japanese victory at Tsushima, the SUP was concerned about how the war's aftermath could affect Japanese immigration to the West Coast, arguing that "[a] peaceful invasion after the conclusion of the Russian war is not only probable, but it is certain unless we learn in time to stem that disastrous flood."[90] Indeed, the idea of a Japanese "invasion," peaceful or otherwise, was something increasingly on the minds of the SUP and the broader exclusionist factions of organized labor. The SUP pointed out that between "twelve to fifteen thousand Japanese have landed in the Pacific Coast ports during the last year. During that time, Japan was engaged in the greatest war of modern times."[91] Additionally, the sailors argued that in the aftermath of the war, "fully three-quarters of a million soldiers have returned to Japan and have been discharged . . . and a great many thousands will find themselves unemployed."[92] The SUP concluded that "Japanese immigration will be doubled and possibly trebled this year [1906]."[93] Moreover, believing the majority of Japanese immigrants in the immediate future to be veterans of the war, the SUP warned: "we will have an army of ex-Japanese soldiers in the Pacific States."[94] The idea that the Japanese were "colonizing" the nation's insular territories, as well as the West Coast, went hand in hand with such militarized discourse. For example, a resolution introduced by Andrew Furuseth and Walter Macarthur in meetings of both the San Francisco Labor Council and the Asiatic Exclusion League pointed to the "systematic colonization by these oriental races of our insular territory in the Pacific, and the threatened, and partly accomplished, extension of that system to the Pacific Coast and other western localities of the United States."[95] Yet despite the focus on the military aspect of Japanese immigration, for the SUP and the AEL, labor remained their central concern.

The SUP and the AEL's rhetoric still reflected the discourse of imperial competition and conquest even when the focus was placed back upon labor competition. In August 1907, after the hysteria of the Russo-Japanese War began to subside, the SUP pointed out that the main danger confronting the U.S. West Coast was not an "army designed for military purposes but an army of equal, or even smaller numbers, designed for the conquest of the United States by the arts of peace. In other words, the danger of the white race lies in an invasion of laborers, rather than an invasion of soldiers."[96] Labor would be the first battle in what the SUP and the AEL saw as an impending long-term conflict with imperial Japan to control the world's largest ocean and its territories. If Japan managed to wrestle control of the Pacific from the United States, they could potentially threaten the West Coast. Such an eventuality might be made easier by the presence of a sizable Japanese settler population in the Pacific states.[97] The nation's leaders during the Second World War shared this sentiment when thousands of Japanese residents, many of them citizens, were sent to internment camps. Former California assemblymen Frank McGowan echoed these thoughts in a speech to the Asiatic Exclusion League on August 26, 1906, pointing to the "peculiar position" the people of California occupy as the "vanguard of the Civilization of this Republic." "As sentinels," McGowan continued, "we look across the pacific [*sic*] to the Far East to observe the countries teeming with ignorant and degraded labor, where harsh environment has made labor slaves."[98] However, as was becoming apparent, the sentinels of the West Coast would not have to look across the entire Pacific.

Hawai'i served as an exemplar of where the SUP thought the United States could end up if Japanese immigration remained unchecked, and began referring to Japanese immigration to the islands as the "Japanese Conquest of Hawaii [*sic*]."[99] With the rapidly expanding Japanese population on the islands—which by 1905 constituted the territory's largest ethnic group—the SUP asserted that Hawai'i was "American in name only."[100] If this influx continued, the SUP opined, the paradise in the Pacific "will become a Japanese Colony."[101] The SUP argued that the Russo-Japanese War suggested that eventually the Japanese will "not allow themselves to be dominated by a minority population" and might rise up and take over the islands, pointing out that, "[r]ecent events [Russo-Japanese

War] in the world's history have clearly demonstrated that the Japs are not as docile as their yellow cousins, the Chinese."[102] By focusing on Hawai'i, the SUP hoped to demonstrate what could happen in California if Japanese immigration was not restricted, stating that the "conquest of the mainland will, of course, take longer" and only federal action could stop it.[103] Furthermore, the SUP argued that once the Japanese settled in great numbers, they would "swarm into our large cities" where there would "either be a revolution or an exodus back to Europe of our white laboring population."[104] As the *Coast Seamen's Journal* argued, the exclusion "movement must prevail if the Caucasian race is to continue to predominate upon the American continent."[105] The Asiatic Exclusion League was even more explicit in its view that the Japanese intended to settle or "colonize" the U.S. Pacific Coast. In December 1908, California state senator Marc Anthony told the League's meeting that the "great state of California . . . can readily support twenty times its present population," and that "[t]he Japanese know this and they openly declare that we do not know how to use these lands to which we have migrated and settled, but that they do."[106] Without some form of immigration restriction, the SUP believed that Japanese immigration could severely weaken America's hold on its Pacific colonies and the West Coast. Though the SUP, the SFLC, the San Francisco BTU (the bodies responsible for the creation of the Asiatic Exclusion League), and the AFL officially opposed annexation in 1898, the threat of Japanese immigration saw them give a passionate defense of U.S. imperial sovereignty on the Pacific and its territories. This further reinforces the fact that labor leaders were not the anti-imperialists they claimed to be, but rather staunch supporters and defenders of white settler colonialism.

Yet the characterization of Japanese immigrants as agents of Japanese imperialism did not mean that the SUP and the AEL ceased to view them as cheap "coolie" labor. In many ways, these two characterizations were mutually reinforcing rather than contradictory. For the SUP and the AEL, the importation of Japanese "coolie" labor by American capitalists would allow the Japanese to gain a foothold in both Hawai'i and North America. Remember, in the immediate aftermath of the Russo-Japanese War, the SUP argued that danger to the white race lies in an "invasion of laborers rather than soldiers."[107] From "coolie" labor, the Japanese would spread beyond the ranks of cheap laborers, into the skilled trades, and eventually, land ownership. Again, Hawai'i was used as a proverbial crystal ball by the SUP and the AEL. In 1908 the Exclusion League pointed out that only 50 percent of Hawai'i's "Asiatic" population was still working on plantations, with "the remaining thousands [but especially the Japanese] being in active competition with the whites in almost every form of industry."[108] Later, the AEL began raising the alarm over the increase in Japanese farms in

California, pointing out that in 1900, there were thirty-seven farms operated by Japanese immigrants, constituting around 1,500 acres.[109] The AEL asserted that between 1900 and 1906 "the number of farms operated by them [Japanese farmers] increased 2600 per cent and the acreage 3100 per cent."[110] From 1905 to 1913, Japanese landholdings increased almost five times "from 61,858 acres in 1905 to 281,687 acres in 1913."[111]

This was particularly troubling to West Coast labor organizations since it meant that from a socioeconomic point of view, the Japanese were beginning to leapfrog white laborers. The Japanese arrive as "coolies," move into other industrial jobs, and eventually buy land and raise crops—the exact reason why many white Americans came west in the first place. This was the ultimate humiliation for white American laborers. The SUP, the AEL, and the rest of America's mainstream labor organizations demanded federal action. Historian Mai Ngai distilled the effect that this humiliation had on whites in California, arguing that "[b]y deciding to become yeoman farmers, Japanese immigrants embraced the quintessential requirement for American liberty and civic virtue, but nativists rejected their endeavors as a foreign conspiracy to take California from white people."[112] Japan's rapidly advancing military helped exacerbate these fears.

However, even though Japan's growing military and imperial power was a useful ally in whipping up public sentiment in favor of Japanese exclusion, Japan's rising power status also gave the Japanese government far more leverage in its negotiations with the Roosevelt administration than the Chinese government ever had. The result was a mutual agreement between two governments rather than unilateral U.S. action. Pressure from the Japanese government allowed the administration and anti-exclusionist business interests to enact a policy of Japanese restriction on their terms, without the input of Congress and thus organized labor and West Coast exclusionists. The so-called "Gentleman's Agreement" of 1907 between the United States and Japan stipulated that if California stopped banning Japanese students from public schools, the Japanese government would not issue passports for their citizens to travel to the United States. In many ways, this agreement was similar to what the SUP and the AFL said about the Foster bill concerning Chinese exclusion. The power to enforce Japanese restriction, according to the SUP, was solely in the hands of the Japanese government. Indeed, this power could be used as leverage anytime the Japanese government felt that the United States was not living up to their terms, or if the United States was persecuting Japan's subjects in America or its insular possessions. Additionally, the agreement was not a formal treaty and, therefore, not subject to Senate ratification. The agreement was drawn up by the administration, issued through an executive order, and executed without ever gaining congressional scrutiny. Organized labor and the rest of the pro-exclusion lobby were completely outflanked by Roosevelt, the Japanese government, and the anti-exclusion lobby.

By keeping Congress out of the equation, the administration was able to diminish organized labor's influence over U.S. immigration policy and reassert its control over the boundaries of the U.S. imperial system. Yet the biggest blow to the SUP and organized labor was that the Japanese government only agreed to stop issuing passports to the United States mainland; it was still free to issue passports to U.S. Pacific imperial possessions, specifically Hawai'i. Hawaiian plantation owners would continue to have a pipeline of cheap labor. The AFL-led faction of organized labor may have been able to disrupt their ability to mobilize cheap Chinese labor, but anti-exclusionists checkmated them on Japanese labor. Furthermore, since there was no law preventing Japanese residents of Hawai'i from moving to the mainland, Japanese individuals could still migrate to California; they would just have to go via Hawai'i. U.S. insular territory, therefore, served as a bridge to the West Coast. Essentially, the agreement had built in a backdoor for Japanese migrants to enter the United States, an ideal outcome for those in favor of unrestricted Japanese immigration.

As a result, the SUP declared that the "Gentleman's Agreement" amounted to "surrender" rather than a settlement because "by far the greater number of Japanese coming to San Francisco arrive from the Hawaiian Islands."[113] Economist John R. Commons confirmed their suspicion in his now-famous *Race and Immigrants in America*—published that same year—when he argued that Hawai'i will continue to serve as a bridge to the U.S. West Coast as long as the agreement was in effect.[114] The SUP liked Commons's assessment so much they printed excerpts of it in the *Coast Seamen's Journal*.[115] AEL member William Temple went even further and stated, "[w]e know that we in California, unless we resist effectively now, will be in the same category [as Hawai'i] and will soon be a Jap colony."[116] Or, at best, if California did not become a Japanese colony, it would be transformed into a plantation "plutocracy" like Hawai'i. Though the fight would continue for exclusion laws that "actually excluded," the struggle over the boundaries of the U.S. imperial system created the basis for an imperial metropole to take shape on the North American continent. It now fell to the SUP and the ISU to ensure that exclusion continued to follow the flag by expanding these boundaries to the deck of U.S. flagged merchant ships in the foreign trade.

CHAPTER 3

Riding the Waves of Empire

Craft Unionism, the La Follette Seamen's Act of 1915, and the Economic Dimensions of U.S. Imperial Power, 1907–1915

The ISU's failure to include U.S. flagged vessels in the Exclusion Act's 1902 expansion meant that while exclusion may have followed the flag of conquest, it did not follow the flag of commerce. As the first decade of the twentieth century was nearing its end, the combined effect of steam technology and the internationalization of the U.S. maritime labor market were taking a heavy toll on America's organized sailors. The transnational reality of the foreign maritime trade limited Congress' ability to regulate it. Even if the ISU had successfully ensured that exclusion followed the flag of U.S. maritime commerce, shipping companies could simply switch their registry to another country and subvert any maritime exclusion law. As a result, the union's last major workplace victory concerned only the coastwise or domestic trade—which was easier for Congress to regulate since it was not open to foreign competition—when the White Act was passed back in 1898. In the foreign trade, 90 percent of all goods were shipped on foreign-flagged (though often U.S-owned) vessels by the eve of the First World War.[1] For the ISU members fortunate enough to find employment in the foreign trade, they had to confront the grim reality of a working environment in which the traditional skills of seamanship were no longer valued. Indeed, from the shipping companies' perspective, these skills were not altogether necessary in the age of steam and cheap foreign labor. By 1911 steam-powered vessels accounted for more than two-thirds of all tonnage in domestic and foreign trades.[2]

The decline of skilled seamanship simultaneously threatened the position of white merchant sailors within the U.S. imperial hierarchy and the SUP and

ISU's status in the AFL-led craft union movement. After all, membership in the American Federation of Labor was reserved only for the skilled trades. Where did it leave them if sailing was no longer considered skilled labor? To add insult to injury, U.S. shipping companies were replacing American sailors with workers the union leadership viewed as utterly incapable of skilled seamanship. What did that say about American sailors and their place within American society? If skill no longer mattered, then they no longer mattered. Besides, so long as shipping companies insisted upon the irrelevance of skill in the steamship era, had access to an international labor market, and were not fixed to a specific national registry, they would continue to replace the more expensive white American sailors with cheaper foreign workers. For shipping company executives, the declining relevance of skilled seamanship expanded the potential pool of workers and allowed ship captains to exploit the cheaper labor markets of China more fully. To reverse these effects, the SUP and the ISU would have to figure how to insulate the maritime labor market from foreign competition without actually passing a new exclusion law, which neither Congress nor both the Roosevelt and Taft administrations had any intention of doing. Indeed, they would need to use more indirect means to achieve racial exclusion. Moreover, the ISU leadership would have to address the transnational reality of the maritime industry because shipping companies could avoid any new laws or regulations by switching national registry.

To accomplish this aim, the ISU moved beyond organized labor's alignment with the idea of empire to actively using U.S. imperial expansion to implement the union leadership's maritime reform agenda. For the ISU, imperial expansion became the means to solve their problems rather than a source of their problems. Initially, the shift from aligning with empire to using empire meant capitalizing on the physical expansion of sovereign U.S. territory into the Pacific as a means of possibly extending the jurisdictional coverage of the Chinese Exclusion Act. The ISU then embarked on a much more ambitious effort, in the form of the 1915 La Follette Seamen's Act, to foist craft union protections on the foreign merchant trade by riding the more abstract, economic forces of U.S. imperial expansion. Using the economic dimensions of American power gave the ISU a reach well beyond the U.S. imperial system's comparatively meager territorial possessions. The SUP and the ISU reasoned that craft union protections could serve the same function as overt racial exclusion by insulating the maritime labor market through the creation of safety and skill requirements that privileged white sailors. This was part of a broader trend in U.S. immigration policy whereby the United States moved from the overt racial discrimination of the exclusion era to the Progressive Era, where the exclusion of undesirable peoples was often achieved without making explicit reference to racial identity.[3]

However, for the ISU, this strategy did not come without its own set of consequences, especially since it had now expanded beyond its northern European–dominated Pacific branch to the more ethnically diverse East Coast—where crews resembled the motley crewed vessels of Melvillian lore. Indeed, the SUP's use of broader and more indirect means to exclude Asian sailors meant the potential exclusion of non-Asian sailors who could not meet the safety and skill standards set by the La Follette Act. Moreover, since East Coast sailors did not face the same level of Asian competition, insulating the maritime labor market there was less of a priority. As a result, the ISU faced opposition from some of its East Coast branch members who questioned the seamen's bill's skill standards as unnecessary and outdated. Many of these members looked to the more radical and inclusive industrial unionism of the recently formed Industrial Workers of the World (IWW) which rejected hierarchies of any kind. The IWW represented an emerging alternative vision of working-class politics and organization that sought to organize all workers, regardless of craft, into "One Big Union."

Additionally, merely insulating the maritime labor market through craft protections did not address the transnational reality of the foreign merchant trade. As long as U.S. shipping companies could flag their vessels outside the United States, they could easily avoid legislative craft protections by switching national registry. To solve this problem, the La Follette Act's jurisdictional coverage applied to all ships destined for a U.S. port, regardless of national registry. Beyond simply insulating the maritime labor market from racial competition, the act would guarantee the "autonomous mobility" of all sailors (foreign or American) by abolishing the last vestiges of the industry's coercive labor practices—creating a free market for maritime labor under craft union rules.[4] The act's effects would finally extend the U.S. domestic or national labor market into the foreign maritime trade. The ISU leadership believed that emerging U.S. economic dominance would force the global shipping industry to adopt American standards. With the La Follette Act, exclusion went beyond following the flag of conquest and commerce. Instead, exclusion would ride the waves of empire by following the long arm of American capitalism and stitch together the transnational legal regime of Chinese exclusion.

Territorial Expansion and the Limits of the Domestic Labor Market

The ISU leadership's shift in strategy from aligning with empire to using empire emerged from its failure to include U.S.-flagged vessels in the 1902 revision of the Exclusion Act. However, in the spring of 1907, the catalyst for the ISU's new strategy arose from an incident in which a Chinese-crewed American steamship began operating in the coastwise trade upon its return from Hong Kong. Before 1907 Furuseth and the union leadership led a strategy that was trying to simply expand the Exclusion Act to American-flagged vessels in the foreign trade. The strategy failed because Congress concluded that the purpose of the Exclusion Act was to protect workers *in* the United States from cheap Chinese competition. Since vessels in the foreign trade were not, according to Congress, *in* the United States, the nation could never apply the exclusion law to sailors.[5] If the act could not apply "outside" the United States, one way forward was to expand the definition of the United States or, more precisely, expand critical protections of the domestic U.S. labor market that insulated Americans from foreign competition into the maritime trade. To accomplish this, Furuseth lobbied the Commerce Department to extend the jurisdictional coverage of the Exclusion Act into the coastwise trade, which after 1900 included the port of Honolulu. The implications of extending the Exclusion Act to Hawai'i, beyond more fully incorporating the coastwise trade into the U.S. domestic labor market, could allow the SUP to challenge the use of Chinese-crewed vessels in the transpacific trade. This shifted the SUP and the ISU's strategy from merely aligning with the idea of empire to using the physical expansion of U.S. territory to further their specific workplace goals.

Indeed, the main obstacle to maritime exclusion had always been the globalized nature of the industry. Even if Furuseth were successful in getting maritime exclusion into the 1902 bill, it would have been nearly impossible to enforce. The regulation of a particular form of capital or industry that was, by definition, internationally mobile would prove difficult for a single national or even imperial jurisdiction. This was largely because U.S. shipping companies could register their vessels under any flag they pleased—a practice that evolved into the "Flag of Convenience" system in the post-1945 era, and still exists today.[6] The Dollar Steamship Line and the Pacific Mail Steamship Company (both dominant in the transpacific trade) registered many of their vessels under the British flag.[7] This meant that any U.S. law, in this case the Exclusion Act, would not apply to their British-flagged vessels.

The globalized nature of shipping capital, more so than the intransigence of American lawmakers, frustrated Furuseth's efforts to extend the Exclusion Act to U.S.-flagged vessels. Even if Congress suddenly prevented U.S. shipping companies from flying foreign flags to get around U.S. maritime legislation, foreign-owned vessels would become even more dominant. The mobility of the workplace environment, combined with the international nature of the foreign trade, allowed shipping companies a virtual veto over U.S. legislation they did not like or found unduly harsh. This was what members of Congress pointed out in opposition to Furuseth's push for maritime exclusion.[8] Ironically, if the law had been successful, it might have made things worse for Furuseth and America's organized sailors. A switch to British registry would most likely have sped up the Asianization process on transpacific routes since the British merchant marine had been using Asian and "lascar" sailors for years, especially in the Pacific and Indian oceans.[9] Any serious attempt to prevent the employment of Asian sailors in the foreign trade would have to find a way around the enforceability problem.

There was no easy way around the enforceability problem, and Congress was not likely to help American sailors. In many ways, the enforceability problem allowed members of Congress to simply wash their hands of the issue by blaming the systemic reality of the international shipping trade rather than their unwillingness to protect American workers. With the defeat of maritime exclusion in 1902, there was not much the sailors could do to combat the Asianization of the merchant marine beyond making a lot of noise and a continued lobbying presence in Washington. As a result, the ISU spent the next several years mostly on the defensive, working with the AFL to ensure (as chapter 2 argued) that the government properly enforced the 1902 exclusion law.[10]

However, in 1907, the ISU achieved a small, though mostly symbolic victory in its fight—a victory that would mark the beginning of an alternative route to, in Furuseth's words, "keep the sea for the white race."[11] The new strategy emerged out of Furuseth's and the SUP's efforts to force the Commerce Department to clarify the jurisdictional coverage of the 1902 Exclusion Act. Specifically, did the Chinese Exclusion Act extend to the coastwise or the domestic trade? Before 1898 this question never came up because U.S. vessels operating in the coasting trade lacked the same kind of access to international labor markets that vessels in the foreign trade had. As a result, domestic crews were usually white Americans or recent American immigrants of European background. This primarily owed to geographic reality rather than any specific legal prohibition. Since the domestic trade was defined as maritime commerce between U.S. ports—whether on the oceanic coasts, the Great Lakes, or the nation's thousands of rivers—it was not possible for domestic trade shipping lines to source labor from the other side of the Pacific.[12] Additionally, Congress had long ago insulated the domestic trade from international competition. Only U.S.-flagged vessels were permitted to operate in the coasting trade; shipping companies did not have to worry about foreign firms using cheaper foreign labor. In 1898 the White Act expanded the definition of the coastwise trade to include "nearby foreign ports" in Canada, Newfoundland, Mexico, and the West Indies.[13] A year later, after Hawaiian annexation, the coastwise trade was extended to the islands despite "foreign and Hawaiian protests."[14] If the exclusion law did apply to the coasting trade, then the law's jurisdictional coverage potentially extended to the middle of the Pacific Ocean, well beyond the water's edge of the West Coast.

In the spring of 1907, the SUP began pushing the limits of the exclusion law by protesting the use of Chinese crews on the steamship *Lyra.* The *Lyra* was unique in that it began its journey in the foreign trade before entering the coastwise trade, which meant it had access to foreign labor markets. The crew in question were shipped on the *Lyra* from Hong Kong, sailed to Seattle, and then to Nome, Alaska, via Vancouver, British Columbia. In a June 10 letter to Commerce Secretary Oscar Strauss, Andrew Furuseth argued that shipping companies' ability to ship foreign crews from foreign ports "deals distinctly with the shipment of seamen in the foreign trade, and cannot be employed in the coasting or 'domestic trade'."[15]

For the Commerce Department, the question boiled down to how exactly it defined "landing" in (or gaining admission to) the United States. In reply to Furuseth, Secretary Strauss forwarded him his decision based on Commerce Department solicitor Charles Earl's interpretation of what "landing" in the United States actually meant. Specifically, Earl distinguished "landing" or "gaining admission to the United States" with the "temporary absence of the men from the vessel during her presence in port."[16] The latter, according to Earl, did not constitute "landing" in the United States so long as the sailors in question were "bona fide members of the crew of a vessel engaged in the foreign trade" and go ashore "only in connection with the loading and unloading of the vessel's cargo."[17] In that case, Earl stated the crew would not be in violation of the country's immigration laws. However, for the *Lyra,* the question was "whether alien seaman may be permitted to become members of the private crew of a private American vessel engaged in the domestic trade of the United States without complying with the requirements of the immigration laws regulating the admission of aliens."[18] In other words, did working on a vessel engaged in domestic commerce mean that the *Lyra*'s Chinese crew had gained "admission into the United States within the meaning of the [country's] immigration laws?"[19] To this question, Earl answered in the affirmative. In his and the Commerce Department's opinion, "the employment of an alien crew upon a vessel engaged in the coasting trade, *would* [emphasis added] necessitate the admission of such crew into the United States."[20] Since the Commerce Department considered the coasting trade inside the United States, it fell under the jurisdiction of the nation's immigration laws, which included the Chinese Exclusion Act.

Just over ten years after the Maguire Act abolished imprisonment for desertion in the coastwise trade, the Commerce Department had more fully incorporated it into the domestic or metropolitan boundaries of the U.S. labor market by bringing the domestic trade under the protection of the Exclusion Act. This was a crucial victory for the ISU, especially the SUP. As the *Coast Seamen's Journal* stated, "[f]or the first time, it is held that the Chinese Exclusion Act extends to at least one branch of America's seafaring craft."[21] However, the victory was more symbolic considering the *Lyra* was likely the first and only instance of a Chinese crew working in the domestic trade between Pacific coast ports. In other words, the employment of Chinese crews on coasting vessels had never really been a problem for the sailors' unions. Luckily for the SUP, the *Lyra* case was part of a broader strategy by Furuseth and the union leadership to strike a blow against the use of Chinese crews on transpacific routes.

About a month after the June 14 ruling, Furuseth again wrote the Commerce Department and attempted to use the logic of the *Lyra* ruling to challenge the Pacific Mail Steamship Company's use of Chinese-crewed vessels between Asia and the West Coast that went via Honolulu. Now, much of the substance of Furuseth's challenge reiterated his and the SUP's long-held belief that the Exclusion Act should apply to all U.S.-flagged vessels, stating that an American ship was American soil.[22] However, it is unlikely, given the enforceability issue, that Furuseth and the union leadership were expecting the Commerce Department to affirm this position. Regardless, the key point in the letter of protest argued that the Pacific Mail Steamship Company's transpacific vessels exited the foreign trade once they entered the port of Honolulu. Furuseth asserted that if Honolulu was a domestic port, then "under the opinion of the Solicitor [of the Commerce Department] of date June 14, 1907, vessels so manned [with Chinese crews] can not [*sic*] carry passengers, or mails [*sic*] between the port of San Francisco and Honolulu, as that is coastwise trade."[23] Furuseth based his logic on the fact that, in the June 14 decision, the Commerce Department ruled that employment in the domestic trade constituted "landing" or "admission to the United States." This meant that the crew of vessels in the domestic trade were, therefore, subject to the immigration laws of the United States, including the Chinese Exclusion Act. If the Commerce Department accepted the argument made by Furuseth and the SUP, the Exclusion Act's jurisdictional coverage of U.S.-flagged vessels would extend almost four thousand kilometers from the West Coast to the middle of the Pacific Ocean.

By pushing for the extension of the Exclusion Act to Honolulu—the farthest outpost of the coastwise trade—Furuseth and the union leadership were moving beyond its alignment with empire in the wake of 1898 annexation to explicitly using the expansion of U.S. territory to further their workplace goals. Hawai'i's status as a domestic American port was only possible because of America's 1898 imperial expansion into the Pacific. Indeed, the SUP, ISU, and Furuseth (like the AFL) all opposed the annexation of Hawai'i in 1898, with the SUP referring to Pacific annexation as a "leak in the ship of state."[24] Nevertheless, by 1907, America's organized sailors had found a way to use one of the recently annexed territories to their advantage.

Furuseth's challenge got around the enforceability problem (at least for this specific route) since only American-flagged vessels were allowed to operate in the coastwise trade—switching to British registry was not an option. However, this hinged on how the Commerce Department would respond to the SUP's protest. Were Oscar Strauss and the Roosevelt administration willing to help the SUP strike a blow against the Pacific Mail Company's bottom line? Were they willing to expand a critical domestic labor market protection to the middle of the Pacific? That is essentially what Furuseth and the SUP were asking. Such a ruling would more explicitly incorporate the space between Hawai'i and the Pacific Coast into the domestic boundaries of the United States by extending into it a vital protection of the domestic U.S. labor market.

If Furuseth's challenge were successful, it would frustrate shipping companies' efforts to use Chinese crews on the entire transpacific trade, even the leg between East Asia and Hawai'i. If the Commerce Department accepted the logic of the SUP's challenge, it would mean a vessel that stopped in Honolulu would have to offload their Chinese crew, ship them back to their port of origin on another vessel, and reship a white crew (assuming there were sufficient white sailors in Honolulu) from Hawai'i to the West Coast. In that case, the Pacific Mail Company would have to use two ships and two crews in place of one crew on one ship, or they would ship a white crew for the entirety of the transpacific voyage. Unfortunately for the SUP, the Commerce Department ruled that using Honolulu only as a stopover point between Asian and West Coast ports did not mean that ships had "entered" the coastwise trade. Strauss's view of the situation neutralized the SUP's efforts to stop the employment of Chinese crews in the transpacific trade.

The logic behind this decision echoes some of Department solicitor Charles Earl's June 7 opinion in that it hinged upon what it meant to "enter" the domestic trade from the foreign. Or, as Strauss himself argued, "does the fact that the vessels in question are not exclusively engaged in the foreign trade, but are also engaged in some measure in the coastwise trade . . . operate to withdraw from them the privileges granted" from the foreign trade?[25] Strauss stated that it "does not."[26] He argued that the "vessels do not cease to be 'in the foreign trade' during any part of their voyage."[27] Strauss continued, stating that, "although they [the vessels] are incidentally engaged in the coastwise or domestic trade, so long as they preserve their status as vessels 'in the foreign trade' " they retained the privilege of "engaging foreign crews."[28] The key point in Strauss's argument rests upon the meaning of the phrase "so long as they preserve their status as vessels 'in the foreign trade'."[29] What Strauss meant by preserving "their status as vessels in the foreign trade" was that so long as an alien "crew of a vessel in the foreign trade . . . go[es] ashore in a port of the United States only in connection with the duty of loading or unloading the vessel's cargo, the immigration laws are not violated."[30] Strauss contended that "such action on the part of the seamen does not constitute landing or entrance to the United States within the meaning of the Immigration [*sic*] laws."[31] Essentially, Strauss was arguing that the vessel preserved its status in the foreign trade if the crew went ashore only in connection with a ship's business and "made no attempt to enter the United States and become part of its population."[32]

Indeed, the question of what constitutes "landing" in or "entering" the United States remains a critical issue in twenty-first-century America. From refugee camps on the southern border to airport/immigration control centers and guest worker programs, the United States has dramatically expanded the instances whereby individuals can physically exist within the nation's boundaries without gaining legal or permanent admission to the nation. Whether in the early twentieth or twenty-first centuries, the legal ambiguity over the meaning of "landing" provides the means to both exclude or exploit vulnerable groups of people. Anti-immigrant proponents can use this legal ambiguity to exclude "undesirable" groups of people from gaining "lawful" admission to the United States. Alternatively, corporate interests can use this ambiguity to gain access to guestworkers from lower-wage labor markets who lack full access to the institutions of American labor and democracy—a situation similar to the Pacific Mail Steamship Company's use of all-Chinese crews between Honolulu and the West Coast.

In any event, Strauss's decision neutralized the SUP's challenge by giving shipping firms a loophole that allowed them to retain their status in the foreign trade even as their vessels traveled between two domestic U.S. ports. The SUP was obviously not happy with this decision. From their perspective, Strauss's ruling contradicted his earlier decision in the *Lyra* case, where he forced a vessel that entered the coastwise trade from the foreign trade to comply with the Chinese Exclusion Act. Moreover, the SUP pointed out that the *Lyra* was "engaged but temporarily in the coastwise trade."[33] Whereas "the vessels of the Mail

Company [the Hawai'i ruling] are engaged regularly in that trade."[34] This was true because the Mail Company steamships often traveled from East Asia to the West Coast via Honolulu, which is likely why the Commerce Department sided with the shipping company. If the Commerce Department had sided with the sailors, the decision could have significantly disrupted the operations of the Pacific Mail Company's and others' transpacific routes. Or, as the *Coast Seamen's Journal* stated, "the department prohibits the employment of Chinese in the case of the *Lyra* and permits, even justifies, that practice in the case of the Mail Company."[35] So while Andrew Furuseth and the SUP were finally able to get the Exclusion Act applied to, in their words, "one branch of America's seafaring craft," it was mainly a symbolic victory that succeeded only in prohibiting Chinese sailors from a labor space they had never entered.[36]

Despite the mixed success the union leadership achieved in using the coastwise trade to expand the scope of the Exclusion Act, the ISU leadership was beginning to use recent U.S. expansion to their advantage. Before 1907 the SUP resisted the effects of empire by aligning with the idea of an imperial hierarchy. After the *Lyra* decision, the SUP and Furuseth had moved beyond a conceptual alignment with empire to actively using the expansion of U.S. territory to their advantage. Unlike the Roosevelt Republicans and their allies in big business who used empire and imperial expansion to access new markets and cheap labor, the ISU (with AFL support) sought to use imperial expansion to protect their jobs and fortify the U.S. metropole from racially undesirable immigrants in and beyond the U.S. imperial system. From a laboring point of view, they were also seeking to expand the parameters of the U.S. white settler empire into the middle of the Pacific Ocean via the merchant marine. Though they were ultimately unsuccessful in their initial efforts, this would not be the last time they attempted to do this. Using empire was the right strategy, but the ISU was using the wrong dimension of U.S. imperial expansion. Moreover, it was increasingly evident that the executive branch would be indifferent or hostile to attempts by the ISU to expand the Exclusion Act, particularly since, as chapter 2 argued, the Roosevelt administration was constantly trying to loosen the Exclusion Act's enforcement mechanism.

If the SUP wanted to insulate U.S.-flagged vessels from Chinese competition, they would have to do it indirectly, without explicit use of racially exclusive legislation. Second, they would have to solve the problem of international competition that rendered any new law or regulation of the foreign trade void if U.S. shipping firms simply switched registry. Just more than eight years after the *Lyra* incident, the SUP was able to solve both of these issues with the passage of the 1915 La Follette Seamen's Act.

Craft Unionism, ISU Expansion, Asian Exclusion, and the La Follette Seamen's Act

The La Follette Seaman's Act was an ambitious attempt to insulate the maritime labor market from foreign labor competition and preserve the skill of seamanship just as the industry had completed the long and uneven transition from sail to steam. It is a remarkable piece of legislation that attempted to reform the maritime industry in one fell swoop. If successful, the La Follette Seamen's Act would create barriers against the employment of Chinese laborers without directly referring to racial identity. The bill and eventual law did not explicitly restrict Chinese, nonwhite, nor foreign workers from employment on U.S.-flagged vessels in the foreign trade. Ostensibly, the ISU leadership argued that the bill was necessary to improve the safety conditions at sea for the protection of the crew as well as the passengers and cargo. This was not necessarily cynical. In fact, it was the principal reason why progressives such as Robert La Follette (the law's namesake) supported the bill. Even though excluding Chinese sailors was one of the ISU's primary motivations, Furuseth and the union leadership had long argued for the importance of skilled seamanship. Indeed, the decline of skilled trades was a concern that went far beyond the merchant marine. It was a central dynamic of turn-of-the-century to mid-twentieth-century labor history. However, it was the racial component that often set the sailors' experience—but especially West Coast sailors—with the decline of skill apart from the rest of the labor movement. For these sailors, being replaced by less-skilled workers hit harder because of who was replacing them.

After the *Titanic* disaster in 1912, the issue of maritime safety took on much greater urgency. The bill addressed, through legislative action, the maritime safety issue by institutionalizing the training, skill, and qualifications necessary to be considered an able seaman.[37] The intended effect was to insulate the maritime labor market from Chinese competition. Only, instead of overtly restricting Chinese workers, the law shifted the rules of the maritime labor market into the ISU's favor by legislating a craft union trade agreement on the industry—creating labor and safety standards they believed Chinese sailors could not meet. The La Follette Act's standards of skill, training, and efficiency, therefore, performed the same function as Chinese exclusion.[38] Through craft union work rules, the Seamen's Act created an environment in which exclusion would exist in fact, if not explicitly in law. This is not to say that skill and race were synonymous, but rather that skill held race within it.

The messy overlap between skill and race meant that the ISU's legislative strategy came with some serious organizational consequences. Since Furuseth and the SUP leadership were attempting racial exclusion without using explicitly racialized laws, regulations, and standards, mechanisms designed to "keep the sea for the white race" were far broader than race and meant the potential exclusion of many non-Chinese sailors. As a result, when the ISU, led by the SUP, began their push to pass what would eventually become the 1915 La Follette Seaman's Act in 1910–1911, they faced significant opposition from their newly expanded East Coast branch. This opposition was especially pronounced from members who did not so easily fit into the binary racialized thinking of Asian and white (or more broadly white and nonwhite) that characterized West Coast racial thinking.[39] Many of these sailors would leave the ISU for the more egalitarian industrial unionism of the IWW. Indeed, since its founding in 1905, the IWW was slowly making progress among maritime workers of the East Coast and would become a serious challenge for the ISU beyond the coast in the postwar era.

Efforts to pass the "Seamen's Bill" were partly a reaction to what the union leadership viewed as the deskilling of the shipping industry in the steamship era. As Shipowners Association spokesman and Dollar Steamship President Robert Dollar told Congress, "[i]n the old days of sailing . . . [skill] was necessary; but on modern steamers such experience is altogether unnecessary. A sailor now is a man who washes the deck, scrubs paintwork and does any work that an ordinary laborer can do."[40] By reducing the level of skill necessary to operate a vessel on the high seas, the industrialization of the merchant marine allowed shipping companies to draw on a much wider range of unskilled laborers. As a result, ship captains were better able to exploit the internationalization of the maritime labor market.

These changing dynamics within the shipping industry also were a blow to a sailor's masculinity. The SUP had long argued that "shipowners have so arranged maritime affairs as to make the calling of the seamen repellant to the American sense of manhood and decency."[41] Replacing white American sailors with workers the *Coast Seamen's Journal* described as a race "whose servility is beneath all Western conceptions of manhood" exacerbated this eroding sense of masculinity.[42] This view of Chinese workers was hardly unique to the SUP. Indeed, Lisa Lowe pointed out that there was a powerful strain in orientalist thought that feminized Asian men. Lowe argued that "[f]rom the 1850s until the 1940s, Chinese immigrant masculinity had been socially and institutionally marked as different from Anglo- and Euro-American 'white' citizens."[43] Part of this characterization stemmed from the fact that white Americans often saw Chinese men working in trades and businesses they viewed as woman's work, such as "laundry, restaurants and other service-sector jobs."[44] Indeed, the AFL pamphlet put out in support of the 1902 exclusion law was subtitled, "American Manhood Against Asiatic Coolism."[45] How could the sailors maintain the pride of their trade if their jobs were going to people who white Americans viewed as inferior, effeminate workers? What did that say about the nature of their trades? The La Follette Act, therefore, was about more than just protecting their jobs. It was also about protecting and maintaining their identity and claim to American manhood.

To say that the SUP's renewed push to pass a "Seamen's Bill" faced an uphill climb is an understatement. They battled a powerful shipping industry in a fiercely competitive international environment as well as a skeptical and often hostile attitude from all three branches of government. More than that, changes in the composition of the ISU's membership also posed a problem for Furuseth and the union leadership's legislative strategy. The ISU of 1910–1911 was different from the ISU of the late 1890s and early 1900s.

As the ISU grew beyond its stronghold on the Pacific Coast, its membership was increasingly more ethnically diverse, especially on the Atlantic. Newer members, many of whom were non-English speakers, felt less of an attachment to the union leadership's strict craft union philosophy. Many of the newly organized sailors on the East Coast expressed skepticism toward the ISU's legislative strategy that emphasized what they saw as outdated standards of skill to insulate the maritime labor market in the foreign trade. More significantly, the Atlantic Coast unions objected to the Seamen's bill's language clause as discriminatory toward non-English speakers. The language clause was the key weapon in the SUP's fight to drive Asian sailors from the sea by mandating that at least 75 percent of the crew be able to understand the language of the officers. The Atlantic Marine Firemen's Union, whose membership was majority Spanish-speaking (made up of both Spaniards and Latin Americans), led the objection to the language clause.[46] These ethnic tensions boiled over between 1911 and 1913 and led to the Firemen's Union's defection to the IWW's recently formed Marine Transport Industrial Union (MTIU). To prevent the loss of more East Coast members, Furuseth exploited ethnic tensions within the Atlantic branches to maintain control of them. His machinations ultimately lead to the collapse of the Atlantic unions in 1913.

In a broader sense, as the ISU began organizing and incorporating sailors on the Atlantic Coast, its near twenty-year craft union consensus faced its first real challenge. Almost immediately after the ISU's expansion to the East Coast, the Atlantic unions, led by the largely Spanish-speaking Firemen's Union, took issue with ISU orthodoxy and its broader legislative strategy to insulate maritime labor markets. During the 1911 ISU convention, Firemen district leader James

Vidal and other leaders of the Atlantic Coast unions introduced Resolution No. 11, which explicitly condemned what would become the La Follette Act's language clause. The resolution asked that the International Seamen's Union of America "oppose and use its best efforts to prevent the passage and enactment into law of . . . section 13" (the language clause) of the La Follette Seamen's bill.[47] Given that almost 80 percent of the Atlantic Firemen's membership was Spanish speaking, Vidal knew that if the language clause became law it could prevent the vast majority of his members from working.[48] Additionally, Vidal questioned the need for specific standards of skill, particularly the idea in the Seamen's bill requiring "that able seamen before obtaining employment must show at least three years sea experience, at least one of which must have been on a sailing vessel."[49] Though, as Furuseth pointed out to the Committee on Merchant Marine and Fisheries, a two-thirds majority at the convention out-voted the resolution, with the remaining third coming mostly from the Atlantic unions.[50] Yet despite the defeat of resolution 11, the linguistic divide between Atlantic and Pacific branches persisted.

Given the divisiveness of the ISU's legislative strategy on the East Coast, Atlantic union officials began questioning the potential efficacy of such an approach. Atlantic Coast Seamen's Union secretary George Bodine testified before Congress against the Seamen's Bills. A lawyer by training, Bodine stressed that the ISU leadership had framed the language provision far too broadly and argued that there was a difference between speaking a language and understanding "lawful commands."[51] To make the point, he conceded that the majority of Atlantic firemen "can't talk [*sic*] the English language" but "as to whether they understand lawful commands they get from the officers—the proof of the pudding is in the eating—presumably they must understand the orders."[52] Additionally, Bodine was skeptical about the practicality of enforcing a language requirement: "[h]ow are you going to decide whether a man knows the language sufficiently to understand a lawful order?" he asked. Bodine continued by pointing out, "there is no specific amount of knowledge that the man must have according to this bill."[53] Furthermore, he argued that at the very least, enforcement of the language clause would require that every port retain inspectors capable of understanding dozens of languages. Otherwise, how would the shipping commissioner know if the crew understood the officers?

Beyond that, Bodine was skeptical that the language clause would actually work and argued that if the bill lacked specific language requirements, assessing a sailor's proficiency would be open to interpretation and possibly nullify the effect of a language clause. In that case, he argued, "[y]ou could not prove that they were qualified and you couldn't prove that they were not."[54] The effect would be that inspectors could say whatever they wanted or simply take the captain's word that the crew understood the officers' orders. To make his point, Bodine drew the committee's attention to Chinese sailors who were "the main complaint on the Pacific Coast."[55] Bodine opined, "I don't think it would take a Chinaman any length of time to pass an examination to be able to understand the orders."[56] This was the crux of Bodine's criticism: what constituted understanding a lawful order? Was it fluency in the language of the officers? Or was it enough to simply understand basic commands, whether a sailor could actually speak the language of the officers or not? In any event, Bodine believed that the lack of specificity would present a problem. These criticisms proved prescient, since the final version of the La Follette Act passed in 1915 stipulated only that sailors "understand any order given by the officers."[57] This gave the Commerce Department broad legal authority to set the enforcement parameters the law itself lacked (but more on that in chapter 5).

Bodine further undermined the ISU leadership's position when he expressed his skepticism over the skill requirements of the Seamen's bill, arguing that they were largely out of date. At one point, an exasperated Furuseth challenged Bodine in front of the Committee on Merchant Marine and Fisheries and demanded he explain his position, barking, "[a]re you still opposed to that section of the bill or are you in favor" of "individual efficiency on the part of the sailors?"[58] Bodine replied, "I don't think that the bill as to efficiency fits modern conditions," though "if the bill had been passed 25 or 30 years ago . . . it would have fitted [*sic*] sailing ships," but "I don't think it fits modern steamers."[59] For Bodine, the issue was that three years' experience was an "unnecessary" "prerequisite" for "an American boy to-day for serving as an able seamen."[60] Whereas thirty years ago, sailors had to learn how "to splice and make sails and do a hundred other things," today, "there isn't the demand for that kind of labor . . . on modern ships."[61] He then somewhat sarcastically asked why it would take "three years" for a sailor "to learn how to steer . . . [or] have the lead and to handle small boats?"[62] These were the same criticisms shipping company executives made against the Seamen's bill—though they, of course, went further in insisting that skill did not matter at all in the steamship era.[63] Bodine, however, was not saying that skill no longer mattered, but that Furuseth and the ISU leadership based their definition of a skilled sailor upon outdated standards relevant only on sailing ships. By this point, Furuseth was increasingly losing patience with the Atlantic Coast Seamen's secretary and was plotting to have him thrown out of the union.

With Furuseth and the ISU leadership's refusal to allow any deviation from its strict craft union principles as well as their unwillingness to modify a legislative strategy that used skill standards and language requirements to insulate the maritime labor market, the Spanish firemen began defecting to the IWW. When Vidal himself finally lost patience with the ISU and joined the Wobblies in 1913, nearly every Spanish-speaking firemen followed.[64] Furuseth made no effort to entice the Spanish sailors back and instead saw an opportunity to double down on a legislative and organizing strategy built around defending white sailors by focusing his attention on retaining the 20 percent of the membership who were not Spanish speaking and had long resented their minority status within the Firemen's Union.

The ethnic tension between the minority of "Anglo-Saxon" firemen and the Spanish majority ensured that the ISU would not lose the division's entire membership to the IWW.[65] Such tension was on display during the 1911 convention when the Spanish firemen called for the removal of the ISU's Philadelphia agent, Oscar Carlson, when he referred to the Spanish firemen as "Degoes."[66] Yet Furuseth and the leadership refused to expel Carlson because they thought it would engender hostility among the "Anglo" firemen.[67] What is more, during an Atlantic Coast strike in 1912, the "Anglo" firemen jumped at the opportunity to scab on the striking Spanish firemen.[68] As a result, when the Spanish-speaking firemen left for the IWW, Furuseth was able to retain the "Anglo" firemen by chartering a new organization under Carlson's leadership.[69] Furuseth and the ISU leadership chose "whiteness" over solidarity.

Fortunately for Furuseth and the ISU leadership, George Bodine's actions in the aftermath of the Spanish firemen's exit provided the perfect pretext for his removal from both the ISU and the Atlantic Seamen's Union. Bodine attempted to bring some "order" to the Atlantic Coast by calling on all the ISU's East Coast unions (the Firemen, Cooks and Stewards, and Seamen) to consolidate within a "single organization."[70] This went against the policy of the ISU and represented a borderline cardinal sin in the eyes of Furuseth, who believed in strict organizational boundaries between crafts, among even the different shipboard maritime workers of the ISU. As a result, Furuseth had Bodine expelled from the ISU shortly thereafter. Bodine then went to the AFL directly, hoping they might recognize his organization as an independent AFL union. However, Furuseth convinced the AFL leadership to refuse recognition. Shut out of the AFL, Bodine made one final move by attempting to affiliate with the International Longshoreman's Association, but again, Furuseth blocked these efforts.[71]

Furuseth saw Bodine's actions as a removable offense because they threatened the ISU's craft union ideology, which emphasized shared skill sets rather than general experience as workers. If Bodine's machinations had been successful, they would have lumped cooks, stewards, firemen, and seamen into one broad category of maritime worker. Now, Bodine was no Wobbly, nor did Furuseth ever imply that he was one. However, the union leadership's central problem with industrial unionism was its apparent indifference to skill as well as a flattened view of labor that subsumed qualitative distinctions of individual workers and trades into a monolithic mass. Indeed, while firemen, cooks, and stewards were part of the ISU, Furuseth did not see them as equal to or as important as seamen. In fact, Furuseth's biographer believed that the only reason he and the ISU expanded beyond the deck crew was to prevent land-based unions from gaining a "foothold on the ships."[72] If the ISU did not organize these trades, they could end up affiliating with their equivalent land-based union. Moreover, in remarks made a few years later on the IWW's constitution, Furuseth observed, "[a]s a basis for the whole philosophy it assumes that the people are divided into two classes: The [*sic*] employing and the working class."[73] The ISU president believed that "pride in production, in skill, in work well done and consciousness of their creative capacity . . . serve[d] as a foundation for class solidarity."[74] For Furuseth and the ISU leadership, skill type and skill level were the basis for class solidarity. This view of class solidarity was rooted in hierarchical divisions within the working class rather than a common experience as workers. With industrial unionism, or syndicalism as Furuseth tended to call it, the ISU president argued that "there is no pride in production, in skill, in work well done; hence, no foundation for any class feeling or class pride."[75]

Furuseth's objections to the IWW's organizational philosophy was precisely why it was so attractive to both younger and less experienced sailors as well as those who did not so easily fit into the ISU's definition of whiteness. In the IWW, younger sailors were not subjected to the condescension of "old timers" like Furuseth who came of age on sailing ships and fetishized the traditional skills of the trade associated with that era. With the declining importance of skill in the age of steam, Furuseth and the ISU were trying to protect their members by entrenching traditional sailing skills through legislation. Conversely, the IWW was offering an alternative more expansive and inclusive form of industrial organization that could potentially prevent shipping companies from outflanking them by looking for less skilled labor beyond the U.S. metropole. Under the leadership of Big Bill Haywood, the IWW would organize anyone.

Furuseth and the ISU leadership's narrow and hierarchical view of solidarity was effective within an ISU dominated by the more ethnically homogenous SUP that consisted primarily of northern Europeans (whether they held citizenship or not). However, in the larger, more ethnically and linguistically diverse Atlantic unions, strict craft union principles were harder to maintain. Moreover, the West Coast's proximity to Asian labor markets and the common enemy of cheap Chinese competition ensured that any potential ethnic fissures within the SUP stayed beneath the surface. More generally, the West Coast encounter with race often collapsed the ethnic fissures from the East into a broader category of whiteness.[76] There was no equivalent common enemy on the Atlantic Coast. The resulting tension between the SUP-dominated ISU leadership and the Atlantic unions that culminated in the Spanish firemen's defection to the IWW and Furuseth's machinations against George Bodine led to the collapse of the Atlantic unions. In the IWW, Spanish firemen would not be subject to Furuseth and the ISU leadership's racial chauvinism.

The fall of the Atlantic unions was actually a blessing in disguise, at least in the short term. Without these unions, Furuseth and the ISU leadership could continue an organizing strategy based around whiteness and a legislative strategy that sought to insulate the maritime labor market through skill and linguistic standards. However, this strategy would come back to haunt them after the war, when the postwar shipping environment made the Wobblies' industrial organizational strategy more attractive, especially for the thousands of new members who became sailors during the massive wartime expansion of the merchant marine. In the meantime, despite the Spanish firemens' defection, the IWW achieved limited success in the ISU, especially on the West Coast. In fact, contemporary labor historian Paul F. Brissenden estimated that in a 1914 report for the United States Commission on Industrial Relations a San Francisco local had 247 paid members.[77] This is compared to about three to five thousand SUP members. Moreover, the 247 consisted of both sailors and longshoremen.

In any event, the combination of the 1912 sinking of the supposedly "unsinkable" *Titanic* and the Atlantic unions' collapse in 1913 provided an opportunity for the ISU leadership to turn both the shipping industry's and their internal critics' arguments about the irrelevance of skill on its head. Additionally, without the ethnically mixed Atlantic branches, the SUP leadership intensified their link between race and skill. Moreover, the *Titanic* disaster placed a renewed focus on safety at sea.[78] After all, if the "unsinkable" ship could go down, what about older ships that had been afloat for decades? Public concern grew so acute that in 1913, an international conference on safety at sea took place in London, with Furuseth attending at the appointment of President Wilson. For Furuseth and the union leadership, the *Titanic* disaster was proof that skill did still matter in the steamship era. Indeed, the National Consumers League supported the bill because of the ISU's emphasis on the need for safety standards.[79]

In 1914 the ISU made its case for the skilled sailor to Congress by arguing that safety and the financial interest of shipping capital were no longer aligned. The union leadership based its argument on the combination of "modern insurance" and limited liability laws that allowed shipping firms to mitigate the risk of a maritime disaster.[80] According to the ISU, the problem was that the insurance was often of value greater than the vessel and its cargo. In a memorial written to the House Committee on Merchant Marine and Fisheries, Furuseth and ISU vice president Patrick Flynn pointed out that, "[m]any years ago the shipowner was responsible to the traveling public for any failure to provide either an efficient crew or a proper vessel."[81] The memorial continued, stating, "any failure resulting in loss of life, health or limb of the traveler was subject to damages which might bankrupt the shipowner."[82] "A carefully worked out system of insurance abolished that," Furuseth added, whereas "when the shipowner was liable to lose his all, self-interest was sufficient to cause him to have a stanch vessel and an efficient crew."[83] Limited liability and modern insurance, according to the ISU, had caused an erosion of safety standards.

The ISU alleged that protection from the potential losses resulting from a shipwreck lowered shipping firms' incentive to ensure a safe vessel. In fact, Furuseth and Flynn argued that this was partly "recognized by the enactment of laws compelling vessels to be well built and properly equipped."[84] Even then, Furuseth stated, shipping companies routinely "evaded those laws or simply disregarded them," causing the government to create an inspection service to keep the shipping companies in line.[85] Though there were legislative standards to ensure vessels were kept safe, Furuseth and Flynn believed that there was no "standard of efficiency required in the men who are suppose" to man these vessels.[86] This was consistent with Furuseth's and the ISU's long-term argument concerning the importance of the skilled sailor to the sailing trade. Shipping companies could render a vessel unsafe since the "shipowner may take his vessel to sea with a crew of not one of whom has any experience or can understand the orders" of the officers.[87] Though not explicitly stated, Furuseth and Flynn were referring to Chinese sailors. Furuseth and the union leadership were cloaking a racial argument in the language of craft union principles that used standards of skill and experience in place of overt racial restriction. This had long been a tactic of the craft-centric AFL-led labor movement.[88]

However, despite the racially neutral language, the ISU and Furuseth seldom hid their argument that the racial characteristics of Chinese workers rendered them inherently unskilled, and thus unfit to serve on America's merchant vessels. As early as 1898, Furuseth stated that Asian "fatalism" disqualified them as potential sailors.[89] While testifying before Congress in 1914, Furuseth argued, "the general opinion among seamen, among people generally is that the oriental is a very poor man as compared with the white man in efficiency."[90] Additionally, the ISU president made a direct connection between the deskilling of the industry and the increasing Asianization of the merchant marine, stating: "in the last twenty years the efficiency of the men sailing the sea, taken as a whole, has been reduced by fifty per cent, and the number of orientals [*sic*] has doubled more than twice."[91] The *Coast Seamen's Journal* advanced this reasoning that same year, arguing that "efficiency and competency are freely sacrificed at sea in order to assure cheapness."[92] Without standards of skill for maritime labor, there could be no safety at sea.

Central to Furuseth's and the ISU's racialization of the Chinese sailor was a belief that they were not "real sailors." That is, they were not in the view of the union leadership, *qualified* sailors. Or, as Furuseth said, "[n]ow, then, I do not want to have anybody believe that everybody who sails as a sailor is a sailor today."[93] Adding, "the fact of the matter is that altogether too great a number of the men who are called sailors are not sailors, at all, because they are picked up from anywhere."[94]

Unsurprisingly, shipping companies rejected this characterization of Asian crews and instead argued that it was white American sailors who were not only inefficient but also undisciplined. Robert Dollar defended Asian crews by stating that they could "get more work out of them" than white American crews.[95] To support his point, Dollar criticized a section of the Seamen's bill that forced captains to produce 50% of a sailor's earned wages on demand while at port, by stating, "[n]o worse provision for the American sailor than this could have been devised, as I am quite safe in saying that 80 per cent of them drink every cent they have."[96] This long-held, popular image of the American sailor continued to haunt them and was being used to undermine their skill and safety argument.[97]

The ISU countered this by painting a racial image of Chinese sailors as docile, unthinking, opium-addicted drones, and panic-stricken children. This was not the first time the sailors had characterized Chinese sailors this way. As early as 1905–1906, the union argued that Chinese sailors were more machine than worker—unthinking automatons utterly dependent on the master.[98] During the lobbying campaign for the Seamen's Act, the union leadership argued it was this docility that made Chinese crews desirable in the eyes of shipping firms. As the *Coast Seamen's Journal* pointed out in 1912, "the Asiatic is a most desirable seamen because he is the cheapest and most docile," and does not agitate for nor care about their "rights."[99] Additionally, Furuseth actually implied before Congress that shipping companies cultivated this docility and dependency by supplying their crew with opium.[100] The *Coast Seamen's Journal* was less subtle, stating in 1913, "Congress ought to prohibit the practice of permitting Chinese crews to be drugged with opium."[101]

According to the ISU leadership, Chinese laborers' docility and opium use combined with their general lack of skill and efficiency, while perhaps not problematic under ideal conditions, would have catastrophic consequences in a crisis. Both the *CSJ* and Furuseth pointed out that during the *Titanic* disaster, everything was exacerbated by the confusion of the crew.[102] A skilled crew, therefore, was necessary to navigate a potential crisis. The ISU argued that Chinese sailors lacked the skill and disposition necessary to handle a crisis while at sea, leading to potential losses of cargo and loss of life for the passengers and crew.[103] Yet according to Furuseth and the union leadership, shipping companies need not worry about such eventualities because the insurance would cover the losses and then some. This discouraged shipping firms from hiring a skilled crew capable of performing in a crisis. Because there was no incentive for shipowners to care about the skill of the crew and thus the safety of the ship, the ISU argued that the Seamen's bill was necessary to "assist the conscience of the shipowner, since his self-interest had been so much reduced."[104] The ISU was able to use the public fear of maritime disasters as a means to enact standards of skill and training that would give white American sailors a leg up on their Chinese counterparts. Through the La Follette Act, the ISU leadership was attempting to provide a legislative definition of the requirements necessary to be considered a skilled and qualified sailor, specifically an "Able Seamen"—a definition they believed Chinese sailors would not be able to meet.

By framing the La Follette Seamen's bill as an effort to improve the safety of life at sea, the ISU attempted to use increased safety standards to create a more protected labor market that privileged the skilled white sailor without explicitly racializing the law—even though racial exclusion was central to the logic of the La Follette Seamen's Act. After all, Furuseth had testified before Congress that the act's purpose was to "keep the sea for the white race."[105] The key to these craft protections was an explicit legislative definition of an able (or A.B. rated) seaman, as well as the exact percentage of able seamen required on all ships. This legislative definition was seen as necessary because, without it, shipping companies could hire anyone and define them as sailors.

To correct this, the Seamen's Act institutionalized the training and experience necessary before a sailor could be considered an able seaman. For instance, the La Follette Act specified that four years after the passage of the law, "sixty-five percent of the deck crew, exclusive of licensed officers and apprentices, be of a rating not less than able seaman."[106] According to the Seamen's Act, to get the rating of able seaman, a candidate must be nineteen years of age and have at least three years' experience or be a graduate of "school ships approved by and conducted under the rules prescribed by the Secretary of Commerce" and "may be rated able seamen after twelve months' service at sea."[107] To acquire the certification of able seaman, applicants may apply for a certificate with an affidavit showing "nationality and age of applicant and the vessel or vessels on which he has had service."[108] This did not, strictly speaking, bar Chinese sailors from acquiring an able seaman rating.

However, given that Furuseth and the ISU believed and argued that many sailors—especially foreign nonwhite sailors—lacked any skill whatsoever, the certification was aimed at boosting white American sailors and discouraging Chinese or foreign nonwhite sailors. In addition, the La Follette Act also addressed Furuseth's and the ISU's concerns that ships were "sent to sea manned by crews the larger part, perhaps all of whom, are unable to speak the language of the officers."[109] This was the key logic behind the language clause that at least 75 percent of the crew are "able to understand any order given by the officers of such vessels."[110]

Again, the act never mentions race. However, given the ISU's argument that Chinese workers often did not understand the officers' orders, the language clause was seen as the law's most potent weapon to exclude Chinese sailors.[111] Furthermore, since the ISU did not explicitly write race into the Seamen's bill, these legislative, craft protections were tantamount to making the sailing trade (more specifically able seamen) synonymous with whiteness. Indeed, linking whiteness and racial identity with specific vocations has a long history in the United States.[112] Moreover, with the collapse of the Atlantic unions in 1912–1913 and the northern European-dominated SUP firmly in control of the ISU, the link between whiteness and skill was less complicated.

With the Seamen's Act, the ISU thought they had finally found a way to effectively exclude Asian sailors without having to force an extension of the Chinese Exclusion Act to American ships, which had little chance of ever getting through Congress. American lawmakers had argued in 1902 that the Exclusion Act was meant to protect workers inside the United States from racial competition, noting that ships in the foreign trade were not inside the United States. However, improving safety at sea was something that shipping companies would have a hard time arguing against, at least in principle, especially in the wake of the *Titanic* disaster and a wave of public concern and conferences on the safety of life at sea. Additionally, the collapse of the Atlantic unions meant that the ISU was far more united in their fight and did not have to worry about internal dissent. However, craft union protections could not, by themselves, get around the international enforceability problem. Indeed, shipping companies could simply stop flying the American flag to avoid them.

The La Follette Act, the Domestic Labor Market, and the Economic Dimensions of U.S. Power

The La Follette Seamen's Act harnessed the economic dimensions of U.S. imperial expansion to deal with the international enforceability problem. Using the economic sphere of U.S. power allowed the sailors an imperial reach that extended well beyond the nation's territorial possessions. Specifically, the La Follette Seamen's Act used the United States' growing preponderance of economic power against the international shipping industry and nonwhite sailors to create a free labor market for maritime labor. The act circumvented the problem of regulating the foreign trade by applying to all ships, regardless of national registry. If a ship was entering a U.S. port, whether it flew the American flag or not, it had to conform to the La Follette Act's specifications. The ISU leadership designed the act to drive Asian sailors from the trade, liberate foreign sailors from the financial and legal shackles of the trade, and raise industry wages on a global scale. If successful, the act would globalize Asiatic exclusion through U.S. imperial trade power by extending an American-style domestic, free labor market to the water's edge of the Asian mainland, protecting white sailors in and beyond the United States from racialized foreign labor competition. Or, as Andrew Furuseth said, the act would provide the promise of "free soil" for seamen.[113]

The central feature of the La Follette Act was its extraterritoriality; the ISU leadership did not limit the act's jurisdictional converge to the mere physical expansion of U.S. territory. Indeed, a key motivation behind the ISU's 1907 attempt to extend the Exclusion Act to the farthest reaches of the coastwise trade was that only American flagged vessels were permitted to operate in the domestic trade. As a result, whatever regulations Congress enacted concerning the coastwise trade could not be undercut by international competition, nor could American shipping firms register their vessels under foreign flags to get around new regulations.

The transnational application of the act would prevent American shipping firms from switching to foreign registry to get around any legislation the ISU was able to get through Congress that might place limitations on who shipping firms could hire. The La Follette Seamen's Act got around this problem by applying to all ships, regardless of national registry, that entered a U.S. port. If a shipping firm wanted to do business in the United States, their vessels had to conform to the La Follette Act's regulations. Foreign governments, but especially the British, were not happy about this feature.[114] As Robert Dollar—who registered the majority of his vessels under the British flag—told Congress, the Seamen's bill would violate "some 21 treaties, causing ill-feeling between foreign nations and ourselves."[115] Luckily for the ISU, by the time the Seamen's bill was passed and signed into law, the major European maritime powers were too busy with World War I to mount much opposition.

The La Follette Seamen's Act leveled the playing field between U.S. and foreign-flagged vessels and neutralized a key argument in favor of Chinese crews. U.S. shipping companies could no longer blame their shift away from white American crews on the abstract forces of market competition. The craft union protections embedded within the bill that the ISU designed to drive Asians from the sea applied to foreign-flagged vessels as well as American.[116] For instance, the act required both foreign firms and foreign-flagged vessels to conform with the law's language clause and ensure that 75 percent of the crew could understand the orders of officers.[117] Note that the act is careful not to demand the crew speak English. The idea was to force foreign shipping firms to rely on their own nationals rather than Chinese, or other foreign racialized laborers. By prohibiting all vessels doing business in American ports from shipping a Chinese crew, the La Follette Act halted the continued downward spiral of maritime wages. However, this was not necessarily enough by itself to achieve the SUP's more ambitious goal of raising wages on a global scale up to the U.S. standard. To achieve this, the La Follette Act had to protect and guarantee the "autonomous mobility" of maritime workers in U.S. ports.[118]

By severing the legal and financial shackles that bound sailors to their ship, the La Follette Act created a free market for maritime labor in the United States. Though the 1898 White Act may have abolished the criminal punishment for desertion in U.S. ports, it did not apply to foreign sailors on foreign-flagged vessels. The same was true of the White Act's provision that prevented ship captains from withholding wages until the end of a sailor's contract; it only applied to American-flagged vessels.[119] This meant that foreign sailors were segmented into different wage scales according to their country of origin, ensuring that there was no free market in labor. Moreover, it prevented sailors from low-wage labor markets from deserting and reshipping in higher-wage ports.[120] In other words, vessels under foreign flags with foreign crews could avoid the high wages of American ports. As a result, U.S. shipping companies, using foreign registries, would sign up their crews in foreign ports. The wages for Chinese sailors may have been the lowest, sometimes as low as $9 per month, but the prevailing wages in Britain were $20 to $25 per month—well below the $40 American average.[121] On transpacific routes, this meant shipping crews from Hong Kong or Shanghai. For vessels on the Atlantic side, U.S. shipping companies flying the British flag would often use sailors hired in Manchester or Liverpool rather than New York or Boston. The La Follette Act removed this incentive by extending the provisions of the White Act that ensured a free labor market in the coastwise trade into the foreign trade by applying to all ships that entered U.S. ports. It legalized desertion for foreign sailors on foreign ships, stipulated that ship captains of all vessels could not withhold wages until the end of a contract, and guaranteed sailors the right to receive earned wages on-demand within forty-eight hours of arrival in a U.S port.[122] This effectively ended the crimping system in U.S. ports for all sailors, foreign and American.

By removing these financial and legal constraints, the ISU was betting that rapidly expanding U.S. economic power would create a new global standard for maritime wages and extend the free labor market of U.S. ports to the rest of the world. In a 1912 letter to President Wilson, Andrew Furuseth and ISU vice president Patrick Flynn explained how this worked in the coastwise trade: "[s]eamen on American vessels are free to leave their vessels in any domestic port" and "the result is that seamen on American vessels engaged in the domestic trade are paid wages and given conditions more nearly conforming to the American standard of living than those engaged in overseas trade."[123] With the La Follette Act, the idea was to encourage foreign sailors to desert in U.S. ports so they could be hired back at the wages of New York or San Francisco. In the words of Dollar Line president Robert Dollar, the Seamen's Act "would cause every crew to desert, whenever they come to an American port, and we would have to ship a new crew."[124] To retain their crews, foreign shipping companies would have to offer wages competitive with American rates. Otherwise, their crew would desert, and they would have to either hire them back at those higher American rates or hire a different crew at the same wages of port. Instead of a race to the bottom, it would become a race to the top; at least that was the idea. Furuseth even predicted that if the law was passed, "England, Germany, France and foreign nations, would, in less than two years, be on the same [wage] basis" as the U.S. shipping industry.[125] The size of the U.S. economy by 1915 was such that it might exert considerable influence over the wages of the international shipping industry. This was not an unreasonable calculation considering, by 1913, the United States produced 36 percent of the world's goods, more than Britain and Germany combined.[126] Moreover, the outbreak of war in August 1914 meant the British and French demand for American goods increased dramatically.

The La Follette Act rode the expansionary forces of U.S. economic power beyond its shores, marshaling them into the service of a labor union. Indeed, labor historian Leon Fink recently argued that "the La Follette Act presumed nothing less than a *nationalist* [emphasis added] solution to the problem of discouragingly cheap, international maritime labor," which is indeed correct.[127]

However, I would push Fink's analysis further and argue that it was a nationalist solution necessarily underpinned by U.S. economic power if it had any hope of actually working.

A more apt description of the La Follette Act was that it presumed an *imperial* solution to the international problem of cheap maritime labor. Secretary of State John Hay understood the imperial potential of U.S economic power when he issued the famous "open door" notes on China in 1901.[128] Hay's "open door" policy called for an open market in China rather than the prevailing spheres of influence that the more established imperial powers such as Britain, France, Germany, and Japan already enjoyed.[129] Hay was betting that emerging U.S. economic dominance could serve as an effective repertoire of imperial power (mitigating the absence of a U.S. sphere of influence in China) and overwhelm its competitors in open, free-market competition. As the late great historian William Appleman Williams first argued, "the policy of the open door was designed to establish the conditions under which America's preponderant economic power would extend the American system throughout the world without the establishment and inefficiency of traditional colonialism."[130] The ISU leadership was making a similar calculation, that emerging U.S. economic dominance would allow the La Follette Act to extend the ISU's vision of how the maritime labor market should operate throughout the world. This vision stipulated whom shipping firms should hire, how they hired them, the kind of qualifications sailors needed, and, most importantly, the type of labor market under which the industry should operate.

For the ISU and the SUP, the La Follette Act's craft union protections, combined with the free labor market it created, provided the promise of "free soil" for America's white merchant sailors. Or, as the union leadership instructed its members to tell their congressional representatives, "[l]et American soil become free soil for seamen as it is for all other men."[131] Indeed, part of the promise of free soil was a labor environment that enjoyed the same protections that white workers within the United States were guaranteed. Chief among those protections was insulation from competition with nonwhite populations and the working conditions that came with them.

Similar to the free-soil vision of westward expansion, the freedom of white Americans was conditional upon the exclusion and often violent erasure of nonwhites. Indeed, historian Jerold Aurbach first pointed this out in his 1960 analysis of the La Follette Act. Aurbach argued that despite the act's progressivist pedigree—sponsored by the era's most famous progressive, Wisconsin senator and key Furuseth ally Robert La Follette—"Furuseth's cry for seamen's rights" was "indistinguishable from Nordic racism."[132]

The La Follette Act is an almost perfect exemplar of the apparent contradictions at the heart of Progressive Era reform efforts. It offered white sailors higher wages, better safety standards, and, most importantly, the freedom to quit their jobs. At the same time, it promised to drive Asian sailors from the trade entirely. Even Robert La Follette was not above these apparent contradictions. During debate over the various Seamen's bills that were submitted between 1911 and 1915, the Wisconsin senator emphasized the bill's safety standards and emancipatory potential.[133] Nevertheless, his understanding of safety was steeped in racial essentialism. In defense of the language clause, he pointed out to his fellow senators that ships were often manned by Chinese sailors "stupefied by opium."[134] He also argued that the law would reverse the decades-long U.S. maritime policy that had "handed over the American merchant marine to the Chinese and the Japanese."[135] A month after the bill was signed into law, La Follette wrote a tribute to his friend Andrew Furuseth and noted how the ISU president "had witnessed the blighting effects of the world wide Shipping Trust upon the seapower of the white race." La Follette continued, stating that in an effort to "swell its enormous dividends," the shipping trust began to "supplant white sailors with the low waged, cheaply fed Orientals, until they swarm the merchant marine of every maritime nation."[136] He then praised Furuseth for recognizing "the future peril to Christian civilization as the sea power slowly but surely passes to the Oriental races."[137] It is no wonder that La Follette was able to find enthusiastic support and key allies among southern democrats, who were well aware of the law's true purpose.[138] Senator Duncan Fletcher of Florida—who was second only to La Follette in his support for the law—argued that the true purpose of the language clause "is not so much intended to promote safety at sea as it is to effect wages and secure the employment of other than Asiatic Seamen on the Pacific."[139]

However, these seeming contradictions make more sense when viewed through a settler colonial analytical lens. Indeed, Marilyn Lake recently argued that in settler societies such as Australia and the United States, progressivism was inculcated with settler colonialism's "regime of race."[140] As a result, we should understand American progressivism as a reform movement that was grafted onto the pre-existing racial order of U.S. settler colonialism—an order that sought to exclude those who did not fit the prevailing definition of whiteness. By attempting to drive nonwhite sailors from the world's merchant vessels, the ISU and the SUP were trying to extend the U.S. domestic labor market far beyond Honolulu, and beyond the space where the United States held direct imperial sovereignty. As Furuseth himself said, "this act gives freedom directly to fully 150,000 American seamen, and indirectly it will affect possibly 2,000,000 other seamen throughout the world."[141] Such freedom, according to Furuseth and the ISU, was necessarily contingent upon the exclusion of nonwhites.

Before the Seamen's Act, the domestic boundaries of the United States labor market—though far from static—ended with the coastwise trade on the Pacific Coast, despite the Commerce Department symbolically extending the Exclusion Act to Honolulu in 1907. However, in the foreign trade, once white American sailors stepped aboard their vessels in San Francisco harbor, they had essentially left the United States domestic labor market and entered a coercive, unfree, imperial labor regime where they were bound to their ship by law, contract, and financial penalty.[142] Conversely, Chinese sailors hired by shipping companies in ports outside the United States were physically held to their ships because the Exclusion Act prevented them from entering the nation.[143] For non-Chinese foreign sailors, the threat of lost wages and the potential of being hunted down and imprisoned or returned to their ships bound them to their ship without the need of actual confinement. In the foreign maritime trade, the interstitial space between ship and shore served as the boundary between the (mostly) free soil national labor market and the unfree, imperial world of international shipping. On the West Coast, this was tantamount to the labor markets of the Far East extending all the way to San Francisco harbor. Moreover, elements of the unfree maritime labor market trickled into the nation because it was the local, state, and federal governments' responsibility to hunt down foreign deserters and return them to their ship. Furuseth and the ISU compared this practice to the Fugitive Slave Law of the antebellum era, even calling it the "fugitive slave law of the sea."[144] The Seamen's Act was an attempt to reverse this arrangement by incorporating the foreign maritime trade, regardless of national registry, into the domestic labor market of the United States.

By incorporating the foreign maritime trade into the domestic U.S. labor market, the Seamen's Act moved the line between domestic and foreign labor markets from the water's edge of American ports to the water's edge of foreign and imperial ports (the government did not consider the Philippines as part of the domestic trade). No matter where a ship was departing from, it had to conform to the Seamen's Act regulations if its destination was the United States.[145] As a result, U.S. sailors would not exit the domestic labor market until they stepped off their U.S.-flagged ships in foreign ports. For West Coast sailors, this meant that the U.S. domestic labor market extended all the way to the water's edge of the Asian mainland, whether in British-controlled Hong Kong or in internationally divided Shanghai.[146] Conversely, when a foreign sailor stepped aboard his vessel in a foreign port that was bound for the United States, it was tantamount to entering the rules and regulations of the U.S. domestic labor market. Given America's emerging economic dominance, the hope was that the La Follette Act would force other nations to adopt its standards across the board. The intended effect was to create what we might call a maritime metropole of whiteness that transcended national boundaries and kept the "sea for the white race."[147]

Viewed in this light, the La Follette Seamen's Act had the potential to stitch together the anarchic (though interconnected) process of nonwhite immigration restriction that characterized the immigration policies of white settler descended nations in the late nineteenth and early twentieth centuries—a process that historians Marilyn Lake and Henry Reynolds called "drawing the global color line."[148] Nations and settler colonies from the United States, Canada, Australia, and New Zealand were all attempting to draw the global color line. Australia had the White Australia policy; New Zealand had a head tax; and Canada had a head tax and a series of legal loopholes to ensure insulation from the "other" nonwhite parts of the British Empire, namely India.[149] Underpinned by emerging U.S. economic hegemony, the La Follette Act threaded these policies together by incorporating a large segment of the shipping trade into a U.S. domestic labor context, which privileged white sailors. For the United States, as Andrew Furuseth told Congress, the law would protect the nation from the 35,000–45,000 Chinese sailors that entered U.S. ports each year.[150] By creating the potential to stitch together the racialized immigration policies of the emerging nations of the Pacific Rim white settler colonies, the La Follette Seamen's Act was one of the most ambitious efforts of racial exclusion ever attempted, though its success necessarily depended on the economic dimensions of U.S. imperial power.

CHAPTER 4

Agents of Empire

Merchant Sailors, the Great War, and the New American Merchant Marine, 1898–1919

The SUP and the ISU justified their various efforts to insulate the maritime labor market from foreign competition by a broader and deeper belief about the proper role of merchant sailors in the history of empire—a view at odds with U.S. maritime policy that since 1884 had emphasized access to cheap labor. Andrew Furuseth's and the union leadership's various tactics were particular examples of their larger ambition of amalgamating merchant sailors with the national interest. The SUP and ISU leadership, led by Furuseth, viewed the merchant marine, specifically merchant sailors, as a valuable and strategic national resource. Furuseth's views were rooted in his reading of naval theorist Alfred Thayer Mahan, especially his most famous 1890 work, *The Influence of Sea Power Upon History*. Furuseth was not the only individual of his era to embrace Mahan. Indeed, Mahan's theories on sea power were widely read among policymakers, military officials, and world leaders.[1] However, Furuseth was unique in his focus on the specific role of the merchant sailor in Mahan's work and maintained that an adequate supply of experienced sailors was just as important as the number of ships a nation counted in its navy and merchant fleet.[2] As a result, the SUP and the ISU leadership believed that insulating the maritime labor market from foreign competition was necessary to cultivate a skilled and experienced reservoir of American sailors. However, amalgamating merchant sailors with the national interest had to be achieved on their terms, as free and independent workers who prescribed the rules and parameters of the maritime labor market. In short, Furuseth and the ISU leadership reimagined sailors as agents of empire rather than a cheap, commodified, and dependent maritime proletariat.

The First World War temporarily affirmed but ultimately subverted these ambitions. Amid a maritime crisis brought on by the withdrawal of the European belligerent power's merchant fleets from normal commerce, the United States government scrambled to meet the demands of foreign trade. With only about 10 percent of goods shipped to and from the United States carried on U.S.-flagged vessels, the government needed ships and, more importantly, men to sail them.[3] This turn of events provided exactly the kind of crisis Furuseth and the union leadership had been warning could happen without a U.S.-flagged merchant marine and an adequate supply of skilled white American sailors. In the short term, the government and even shipping company executives agreed to shift U.S. maritime policy away from access to cheap labor and over to cultivating a reservoir of skilled and independent American sailors and even to prioritize union members in the hiring process. Moreover, the Wilson administration created and invited the ISU to join an institutional apparatus that would build and manage a new American merchant marine. As a result of this expansion, the ISU's numbers ballooned from thirteen thousand in 1914 to more than one hundred thousand by war's end. This facilitated the successful reorganization of an Atlantic branch that had collapsed in 1913–1914.[4]

However, in the long run, structural changes in the U.S. and international shipping industry brought on by the war subverted these gains. The shipping industry emerged from the war consolidated, highly capitalized, and about to face stiff competition from the British merchant fleet's return to normal commerce. As a result, access to cheap labor again was prioritized. When the wartime emergency dissipated, so did the ISU's leverage. Instead of becoming agents of empire, the ISU and the SUP were entangled within a corporatist state structure that left them with little bargaining power in the postwar era. Moreover, the Paris Peace settlement created an international regime of regulation in the form of the League of Nations and the International Labor Organization that Furuseth believed undermined the unilateralism of the La Follette Act, which was already under siege from lawsuits within the United States. Furthermore, Furuseth was unable to gain the support of European sailors' unions in his efforts to salvage and extend the La Follette Act because they held fundamentally different views on the nature of maritime labor relations—views at odds with the law in both letter and spirit. In the end, the shipping industry became more intensely amalgamated and integrated with the national interest, but white American merchant sailors did not. The First World War helped the

ISU reach the peak of its power while simultaneously laying the seeds for its downfall.

From Objects and Instruments to Agents of Empire

The outbreak of war in August 1914 changed everything. With the major imperial powers mobilizing their merchant fleets and economies for what would eventually become a totalizing armed conflict, the U.S. shipping industry entered a crisis. Current U.S. maritime policy whereby the vast majority of American manufactured goods were shipped on foreign-flagged vessels quickly was exposed as untenable. Indeed, since the Spanish-American War, the union leadership had been arguing that this type of policy was prone to precisely this kind of crisis. At least for a moment, it seemed that Andrew Furuseth and the ISU leadership had been vindicated. The United States needed a large merchant marine that sailed under the American flag, manned by "Americans," and it needed it as soon as possible. By 1916 the United States began a massive shipbuilding program.

Additionally, the government created large corporatist institutions to build, manage, and recruit the labor necessary to man the new merchant marine. Within a few short years, white American sailors went from a desperate group of laborers in a decaying trade to a sought-after labor force. This unexpected turn of events created the conditions for U.S. merchant sailors' amalgamation with the national interest. The war compelled the government to temporarily incorporate white American maritime labor into its desired place within the U.S. imperial hierarchy. This new reality made the La Follette Act's ambition of building an American merchant marine remarkably prescient. As the war raged, the Seaman's Act began to affect the wages of British sailors, helping to level the playing field by bringing up British wages to the American standard. The war had, at least for the moment, transformed white American sailors from largely undesirable objects or instruments to agents of U.S. empire.

Maritime labor long has occupied a dual role within the history of empire, similar to military labor. "Soldiers," as historian Peter Way posited, "constituted both instruments and objects of imperial authority."[5] This meant that soldiers helped drive imperial expansion but also were subjugated by the empire they served. Soldiers "freely enlisted in an occupation that involved taking from others their lands, their freedom, and their very lives."[6] But as "workers in the war industry, they were regimented and rendered unfree for the duration of their enlistment, subordinated as laborers, and subjected to cruel work discipline."[7] The life of a merchant sailor followed a similar, if not identical pattern. They also were rendered unfree for the extent of their contract and subjected to cruel work discipline. Moreover, the shipping companies subjected sailors to a system of debt dependency that often made it difficult to escape the industry in which they "freely" enlisted, and historically were subject to criminal punishment for quitting their jobs.[8] On the other hand, merchant sailors helped facilitate the rise of vast globe-spanning maritime empires.[9] They carried the fruits of empire from plundered territories back to the imperial center and circulated valuable commodities produced by colonial and imperial subjects, whether as free laborers, indentured servants, or slaves. Soldiers created the possibility of empire, but sailors made it a working reality.

However, the crucial difference between soldiers and merchant sailors lay in the specific source of their dehumanization. Like most forms of routinized labor, the dehumanization of sailors stemmed from their commodification. They were a resource to be exploited that did not possess the same range of rights—such as the right to quit—that other commodified workers enjoyed. For soldiers, their dehumanization emerged not "from their commodification but from their amalgamation with the national interests," reducing them to an appendage of state power that was programmed to serve and obey.[10] This was a difference between sailors and soldiers that the ISU and the SUP leadership were working to eliminate.

The SUP and ISU leadership resisted their commodification by working for their amalgamation with the national interest. In doing this, however, the union leadership was not merely trading one form of dehumanization for another. What made the SUP's and ISU's efforts of national amalgamation different from the dehumanized nature of soldiers was that the SUP and the ISU wanted it under their terms. They wanted to set conditions under which they would be amalgamated. By setting the terms of their amalgamation, the SUP and the ISU were attempting to ensure they would become agents rather than mere instruments and objects of "imperial authority."

The SUP's and ISU's access to an essential institution of empire—the merchant ship—made possible their attempt to amalgamate with the national interest.[11] The SUP and Furuseth maintained that the merchant marine was too important a strategic resource to be manned by foreign workers. To support this belief, Furuseth turned to the theories of Alfred Thayer Mahan to make the case for merchant sailors' amalgamation with the national interest. In 1902 he told Congress that "[c]aptain Mahan informs us that it was English seamen, the plenitude of them, that gave to England her victory over France in two wars."[12] He continued to reference Mahan, stating, "from the merchant marine must come the seamen who shall man and equip the modern battleship."[13] Moreover, Furuseth cited a 1901 report from the commissioner of navigation to the Senate

Committee on Immigration explaining the pitfalls of U.S. merchant marine policy that encouraged "vessels owned by Americans but sailing under foreign flags and manned by foreigners."[14] Reading from the report, Furuseth said, "[f]or all national purposes these vessels contribute to the maritime strength of foreign nations and are training schools for their navies."[15]

The merchant marine's traditional role as a feeder for the navy provided the SUP's and the ISU's most compelling justification to insulate the maritime labor market from foreign competition. They framed Asian encroachment within the merchant marine as a threat to the future of American naval power. The SUP reasoned that if the merchant marine began to rely exclusively on Chinese sailors to man their ships, the U.S. Navy would not have an adequate number of experienced "American" sailors to draw on in a time of war. The *Coast Seamen's Journal* opined that sailors "are men of skill and endurance, requiring long and systematic training," with "naval seamen" being "the highest development of this quality."[16] As a result, the *Journal* concluded: "Every Chinaman and other Asiatic employed on such vessels reduces proportionally the naval strength that may be depended upon in a time of need."[17] Moreover, in the aftermath of the Spanish-American War, the SUP leadership wrote to President McKinley and asked "if the whole merchant marine of the United States had carried nothing but Chinese crews for the last fifteen years, where would the government have obtained the men who fought so valiantly on first day of May" and could the "Chinese have done as those men did?"[18] From the union leadership's perspective, insulating the maritime labor market from foreign competition served the national interest.

The SUP and the ISU framed their attempts to insulate the maritime labor market in the foreign trade—whether through overt racial exclusion or craft union standards—as part of an imperial competition to control the world's oceans. For instance, while testifying in support of extending Chinese exclusion to merchant ships in 1902, Furuseth told Congress that "[u]nder existing law [without maritime exclusion] we shall have Chinese and nothing but Chinese, and shall go on training men for the future navy of China."[19] That same year, the *Coast Seamen's Journal* protested the granting of government mail subsidies to shipping firms that used Chinese crews by asking "if the citizens of the United States wish to pay taxes for the training of seamen for the Chinese Navy."[20] During the campaign to enact the La Follette Seamen's bill, Furuseth warned Congress that, "[a]s it now stands . . . the oriental is going to take control of the oceans of the world."[21] However, Furuseth maintained that if the government passed the Seamen's Act and put white American sailors on an even plane with Chinese sailors, "we can then fight them for control of the world's oceans."[22]

Behind the SUP and ISU leadership's understanding of control of the seas was the logic of white settler colonialism. Obviously, the world's oceans are not territory to be occupied or settled in the same way as land. People do not settle the ocean, nor do they set up farms, homesteads, or even political units. Nevertheless, as Furuseth pointed out in 1915, some two million people, including 150 thousand Americans, made their living on the high seas.[23] At any given moment, there were hundreds of thousands of workers laboring afloat the world's oceans. While it may not be possible to occupy or settle an ocean, it is possible to occupy the jobs and vessels that traverse the sea. Since these jobs were, according to the SUP and the ISU, essential to U.S. commercial and naval power, who held them was vitally important. In the context of colonization or occupation, the spread of maritime and naval power was a logical extension of U.S. westward expansion. The *Coast Seamen's Journal* and Furuseth himself even framed the implications of the La Follette Act as bringing "free soil for" seamen.[24] For the SUP and the ISU, control of the seas was about who occupied the ships. The La Follette Act's passage, therefore, was a critical step on the SUP's and ISU's road from instruments and objects to agents of empire.[25]

Shipping companies rejected the ISU's understanding of control of the sea and argued—perhaps unsurprisingly—that control was about who owned the ships, not who worked on them, or even where the ship was flagged. Indeed, there was a consensus among shipping company executives, administrators, and congressional officials from the 1890s onward that maritime labor was tethered to the national interest. They just had a different understanding of what that meant. From the state and shipping capital's perspective, the only measure of maritime labor's importance to the national interest was its low cost. If that meant American shipping firms had to register their vessels under foreign flags to obtain cheap labor, then so be it. Before the war, U.S. shipping companies with state support argued it was better to have a merchant marine owned and controlled by American capital but crewed by foreign workers on vessels flying foreign flags. Moreover, some of the largest shipping firms in the world were based in Britain but often controlled by American capital. This arrangement allowed the shipping industry to benefit from what might be called the twin pillars of U.S. imperial expansion: access to markets and cheap labor.[26] However, the U.S. government and even shipping company executives were about to rethink these assumptions shortly after the outbreak of war in 1914.

The outbreak of war in Europe quickly led to a maritime crisis on the Atlantic Coast that the ISU had been warning against. This turn of events presented an opportunity to test the policy recommendations that Furuseth, Walter Macarthur, and the rest of the union leadership long had advocated. While war may have precipitated the crisis, the ISU believed that U.S. merchant marine policy, or lack thereof, was the underlying cause. In February 1915, the *Coast Seamen's Journal* pointed out: "[t]he shortsighted [*sic*] policy of our government has for years driven American boys from the ships, and American ships from the seas. We are now confronted with external circumstances both serious and ridiculous."[27] The *Journal* continued, stating, "[w]ith enough raw material and manufactured goods to supply the warring nations of Europe . . . we are compelled to see our commodities shipped on foreign bottoms [vessels]."[28] At the outbreak of war, the vast majority of American exports were shipped on foreign-flagged vessels. In August 1914, 58 percent of the U.S. foreign trade was carried on British vessels alone.[29] As the British Empire, Germany (which possessed the world's second-largest merchant fleet), and the rest of the European belligerents began mobilizing for war, they withdrew their respective merchant fleets from normal commerce. Freight began to back up in major East Coast ports; the shipment rates of wheat quadrupled; and cotton rose from twenty cents a hundredweight in 1910 to $1.30 in 1915.[30] The United States scrambled to fill the "hole" left by the European merchant fleet's redeployment to ensure the continued flow of American exports. Moreover, the simultaneous explosion of allied demand for American arms and supplies exacerbated the situation.[31] Ultimately, the withdrawal of European merchant fleets from normal commercial activity demonstrated the general inability of the American merchant marine to fulfill the demands of foreign trade.[32] As a result, the U.S. government had to come up with a plan quickly.

With the passage of the 1916 Merchant Marine Act, the Wilson administration began taking the necessary steps to build the kind of merchant marine the union leadership long insisted the United States needed.[33] The act created the United States Shipping Board in September 1916 "for the purpose of encouraging, developing, and creating a naval auxiliary and naval reserve and merchant marine to meet the requirements of the commerce of the United States with its Territories and possessions and with foreign countries."[34] The previous sentence is an almost perfect distillation of what the union leadership had been advocating since its inception. The legislation and the agencies the Merchant Marine Act created represented a massive investment in U.S. maritime power. Even before 1916, American shipyards began cranking out ever-greater tonnage. However, it quickly became apparent that a coordinated approach was necessary to fill the gap left by the warring European states. The 1916 Merchant Marine Act would allow the United States merchant marine to finally match the nation's growing economic power and eventually rival the might of British maritime power.

Indeed, Andrew Furuseth, along with *Coast Seamen's Journal* editors Walter Macarthur (now the San Francisco harbor commissioner) and his successor, Paul Sharrenberg, argued that the reliance on foreign carriers left the United States open to just this kind of crisis. As the *Journal* stated, the new shipping board "will have at its disposal the sum of $50,000,000 for the building of an American merchant marine, a fleet of vessels that will be American in fact as well as in name—i.e. ships that will serve the public instead of purely selfish interest."[35] Furthermore, the *Journal* celebrated the appointment of lawyer William Denman of San Francisco, who had successfully argued many important court cases favorable to sailors and noted that "whatever problems there was with the shipping board, the inclusion of Denman ensured that sailors would have a strong ally on the board."[36] In creating the Shipping Board, the Wilson administration used the power of the state to direct and control the building, manning, and operation of the U.S. merchant fleet.

The creation of the Shipping Board was good news for ISU members, especially with an ally in charge of building and manning America's new merchant marine. Additionally, before the United States entered the war, American shipping firms that flagged their vessels under British registry (such as the Dollar Steamship Line) began reverting to U.S. registry to take advantage of American neutrality since the north Atlantic had become a dangerous warzone.[37] By early January 1917, the Shipping Board had banned the transfer of U.S. vessels to foreign flags.[38] After nearly fifty years of decline, the U.S. merchant marine was not merely resuscitated back to life but received a powerful shot of adrenalin. The government designed the building program for speed; this was not a long-term plan that moved gradually. Ships were needed as quickly as possible, and more importantly for the ISU, they needed labor to make the ships sail. This crisis was not just about building more ships, especially since the 1916 legislation conceived of the merchant marine as a naval auxiliary.

The material needs of the war effort (before and after United States entry) finally created a need for "native" American sailors. Suddenly, it seemed that the Wilson administration finally understood what Andrew Furuseth and the SUP had been saying all along about the need for a merchant marine made up of "native" American sailors. Once the United States officially entered the war, a highly publicized campaign to recruit American sailors began. Before the war, the percentage of Americans who manned American ships in the foreign trade was still quite low. On the Atlantic side, the majority of sailors on U.S. vessels were European. On the Pacific side, the decline of "American" crewed vessels resulted from the shipping companies' reliance on cheap labor from China. Indeed, the central ambition of the Seamen's Act was to reverse these trends.[39]

However, some of the La Follette Act's provisions came in gradually. For instance, the quotas of the language clause started with 50 percent, later rising to 75 percent.[40] Furthermore, the act initially only applied to American-flagged vessels. Yet the impact of the war served to weaponize the act by amplifying its effects. For the moment, the war was doing the heavy lifting since the belligerent powers were drafting thousands of European sailors into their respective militaries. It would be a few years before American sailors would feel the true effects of the La Follette Act. Once the United States officially entered the war in April 1917, the need for native sailors accelerated.

With U.S. entry into the war, the problem of maritime labor on the Atlantic Coast morphed into a full-blown labor crisis that the government needed to resolve. As with other strategic industries, the Wilson administration began building on the corporatist institutional framework created in 1916 to better direct and manage the emerging U.S. merchant marine. The idea behind this type of state structure is to involve and incorporate trade union leadership and business organizations into the nation's economic planning.[41] Just over a month after the U.S. entry into the war, the ISU signed the Atlantic Agreement and agreed to join the United States Shipping Board.[42] In exchange, the Shipping Board agreed to recognize the ISU and its affiliates as the sole representatives of maritime labor. The board also agreed to the payment of union wages (which brought Atlantic wages up to the higher Pacific Coast rate) and guaranteed that at least 60 percent of maritime jobs would go first to ISU members.[43]

The Atlantic Agreement laid the groundwork for greater cooperation between shipping capital and maritime labor for the duration of the war. A few months later, the secretaries of labor and commerce invited America's organized seamen to participate in a conference held in Washington designed to solve the crisis with representatives from the Departments of State, Commerce, Labor, the Shipping Board, and the shipowners.[44] Secretary of Labor William B. Wilson argued that manning the ships was a bigger challenge than simply building them, stating that, "[o]ne of our greatest problems will ultimately be the supply of a sufficient amount of skilled labor to man our vessels."[45] Such greater difficulty lay in the fact that as the U.S. had entered the war, the government specifically needed "native" American sailors since, as Wilson pointed out, "[o]ur American merchant marine has been manned by a personnel that is not entirely American."[46] By July 1917, Secretary Wilson estimated that upwards of 30 percent of the seamen engaged on American vessels were from Scandinavian countries (Furuseth's birthplace) that were not yet part of the war effort.[47] If circumstances conspired to drag these countries into the conflict, Wilson argued that their sailors likely would be conscripted into the armed forces of their respective nations, exacerbating the maritime labor crisis. It is interesting to note that the labor secretary's objection to the use of Scandinavian sailors was not their lack of U.S. citizenship, but that this important supply of skilled sailors could be lost if their respective countries entered the war. Additionally, Wilson pointed out that sheer numbers were not enough.

This meant that the problem of maritime labor was qualitative as well as quantitative. Finding sailors was one thing but ensuring that they possessed the training and skills necessary to safely and efficiently operate a vessel in a time of war was another. The labor secretary's opening remarks at the Washington Conference reflected this, stating, "[i]t is essential to safety that we should have not only a sufficient number of skilled men to handle vessels but that those men should be sufficiently experienced in utilizing their skill so that they may do almost automatically and in proper sequence, the things that are necessary for safety."[48] This was music to the ISU's ears. For thirty years, they had argued that even in the steamship era, skill was as important as ever. Wilson's statement and the general attitude of the Washington Conference confirmed this logic. For the moment, the crisis brought on by the war provided the sailors with a bit of redemption. Skill, experience, and seamanship were celebrated once again. As a result, the U.S. Shipping Board created a Sea Service Bureau dedicated to recruitment and training, ensuring newly recruited sailors had the skills necessary to ensure safety and efficiency at sea.[49] Furthermore, the newfound respect for skill seemed to indirectly rebut the central argument of the shipping firms in favor of cheap Asian labor. Finally, the sailors were gaining the respect that they long had craved.

Yet more than a newfound respect for skill, the maritime crisis seemed to cement the sailor's role as an essential component of U.S. imperial power. The *Coast Seamen's Journal* proudly reprinted the kind words of praise from the U.S. Shipping Board's director of recruitment, Henry Howard. In February 1918, Howard stated, "[a]t no other period in our national life has need been greater than now for fearless men to carry our flag through stress of war and storm to foreign ports.... In his hands we trust our trade; but more than this, we trust our honor, too. Neither shall perish so long as our mariners sail the seas."[50] The bureau's call to the sea ended by emphasizing that the war was to be won by ships, and calling for the recruitment of fifty thousand men to crew the "New Merchant Marine."[51] President Wilson pointed out that the sailors who manned the nation's merchant ships had become an essential "factor in our national life."[52] The president added that "[n]o more honorable serviceable tasks can come to any of our people than that of manning our merchant marine."[53] Andrew Furuseth could not have said it better himself. Beyond their newfound respect, the ISU's actions and influence was beginning to affect the global shipping industry.

By 1917 the ISU's efforts to force their way into their desired place within the U.S. imperial hierarchy dovetailed with the effects of the war and began to show results. Part of the La Follette Act's logic to build an American merchant marine was to neutralize the advantages of foreign fleets by creating a more level playing field. During the second half of the war, the La Follette Seamen's Act began to strike at the heart of British maritime power that was as much rooted in low wages as it was in having the world's largest fleet. 1916–1917 is when the La Follette Act's extraterritoriality came into effect. Initially, the law's provisions would apply only to American-flagged vessels, but by 1916–1917, the law applied to foreign-flagged vessels as well. The key provision was the decriminalization of desertion and the abolition of withholding wages, the tools British shipping companies used to remove the temptation for sailors to desert in the higher-wage ports of the U.S. eastern seaboard. Much to London's annoyance, British sailors began deserting their vessels in large numbers, hoping that shipping companies would rehire them on higher-wage U.S.-flagged vessels. Two factors exacerbated this practice. First, before U.S. entry into the war, British sailors often deserted in American ports to reship on U.S.-flagged vessels to take advantage of American neutrality, rather than battle German U-boat attacks on British vessels.[54] Second, since the Atlantic Agreement doubled East Coast wages, British sailors now had an extra incentive to desert in U.S. ports.[55]

As the Atlantic Agreement combined with the La Follette Act's decriminalization of desertion induced thousands of British sailors to desert their ships in U.S. ports, a crisis emerged within the British merchant marine.[56] This caused such a disruption to British maritime labor that Britain complained to the U.S. government that the La Follette Act hindered their ability to ensure a reliable maritime labor force.[57] The British initially responded by increasing the prosecution for desertion, but this was difficult given that most of the deserted sailors were serving under the American flag.[58] When cracking down failed to work, the British government formed the National Maritime Board in November 1917, which stipulated a new wage that essentially doubled the prewar rates, bringing them on par with the new U.S. wages that came out of the Atlantic Agreement a few months earlier.[59] This is exactly what the ISU leadership designed the La Follette Seamen's Act to accomplish. It leveled the playing field between British- and American-flagged vessels, helped remove the incentive for U.S. firms to sail under the British flag, and increased American maritime power at the expense of the dominant British. Indeed, the extraordinary circumstances of the war were also a significant factor. It provided sailors with a tremendous amount of leverage.[60] However, if the La Follette Act had not removed the legal and financial constraints against desertion for foreign sailors in U.S. ports, British captains may have been more successful in holding on to their crew in those ports even under wartime circumstances.

During the war, American merchant sailors were successfully amalgamated with the national interest and achieved their desired status of agents of empire. On top of that, the Shipping Board and the secretary of labor began arguing for the importance of finding skilled and experienced sailors capable of navigating the dangerous waters of the north Atlantic warzone. Finally, the La Follette Seamen's Act began yielding results that directly increased U.S. maritime power. America's organized sailors were incorporated into the U.S. imperial hierarchy while also helping increase U.S. imperial power. By 1918 the SUP held "closed-shop control" over 90 percent of Pacific Coast shipping.[61] Yet questions remained: would this arrangement last when the war was over? How permanent was this new turn of events?

From Agents to Objects

Despite the gains the ISU made from the war effort, the consequences of the conflict ultimately subverted their quest to become agents of U.S. empire. The war provided a perfect storm of circumstance to reverse the gains achieved in the last few years—including the La Follette Act—and reduce the sailors back to "objects and instruments" of U.S. imperialism. First, like almost every other industry, shipping capital hoped to use the war as a means to weaken or repeal labor legislation they argued would hurt the war effort. Conveniently, this was the same legislation that they previously had maintained would damage their bottom line. Second, at the same time, shipping company representatives accused the ISU of taking advantage of the wartime emergency to strengthen their organizations at the expense of the war effort. Third, though the ISU came out of the war stronger, the U.S. shipping industry came out in its strongest position since before the Civil War. Not only were shipping firms making vast sums of money in the absence of European competition, the war led to a massive consolidation of American shipping capital. Consequently, shipping firms were keen to defend their newfound position in the global marketplace knowing that the British aggressively would attempt to reassert their maritime dominance after the war.

However, what most concerned the ISU leadership was that global shipping capital would use the upcoming Paris Peace Conference to dismantle everything they had worked for over the last thirty years.[62] Andrew Furuseth, in particular, was not certain if the La Follette Act would survive the conference given how much the international shipping industry and the British government detested the law.[63] As a result, Furuseth traveled to Europe in the spring of 1919 to defend the La Follette Act and represent America's organized sailors at the peace conference. Specifically, Furuseth viewed the League of Nations and the International Labor Organization as the biggest threat to the unilateralism of the La Follette Seamen's Act. To maintain their position, Furuseth needed the support of Europe's organized sailors to defend the Seamen's Act in the face of an emerging internationalist regime of regulation. This would prove to be a challenge. In his previous trips through Europe before the war, Furuseth had come to believe that European sailors had a fundamentally different understanding of maritime labor relations. Without the support of European sailors' unions, Furuseth argued that the League of Nations would take a hostile position toward the Seamen's Act. As a result, Furuseth opposed the organization as un-American. This position would strain his relationship with both Samuel Gompers and President Wilson. All of this meant that while white American sailors were incorporated into their desired place within the imperial hierarchy, they just as easily could be demoted.

Despite the praise lavished upon America's organized sailors or their newfound status as the vanguard of American democracy, the tension between maritime labor and capital simmered just beneath the surface. The massive expansion of the U.S. merchant marine during the war was obviously a boon to both shipping capital and the ISU. For shipping companies, profits spiked, government money flowed, and competition disappeared. For the sailors, membership exploded, dues increased, and jobs were plentiful.[64] As an allied victory became more or less assured and the end of the war was in sight, U.S. shipping firms and the ISU looked to capitalize on their recent gains and make them permanent. Additionally, U.S. shipping firms and the ISU were trying to ensure that the other side's advantages would not become permanent. Even during the détente of the Washington Conference, shipping company representatives suggested that the ISU was using the war as a means of strengthening their organizations. President of the Puget Sound Shipping Association, Captain James S. Gibson, told the conference that while he did not doubt the patriotism of the ISU, he felt that "they hold with tenacity to the strength of their organizations" too much.[65]

The shipping industry saw the war as an opportunity to dismantle some of the recent gains made by the sailors. Indeed, the war provided an almost perfect pretext for shipping companies to discipline maritime workers by suspending key legislative labor protections. Shipping capital employed a two-pronged strategy to bring labor to heel and maximize the wartime opportunity. First, as the war raged, shipping interests constantly challenged the constitutionality of the La Follette Seamen's Act in court.[66] Second, shipping company representatives suggested that it might be necessary to suspend any law or protection they found intrusive or detrimental to their bottom line. Captain Gibson, for instance, recommended the "suspension of all laws which create any kind of burden or which throw obstacles in the way of finding personnel for this immense fleet being constructed."[67] Attempting to assuage the sailors, Gibson added that any changes to existing maritime law would not be permanent.[68] For the most part, the obstacles Gibson referred to were in the La Follette Seamen's Act. The shipping companies fought it tooth and nail while Congress debated it and still sought repeal after it became law. The sailors responded by arguing that the La Follette Act actually helped recruit and man the rapidly expanding merchant fleet.[69] They maintained that if the shipping companies stopped trying to undermine it and ceased challenging its legality, the act would be an even more effective recruitment tool. By 1918 the ISU was increasingly worried that the government would suspend the act until the end of the war.

Yet the biggest challenge for the ISU was that the war led to a massive consolidation of the American shipping industry that increasingly entangled it within the machinery of the state. Indeed, war has long had a general tendency to consolidate and centralize the merchant shipping industry.[70] Additionally, shipping industry consolidation was exempt from the Sherman Anti-Trust Act because of its strategic importance to the war effort.[71] As a result, the level of consolidation and state cooperation was unprecedented. Indeed, the United States government actually owned many of the ships operated by private shipping firms. Furuseth worried that if this arrangement continued after the war, the interests of the shipping companies and the state would become even more aligned. Even when state and shipping capital were less entangled, the executive branch (through the Commerce Department) always seemed to interpret regulations in the shipping companies' favor. By late 1917, the SUP pointed to a rumor, never actually denied, that the United States government would retain ownership, but private shipping companies would operate the ships.[72]

The wartime corporatist agencies designed to manage the U.S. shipping industry could just as easily work against the ISU. While these structures gave the union leadership a modest role in national economic planning, they ultimately affirmed pre-existing industry hierarchies and served to alienate the leadership from its base by insisting that labor leaders simply manage their membership in exchange for their seat at the table.[73] In the years following the war, this divide would explode into the open (as chapter 5 will examine). Moreover, by creating the Sea Service Bureau, the U.S. Shipping Board could challenge the SUP's and the ISU's control over the labor supply, muting the impact of a strike because the board would have a supply of trained sailors to draw from in the event ISU members walked off the job. Indeed, after the war, the bureau gained a reputation within the ISU as a "government fink hall."[74] With the United States Shipping Board essentially taking control of the merchant marine, a consolidated shipping industry could crush any labor action with the full power of the federal government at war.

Federal control over the nation's merchant marine gave the SUP and ISU little, if any, opportunity to continue their struggle, which was a key benefit of these corporatist institutions from the shipping companies' point of view. Political and economic power was already far more entangled on a merchant ship than in most other industries. Federal control only enhanced it. The close relationship between private shipping capital and the state was a nearly perfect arrangement to break the ISU or to undermine the Seamen's Act, especially since both the shipping industry and maritime labor was gearing up for intense competition after the war. The window of opportunity for America's shipping industry provided by the war was about to end. A victorious British Empire would aggressively fight to reclaim and maintain its dominant maritime position from before the war. This turn of events put more pressure on the Seamen's Act because where both American and British shipping capital were aligned was in their intense opposition to the law. So concerned were the British that the State Department attended the Washington Conference to represent British shipping interests.[75] This alignment of interest regarding the La Follette Act went beyond U.S. and British shipping capital (though Anglo-American opposition was its biggest threat) and convinced the ISU leadership that the act would not survive the Paris Peace Conference.

Additionally, the war was less beneficial for the Pacific Coast trade despite an explosion of jobs and ship construction on the Atlantic. Since wartime supply routes were more profitable during the war, many Pacific Coast vessels had been retasked to the Atlantic. This allowed Japanese shipping firms to take over the majority of the Pacific trade. Moreover, Japan's control was furthered by the Pacific Mail Company's withdrawal from the Pacific trade after the La Follette Act was passed, while other firms sold some of their vessels to Japanese shipping lines.[76] By the end of the war, Japanese shipping companies controlled 55 percent of the Pacific carrying trade.[77] While the ISU may have held closed shop control over 97 percent of the ships on the West Coast, the percentage of U.S. ships had dropped to 2 percent of the trade.[78]

When Furuseth left for Europe in the spring of 1919, his challenge was selling the principles of the Seamen's Act to skeptical European, but especially British, sailors' unions. In his previous trips to Europe, Furuseth became frustrated with what he saw as European sailors' privileging of welfare over freedom. "They do not seem to feel the chains as chains," he wrote from Europe in 1908.[79] Furuseth believed that the Dutch were almost "beautifully unconscious" of their daily oppression.[80] In France, Furuseth felt that the notion of emancipating the seamen of the world largely fell on deaf ears, and he said that "to the [French] seaman himself it comes almost as . . . a blow when you tell him that he also should be under the aegis of the French motto . . . 'Liberte, Egalite, Fraternite [*sic*].'"[81] At the Transport Workers Conference in Vienna, Furuseth said that a German delegate found his ideas preposterous and almost radical, arguing that no one could ever submit such proposals to the Reichstag.[82] On his second visit in 1913, it was more of the same. To Furuseth, it seemed only American sailors were aware of the tyranny and lack of "freedom" on the high seas. Moreover, Furuseth argued that those who did recognize that maritime work demanded the surrender of certain freedoms, such as the French, did not really see this as a problem.

Yet despite past experiences, by 1919, changes in the maritime industry's landscape over the past seven years provided reasons for Furuseth and the ISU leadership to be more optimistic. Because this was a peace conference, only the victorious allied powers would be in attendance. There would be no German delegation to accuse Furuseth of being a radical for suggesting that sailors ought to be free. More importantly, the La Follette Act's abolition of the criminal and financial penalties designed to hold sailors aboard their ships helped to directly raise the wages of British sailors.[83] Even though the British seamen's union leadership were not enthusiastic supporters of the American position, they tended to be the most sympathetic of the European sailors' unions. With the wage increase brought on partly by the La Follette Act reforms, perhaps Furuseth could turn British ambivalence into enthusiastic support.

While the British Sailor's Union (BSU) leadership understood and respected why the Seamen's Act was so important to Furuseth and the ISU, the BSU head—and newly minted Liberal MP—Havelock Wilson believed that extending the principles of the act to the UK would prove detrimental to British sailors. In anticipation of Furuseth's impending arrival at the 1919 World Seafarers Conference in London, Wilson explained the British position to the delegates. Wilson took issue with the Seaman's Act provision that allowed sailors the right to quit their vessels and contracts at any time and receive a portion of their earned wages. Wilson stated that while "American seamen, especially Mr. Furuseth" believe "that it is impossible for seamen to combine, or to obtain any redress of their grievances, unless they have this right to quit," the BSU head said that he and his colleagues "do not share Mr. Furuseth's views on that point." In fact, Wilson said he and the BSU leadership "entirely disagree with him [Furuseth]."[84]

Wilson explained that the UK's vast imperial holdings meant that any "right to quit" legislation modeled on the Seamen's Act would end up benefiting shipping companies, not Britain's sailors. In fact, Wilson argued that it would hurt British seamen and lead to the "destruction of our organization." "We have an Empire," Wilson stated, "and in our Empire we have all kinds of people—black and white. We have also all kinds of conditions of labor." As a result, Wilson explained that if white sailors contracted in Britain arrived at a colonial port like "Colombo [Sri Lanka] for bunker coal," and decided, "we have had enough of this ship, we are going ashore." In such a situation, Wilson pointed out that "the captain would be delighted" since he could "fill the places of those men with Lascars at about 30s. or £2 a month instead of paying £15 a month." Wilson continued by stating that if "you have a couple a dozen ships dropping their crews at Colombo . . . you would soon have 400 to 500 white men on the beach, their money all spent." "[E]ventually," Wilson said, "those men after two or three weeks on shore would get tired of having no work to do, and the would be offering their services to ships bound for European ports at 1s. a month."[85] Essentially, Wilson believed that the "freedom" provided by the La Follette Act would not only bring down the wages of white British sailors rather than raise them, but also leave them stranded in the far-off ports of the British Empire. As a result, Wilson told the delegates that "we will do everything we possibly can to support the American seamen in maintaining their [La Follette] shipping law as long as they wish; but we cannot promise Mr. Furuseth . . . that we shall seek similar legislation in the United Kingdom."[86]

Furuseth's eloquent speechifying about how extending the principles of the La Follette Act would emancipate the world's seamen failed to persuade the conference. In the end, the conference adopted Wilson and the BSU's position and resolved that every effort should be made to support the act in "its entire scope in ports of the United States."[87] However, the resolution also stated that the "extension of the act to all countries might be detrimental to the best interests of the seamen of such countries."[88] While this did not necessarily affect the operation of the La Follett Act in the United States, it was a blow to Furuseth's and the ISU's ultimate ambition of extending the principles of the Seamen's Act around the world.

The lack of tangible support from European sailors' unions, combined with their rejection of the "right to quit" principles of the seamen's law held serious consequences for the La Follette Act and the institutions the peace conference created. For instance, the French government re-emphasized their position that treated the merchant marine as a naval reserve.[89] This circumvented the La Follette Act's regulations that prevented foreign-flagged ships from holding their sailors onboard, essentially removing them from the free labor markets of U.S.

ports created by the law. This basically nullified any effect the Seamen's Act would have on the French merchant marine. It was a significant blow to the La Follette Act's ambition to raise the wages of the global shipping industry. Beyond this, Furuseth was worried that the League of Nations, specifically the International Labor Organization, presented a serious threat to the La Follette Act.

Furuseth saw the ILO and the League of Nations as extensions of British imperial interests, not as the egalitarian international forums that many hoped they would become. As a result, he viewed them as a direct threat to the Seamen's Act. This makes sense given that one of the central ambitions of the La Follette Act was to build an American merchant marine to rival the British. Furuseth based his view on the representative structure of the ILO. The ILO was officially composed of Belgium, Cuba, Czechoslovakia, France, Italy, Japan, Poland, the United Kingdom, and the United States. However, according to Furuseth, the British Empire effectively received the most members because of their dominions: Canada, Australia, New Zealand, South Africa, and so forth.[90] This reality potentially nullified the more imperial ambitions of the Seamen's Act, which relied upon America's preponderance of power in the global marketplace to reorient the labor relations of the global shipping industry to favor U.S. sailors' union ideals. Whereas, under the ILO, the power of the United States to influence the global shipping industry, even if the Wilson administration fought to advance their position, was limited to one country one vote. Furthermore, Furuseth and the American sailors could not count on support from European sailors to advance their positions by lobbying their respective governments to support the American sailors' positions.

As a result, Furuseth saw these institutions as not only hostile to U.S. imperial interests but also as fundamentally un-American in theory as well as practice. At the AFL convention in June 1919, after his return from Europe, Furuseth spoke on the convention floor, where he attacked both the ILO and the League of Nations. He stated, "there isn't a solitary thing here [in the league, ILO and Treaty] that leaves any of the American ideals in this document."[91] Specifically, he was referring to the fact that the Paris Peace Conference refused to add a section modeled on the Thirteenth Amendment to the U.S. Constitution, on the grounds that there was no slavery in Europe.[92] Furthermore, Furuseth pointed out that when he asked the conference to consider adopting the spirit of the Thirteenth Amendment to allow sailors to leave their vessels in safe harbors, the conference voted that down as well.[93] Though the Peace Conference may not have dismantled the Seamen's Act as Furuseth warned, it rejected many of the act's more important principles. Furuseth's stance against the ILO and the League of Nations had serious consequences for his and the ISU's position within the U.S. labor movement, leading directly to a public falling out with Samuel Gompers and President Wilson that exacerbated the divisions beginning to emerge within the union itself. After Furuseth's speech criticizing the ILO and the League, every AFL leader attacked his positions by pointing out that all AFL-affiliated unions had given up some sovereignty; the ILO was no different. Furthermore, as Gompers himself was the first head of the ILO, he had no sympathy for Furuseth's position. The AFL president felt Furuseth had betrayed him and the organization by writing a letter to President Wilson denouncing the treaty. It did not help matters that Furuseth refused to reveal the contents of the letter. Since sailors mainly operated outside the nation, it makes sense that Furuseth would be more hostile to the ILO or the League of Nations than Gompers or even the prevailing views of the AFL as a whole. The international nature of the shipping industry meant that it was more affected by international regulatory bodies such as the ILO and the League of Nations. Especially since in 1917, the Supreme Court ruled that though a U.S.-flagged ship was American soil, laboring on it did not mean that one was laboring within the United States (but more on this in chapter 5).[94]

Yet despite Furuseth's concern, his position divided the ISU and its affiliated unions. Though Furuseth received a standing ovation after his controversial speech, it was largely out of respect for him personally and his past achievements rather than a barometer of the popularity his position held among the membership. Every faction rejected his position when it came time to vote, and the AFL officially endorsed both the League and the ILO. The only faction that supported Furuseth was the many Irish American delegates concerned the treaty could harm the Irish struggle for home rule. Two ISU delegates even voted against Furuseth.

The division within the ISU on display at the AFL convention only worsened in the coming years. Though the war had expanded the ISU's membership by almost one hundred thousand members, many of the newcomers were not as committed to the leadership's strict adherence to its craft union principles. As will become apparent in chapter 5, these new members were increasingly sympathetic to forming greater bonds of solidarity with workers beyond the sailing trades. With the rise of the Industrial Workers of the World as a viable alternative, the ISU would face mounting internal pressure to adapt from its rigid craft union principles.

CHAPTER 5

They Always Choose Exclusion

Internal Dissent, Postwar U.S. Maritime Policy, and the Fall of the Sailors' Unions, 1915–1924

Though the wartime maritime boom led to a rapid expansion of the ISU along with the U.S. shipping industry, shipping capital and organized labor emerged from the war in structurally opposite positions. Indeed, the war provided shipping capital with the economic stimulus necessary to build what by 1919 was the world's second-largest merchant fleet behind only Great Britain. More than that, the U.S. shipping industry was consolidated, highly capitalized, and undergirded by a newly created state institutional infrastructure. By contrast, the sailors' unions came out of the war in a deceptively weak position. While the war helped build the ISU into a much larger organization, the power of the ISU leadership over its expanded membership was far from consolidated. In fact, between the end of the war and 1923, the ISU leadership was constantly being challenged by the rank and file and the district unions. These challenges extended beyond simply replacing longtime leaders such as Andrew Furuseth and Paul Scharrenberg with new blood, but to the very foundations of the ISU's exclusionary craft unionism itself. The ISU leadership was, therefore, caught between an increasingly assertive rank and file and an empowered shipping industry supported by a still extant wartime corporatist infrastructure.

The origin of this structural opposition was rooted in the divergent effects expansion had on shipping capital and the ISU. The problem for the ISU was that there was a tension between expansion and their exclusionary craft unionism. When the ISU expanded beyond its Pacific Coast stronghold, it faced challenges to the leadership's governing ideology, particularly its legislative program. This was true even before the war, when the East Coast Spanish Firemen challenged the ISU's craft union orthodoxy, leading to the collapse of the Atlantic unions. Expansion, therefore, meant that a changing membership was more likely to challenge ISU orthodoxy. When faced with the prospect of choosing expansion over their exclusionary ideology, the leadership chose the latter.

For shipping companies, expansion did not have a downside. This was especially true of the specific type of expansion that took place during the First World War. As chapter 4 demonstrated, the shipping crisis of 1915 that resulted from the European fleets' withdrawal from normal maritime commerce forced the U.S. government to step in and facilitate the creation of a shipping industry that could compete with the might of British maritime power. Additionally, the importance of the shipping industry to the war effort meant that the government did not try to limit its expansion through antitrust legislation.

Additionally, judicial and regulatory changes made during the war laid the groundwork for shipping companies to gain unrestricted access to cheap Chinese labor once the hostilities ended and the government decided it no longer needed highly skilled white American sailors. These decisions effectively reversed the labor market protections established by the La Follette Act and brought the boundaries of the domestic labor market back to the water's edge of the continental United States. When the expanded membership created by the war offered a solution that allowed the ISU to combat cheap foreign labor *through* expansion by potentially incorporating Chinese sailors into the ISU, the leadership refused. Indeed, this was a step the ISU leadership could not take considering their justification for insulating the maritime labor market was to build up American maritime power by creating a ready supply of skilled American sailors that could be called up to the navy if needed. Incorporating Chinese sailors did not serve this goal. Instead, the union leadership tried to use the 1924 Immigration Act to exclude Chinese sailors from ships bound for the United States once and for all. Unfortunately for the ISU, the latest push for exclusion failed. Instead, the 1924 Immigration Act further entrenched the La Follette Act reversal and reaffirmed an imperial division of labor established by the 1902 Exclusion Law (discussed in chapter 2), which placed U.S. vessels outside the domestic labor market and its protections. Only this time, the 1924 law projected that imperial division of labor onto the entire globe—well beyond the limited confines of the U.S. colonial empire.

The postwar challenges presented by the still extant wartime corporatist institutions placed the union leadership in a position of having to choose between expanding beyond their craft union orthodoxy and doubling down on it. As the state began to use these institutions to help U.S. shipping firms destroy the ISU and impose an open shop on the industry, a rank-and-file rebellion emerged. To combat the much more aggressive actions of the shipping companies and the U.S. Shipping Board, the rank and file began pushing for the ISU and its district unions to form bonds of solidarity with maritime workers outside the sailing trades. This push culminated in the formation of the Marine Transport Workers Federation of the Pacific, an umbrella organization for sailors, longshoremen, riggers, and other marine trades. The ISU leadership dealt with this challenge by recommitting to its craft union ideology, centralizing its control over the national organization, and expelling members that challenged its craft union orthodoxy. This further alienated the rank and file and led to a mass exodus from the ISU. By 1923 the ISU had shrunk back to its prewar levels.

Although the challenges from shipping capital and the rank and file came from opposite poles, both threatened the labor market protections the ISU leadership had built over the previous thirty years, which they designed to insulate white American sailors from foreign competition. Moreover, the labor market protections established by the ISU were the foundation of Andrew Furuseth's and the leadership's efforts to elevate the status of U.S. sailors from objects and instruments to agents of U.S. empire. As a result, the combined effects of a consolidated and empowered shipping industry with increasing rank-and-file hostility toward exclusionary craft unionism further jeopardized white American sailors' tenuous hold on their status as agents of empire and their place within the U.S. imperial hierarchy. In the end, the ISU leadership's efforts to maintain its position within the U.S. imperial hierarchy of labor ultimately led to its fall from it. They chose exclusion and lost.

The Sinking of the La Follette Act and the Postwar Return of Cheap Foreign Labor

While the First World War temporarily shifted U.S. merchant marine policy away from cheap foreign labor to highly paid white American labor, two state interventions during the conflict laid the groundwork for shipping companies to gain almost unrestricted access to cheap Chinese sailors by reversing the La Follette Act's incorporation of the foreign maritime trade into the domestic U.S. labor market. In the aftermath of the war and these decisions, the ISU confronted the grim reality that every effort they made to limit shipping capital's ability to source the cheapest labor ended either in failure or reversal. After thirty years of trying to insulate the foreign maritime labor market, an alternative approach emerged from the ISU's reorganized Atlantic unions that took the exact opposite approach. Instead of restricting shipping capital's access to foreign labor markets, members of the Atlantic unions spearheaded a strategy that sought to expand the ISU alongside shipping capital into those markets by helping organize an Oriental Seafarers Union. This approach represented a potential multiracial and internationalist way forward for the ISU. Yet in the end, the ISU leadership led by Furuseth again doubled down on exclusion when they tried to use the 1924 Immigration Act to re-establish the labor market protections of the La Follette Act. This, too, proved unsuccessful. Though they were able to prevent further erosion of the La Follette Act from the bill, the 1924 law ultimately affirmed shipping capital's access to cheap Chinese labor. Moreover, the law permanently shut the door on the ISU's ambition of incorporating the foreign maritime trade into the domestic or metropolitan labor market. Instead, the law projected a metropolitan/imperial divide onto the world that placed the deck of U.S.-flagged ships firmly outside the U.S. metropole and its labor market protections.

In December 1915, the Commerce Department removed the most important guardrail established by the La Follette Act to insulate the U.S. maritime labor market in the foreign trade against cheaper Chinese competition. After the arrival of the S.S. *China* in San Francisco harbor, U.S. officials administered the language test to the vessel's twenty-six Chinese sailors as stipulated by section thirteen of the La Follette Act, which stated at least 75 percent of the crew must be able to understand the orders of the officers.[1] All twenty-six sailors passed because Commerce Secretary William C. Redfield ruled that pidgin English was an acceptable level of proficiency.[2] As the *Coast Seamen's Journal* stated, the acceptability of pidgin English by the Commerce Department "has practically nullified the letter as well as the spirit of the law [the La Follette Act]."[3] Indeed, both U.S. and foreign shipping companies detested the language clause precisely because they knew it would limit their access to cheap Chinese labor. As the *Journal* commented, "[t]he Commerce Department, as conducted by Mr. Redfield, seems determined to so construe and administer the Seamen's Act as to entirely satisfy the owner of every coolie-manned ship touching American ports."[4] George Bodin's predictions (discussed in chapter 3) that the language clause was too vague and open for interpretation proved prophetic.

Beyond nullifying the anti-Asian ambitions of the La Follette Act, the acceptability of pidgin English subverted the law's efforts to create a freer labor market for sailors in Pacific Coast ports. Now that the secretary of commerce offered shipping firms a way around the language test, ships could continue arriving in U.S. ports with Chinese crews signed on in Asia. The Exclusion Act and the Alien Contract Labor law did not allow Chinese sailors to "land" in American ports—that is, leave their ships and enter the United States. Under U.S. landing policy, ships' captains were required to hold excluded sailors onboard. They could disembark only in connection with the operations of the ship, as specified by the treasury secretary's ruling of July 1892 and the Commerce Department's ruling of June 1907, discussed in chapters 1 and 3, respectively.[5] This meant that Chinese sailors could not take advantage of the La Follette Act's decriminalization of desertion. As soon as a Chinese sailor tried to sign new articles before the shipping commissioner, he would be in violation of the Chinese Exclusion law and the Alien Contract Labor Act.[6] The idea behind the abolition of criminal punishment for desertion was to create a freer market for maritime labor in U.S. ports so that sailors could desert their ships and be reshipped on another vessel at higher American wages.[7] As a result, shipping firms had to ensure that they reshipped Chinese sailors on the same vessel they arrived in, or the company would be in violation of the Exclusion Act and the Contract Labor law.

Two years later, a Supreme Court ruling on what became known as the *Bessie Dollar* affair gave U.S. shipping companies even greater flexibility to employ Chinese sailors on trans-Pacific routes. The circumstances surrounding the *Bessie Dollar* affair took place before the war began in January 1914. The incident involved the Dollar Steamship Line's transfer of a Chinese crew from one of their British-flagged vessels, the *Bessie Dollar,* to an American-flagged vessel, the *Mackinaw,* in San Francisco harbor. Initially, former *Coast Seamen's Journal* editor Walter Macarthur acting in his new position as the San Francisco harbor commissioner, formally requested that the customs collector withhold the clearance papers of the *Bessie Dollar* and the *Mackinaw* on the grounds that they violated the law.[8] Additionally, Macarthur refused to sanction the transfer of Chinese sailors to the *Mackinaw*. However, U.S. Shipping Commissioner E. T. Chamberlain overruled Macarthur, stating that he was "not justified in refusing to sign on the crew of the *Mackinaw.*"[9] Chamberlain argued that whether or not the crew violated the immigration laws of the United States was a matter for the Department of Immigration to determine, not the shipping commissioner.[10] The SUP then sued the Dollar Line on the grounds that this action violated the Alien Contract Labor law. By 1917 the case finally had made its way to the Supreme Court.

The decision legalized the reshipment of Chinese sailors in U.S. ports since the Court found that transferring the Chinese workers from the *Bessie Dollar* to the *Mackinaw* in San Francisco harbor violated neither the Exclusion Act nor the Alien Contact Labor law. As the *Coast Seamen's Journal* saw it, the Court's ruling "legalized the unlimited importation of coolie labor for service on American ships."[11] Moreover, the *Bessie Dollar* decision overruled and reversed the treasury secretary's opinion of July 1892 and the Commerce Department's *Lyra* ruling of 1907.[12] In the 1892 decision, Treasury Secretary Charles W. Foster agreed with the SUP that to transfer sailors from one ship to another, they would have to disembark and sign new employment articles before the shipping commissioner, as specified by the Shipping Commissioner's Act of 1872.[13] He also agreed that once a Chinese sailor presented himself before the commissioner, he would be in violation of the Chinese Exclusion Act and face deportation.[14] The 1907 Commerce Department decision was a bit different, but department solicitor Charles Earl did say that "landing" in the United States constituted admission to the United States, and specified that Chinese sailors could legally go ashore "only in connection with the loading and unloading of the vessel's cargo."[15] The narrow window Earl allowed for Chinese sailors to go ashore implied that quitting their vessel and signing new shipping articles would constitute "landing" or entering the United States, though he does not state this explicitly. With the *Bessie Dollar* decision, the Supreme Court contradicted these executive rulings and stated that Congress never meant for the Alien Contract Labor law (and by implication the Exclusion Act, though it was not specifically mentioned) to apply to U.S. ships engaged in foreign commerce.

The *Bessie Dollar* decision effectively drew the line between nation and empire and foreign and domestic at the water's edge of San Francisco harbor. This almost completely reversed the progress of the La Follette Act, which had placed that line between U.S.-flagged vessels and the water's edge of foreign and imperial ports. The legal logic of the decision puts this distinction into sharper focus. The Court declared that sailors were not actually "laborers," but mariners and therefore were not covered by laws meant to protect "laborers."[16] This reasoning was a perversion of the ISU's efforts to amalgamate themselves with the national interest. The court seemed to agree that sailors were part of the national interest but in a way that limited their legal protections rather than expanded them. The *Coast Seamen's Journal* responded to this logic by stating, "[t]he provisions of the contract labor law were intended to prevent bringing American labor into competition with the pauper of other countries, and to say that American seamen must be subject to such competition is, in effect, *a declaration that they are not part of the people of that country* [emphasis added].[17] Perhaps more accurately, it meant that the foreign trade was not part of the national realm, but the foreign and imperial realm. Secondly, even though the Court's decision considered U.S.-flagged vessels in the foreign trade American soil, laboring on them did not mean that one was laboring within the United States. Or as the court said, "equally unallowable [to the idea that sailors were laborers] is the contention that a ship of American registry engaged in foreign commerce is a part of the territory of the United States in such a sense that men employed on it can be said to be laboring within the United States or performing labor in this country."[18] From a labor perspective, the foreign maritime trade was not part of the United States.

This decision, combined with the Commerce Department ruling on pidgin English, provided U.S. and foreign shipping companies with the means to cut white American sailors on the Pacific Coast out of the foreign merchant trade altogether. First, the Commerce Department ruling on pidgin English allowed shipping companies to continue hiring foreign Chinese sailors despite the La Follette Act's language clause. Second, the Supreme Court's decision had firmly placed the water's edge of the West Coast as the line between nation and empire, or more precisely, the line between the domestic U.S. labor market and an imperial or foreign labor market. This legal precedent established by the *Bessie Dollar* decision then provided shipping companies with the means to reship Chinese sailors—or any group of people excluded from the United States—without violating either the Exclusion Act or the Alien Contract Labor law. As a result, the ISU leadership's near thirty-year legislative strategy to insulate the maritime labor market in the foreign trade from Chinese competition lay in shambles.

In those thirty years, the state allowed shipping companies to subvert practically every limit the ISU attempted to place on their ability to access the world's cheapest sources of maritime labor. In 1902 shipping companies successfully defeated the ISU's efforts to extend the Chinese Exclusion Act to U.S.-flagged vessels. In 1907, when the Commerce Department agreed that the Exclusion Act did extend to the coastwise or domestic trade, Commerce Secretary Oscar Strauss provided shipping companies with a loophole that allowed them to use Chinese crews between Honolulu and the Pacific Coast on transpacific routes (as opposed to replacing them with a white crew from Honolulu to the mainland, which the ISU wanted).[19] Now, the Commerce Department had gutted the La Follette Act's most potent weapon against Asian competition by permitting pidgin English as an acceptable level of proficiency under section thirteen of the act. However, between 1919 and 1920, an alternative approach to the problem of cheap Chinese labor had emerged within the ISU.

If it was not possible to prevent the insulation of the U.S. maritime labor market with the rest of the world's, specifically China's, then the logical alternative for the ISU was to expand into those markets itself by organizing Chinese sailors. This is exactly what the Atlantic unions began to do after the strike of 1919.[20] During that strike, as seamen from all "nations were leaving their ships en masse . . . several Chinese crews likewise abandoned their ships, persuaded others of their countrymen to join them and to the number of 400 applied for admission . . . in the local divisions of the I.S.U. of A."[21] However, as the Atlantic unions admitted, this created a problem because "the eligibility clauses of the constitutions of all the Affiliated Seamen's unions, were intended to operate in strict conformity with barriers erected by Federal legislation in excluding Asiatics from participation in American citizenship and from their general admission in competition with enlightened American labor."[22] In an attempt to get around this problem, the Atlantic unions pointed out that the Exclusion Act did "permit . . . the unrestricted employment of Oriental seamen on American ships."[23] Therefore, the Atlantic unions argued, "it would be unwise" and "unjust" to "deny them the right to organize."[24] Despite this, the leadership would not budge on the exclusion of Asian sailors. As a result, the Atlantic unions decided to help organize Asian sailors in an independent union, which had no official affiliation with the ISU or the Atlantic unions, under the leadership of Bill Yak of San Francisco and James S. Alina of Honolulu.

The Atlantic unions understood that by helping organize Asian sailors, they were turning maritime labor relations upside down by ensuring shipping companies no longer could use anti-Asian prejudice against the sailors' unions. As the Atlantic unions pointed out, "[t]he American shipowners have been constantly using race against race, creed against creed, and nation against nation, in the commercial chess game to beat and destroy the Seamen's Unions."[25] Yet by helping and supporting the organization of Asian sailors, the Atlantic unions argued that shipping firms had been "checkmated" because they finally had deprived them of "their last pawns" against the seamen's unions.[26] As a result, the creation of the Oriental Seafarers Union was a milestone in the history of the maritime labor movement. It had the potential to fundamentally upend maritime labor relations, especially if it was part of a larger strategy to organize every source of maritime labor that U.S. shipping companies attempted to access.

Additionally, the leaders and primary organizers of the Oriental Seafarers Association represented a multiracial and potentially internationalist path forward for the maritime labor unions. James Alina was born in Hawai'i to "Chinese-Kanaka [Pacific Islander] parents," spoke "English, Hawaiian, and Spanish as well as Chinese."[27] He was, as the Atlantic unions stated, "invaluable to the polyglot organization."[28] Unlike Andrew Furuseth, Yak was born in San Francisco "more than fifty-years ago."[29] And, unlike most of the sailors on the Atlantic Coast, both Yak and Alina were American citizens, though the majority of the organization's membership was not.[30] Again, the low rate of U.S. citizenship among the SUP and the ISU was a key reason their organizing strategy was built around "whiteness" rather than citizenship. By the summer of 1920,

Yak and Alina had organized four thousand members of various Asian nationalities, "including Chinese, Japanese, Siamese [Thai], Koreans and Malays."[31] With the beginnings of such a broad and diverse organization of Asian sailors, the Atlantic unions taunted the shipping companies by continuing with their chess metaphor and scoffed, "[c]ome on, Mr. Shipowner: the board is waiting, its [*sic*] your next move."[32] Unfortunately for them, the next move came not from the shipping companies but their own union leadership.

Despite the best efforts of Yak, Alina, and the Atlantic unions, the organization of the Oriental Seafarers was an anomalous outlier and did not represent a major shift in ISU strategy or policy. Indeed, as Seattle branch member Peter Gill later pointed out, the Atlantic unions were not reprimanded for violating the spirit of the ISU and affiliated unions' policy of racial exclusion. Still, there is little to no evidence that the ISU or the SUP attempted to organize Asian sailors on the Pacific (where it would have made the most sense), other than a lone article in the *San Francisco Call* from February 8, 1922. The article reported that ISU vice president Paul Scharrenberg announced the union was making plans to organize Chinese sailors in "every part of the Pacific."[33] The article explains that Scharrenberg told the paper a proposal to organize Chinese seamen was discussed "informally" at the annual ISU convention a month earlier.[34] The paper quotes Scharrenberg as saying, "[t]he strike of the Chinese [seamen] in Far eastern waters now in progress shows that they are capable of organization."[35] He further stated that the "[o]rganization of the Chinese will be forced upon white seafarers of Europe and America as a matter of self protection [*sic*]."[36] It is not clear what exactly Scharrenberg meant by "informal" discussions. There is nothing in the 1922 ISU convention proceedings (or subsequent years) about potentially organizing Chinese sailors on the Pacific. Additionally, there is no other reference in the *Seamen's Journal* or any other ISU publication about potentially organizing Chinese sailors on the Pacific. There is also no reference to Scharrenberg's announcement or the *Call*'s article in the *Journal*. Moreover, none of the memoirs written by union officials or published histories of the union make any reference to a proposal meant to organize Chinese sailors on the Pacific, Scharrenberg's announcement, or the *Call* article. The only other reference to this article is from Scharrenberg himself in an oral history interview conducted by Corine Gilb of the University of California, Berkeley, in 1954. In the interview, Scharrenberg confirmed the facts of the *Call* article and justified Chinese organization using the same logic as the Atlantic unions did with the Oriental Seafarers Union. He argued that the "only way to maintain wages and hours and conditions is to take into our Union everybody who's available to the shipowner."[37]

The lack of comment or controversy from the SUP and the ISU is puzzling given the gravity of what Scharrenberg was proposing. For more than thirty years, the SUP leadership tirelessly worked to "drive" Asian sailors from the sea. How is it that the *Journal* and all other sources ignored Scharrenberg's announcement? Surely such a monumental policy reversal would provoke some discussion. Even in the 1954 oral history interview, Scharrenberg offered no further comment or elaboration other than the above quotation. Did the ISU leadership privately and quietly sanction Scharrenberg? There is no evidence to suggest that they did or did not. Maybe it played out like the ISU response to the Oriental Seafarers Union, where the leadership did not support it, encourage it, or amend their constitution to permit it, but neither did the leadership reprimand Atlantic union members who worked with Yak and Alina. Maybe they hoped it would simply fizzle out and go away?

Additionally, was Scharrenberg softening on the Chinese issue? Possibly, but not likely. On the one hand, the Atlantic dispatch article that argued for the Oriental Seafarers Union in 1920 was published during his tenure as editor. On the other hand, Scharrenberg oversaw the publication of more than one hundred anti-Chinese articles full of ugly racist rhetoric before and after the 1920 Oriental Seafarers article. Moreover, in the same oral history interview from 1954, Scharrenberg reiterated his belief that Chinese exclusion was the correct and necessary policy, arguing: "if it had not been for the early labor agitators, I think the pacific [*sic*] Coast would be filled up with Chinese."[38] "It was the hell-raising of the agitators," Scharrenberg continued, "that maintained California for us and our kind of people."[39] Based on the available evidence, it is impossible to say why Scharrenberg made the announcement or why the union never sanctioned him or publicly commented on the article. What we do know for certain is that the SUP and ISU leadership continued to try and ban the use of Asian sailors on U.S.-flagged ships and did not attempt to organize Chinese seamen on the Pacific.

Beyond simple racial prejudice, part of the problem was that Andrew Furuseth, Scharrenberg, and the union leadership's primary justification for insulating the maritime labor market against Chinese and foreign sailors was to build up American maritime power. "Sea power," as Furuseth was wont to say, "was in the Seaman."[40] That is, the nations with the best sailors had the strongest navies and merchant fleets. Moreover, Furuseth had spent thirty years maintaining that Chinese workers were inferior sailors, lacked the proper skills and training, panicked in a crisis, and were often drugged with opium, putting the passengers, crew, and cargo at risk.[41] How could he justify organizing Asian sailors for better pay and conditions if he regarded them as inferior sailors? More than that, if these seamen were subjects of Japan or China, from Furuseth's and the leadership's point of view, helping Asian sailors gain better employment opportunities was tantamount to training sailors for the Chinese and Japanese navies. Indeed, he made this exact argument to Congress in 1902 (as discussed in chapter 4) when he maintained that by relying on Chinese sailors, the U.S. merchant marine was "training men for the future navy of China."[42] The *Seamen's Journal* used this line of thinking again in reacting to the *Bessie Dollar* decision, arguing that the effect of this decision would prevent the United States from "reestablish[ing] our country's sea power."[43] On top of that, organizing Chinese sailors subverted the racialized hierarchy of labor within the U.S. empire that Furuseth and the AFL helped create when both organizations insisted upon applying Chinese exclusion around and through the U.S. imperial system.[44] Luckily for Furuseth and the union leadership, a few years later, a comprehensive immigration restriction bill was moving through Congress that provided him and the ISU a final opportunity to double down on exclusion. The bill in question would become the Immigration Act of 1924, also known as the Johnson-Reed Act.

Furuseth initially became involved with the resurgent immigration restriction lobby because one of the earlier versions of the bill would have destroyed the last vestiges of the free labor market in U.S. ports established by the La Follette Act. The House Committee on Immigration and Naturalization was trying to make sure that sailors who were deemed "ineligible for admission" to the United States by the new law could not enter the country, whether because of explicit racial exclusion or because their admission would exceed the quota for their specific nationality established by the law.[45] As a result, the committee proposed that such sailors post bonds to ensure they returned to their vessels and did not try to enter the United States illegally.[46] First, Furuseth argued, "no bona fide seaman can put up any bond" since all a "bona fide seaman has in the world is perhaps a few dollars."[47] The effect of this, according to Furuseth, would put a "premium on manning vessels of every nation that come to the United States with men that are prevented from landing in the United States" because posting bond prevented these sailors from deserting and reshipping on another ship at higher American wages.[48] Furuseth reiterated this problem in a direct appeal to President Coolidge on January 25, 1924, arguing, "the inevitable result of this [having sailors post bonds] will be the employment of excluded persons on the majority of vessels coming to ports of the United States."[49] Moreover, Furuseth argued that any sailor who could afford to post the bond was not a bona fide seaman and had likely signed on as a sailor precisely *to* subvert U.S. immigration laws.[50]

Furuseth offered an alternative that both neutralized the need for excluded sailors to post bonds and returned the foreign maritime trade within the boundaries of the domestic U.S. labor market, re-extending them to the water's edge of foreign ports. To accomplish this, the ISU president proposed to the committee that "it is hereby made unlawful for any vessel to bring, except in distress, any person ineligible to citizenship in the United States into any port of the United States as a seaman unless he be a national of the country whose flag the vessels flies," (this last part was to ensure that a Chinese vessel could employ their own citizens, for example).[51] This effectively would stop U.S. and foreign shipowners from signing on a Chinese crew (or any other sailors excluded from U.S. citizenship, which after the 1924 law passed would include practically all Asians as well as Chinese) in a foreign port if the vessel was headed for an American port. To enforce this provision, Furuseth suggested that "[a]ny such person so brought shall be taken into custody by the immigration officer in charge and shall be deported as a passenger on some other vessel" "at the expense of the vessel" that brought the sailor in question.[52] When President Coolidge signed the Immigration Act of 1924 into law on May 24h of that year, the sailors' union leadership achieved mixed success.

They were able to keep out of the law the provision that forced excluded sailors to sign bonds; however, Congress ultimately rejected the SUP's latest effort to extend the domestic labor market into the foreign maritime trade. Indeed, section nineteen of the Immigration Act did state, "[n]o alien seamen excluded from admission to the United States under the immigration laws ... shall be permitted to *land* [emphasis added] in the United States."[53] Note, however, that the law only prevented excluded sailors from *landing* in the United States, but did not prevent shipping companies from "bringing" them into U.S. ports like Furuseth wanted.[54] The distinction is subtle but significant because the Supreme Court had determined in the *Bessie Dollar* case that signing new shipping articles before the U.S. shipping commissioner did not constitute "landing" in the United States.[55] While section nineteen might effectively prevent Chinese sailors from entering the general U.S. population, it still permitted shipping companies to hire Chinese sailors in foreign ports and reship them in the United States. This effectively ended the SUP's ambitions of incorporating a defining protection of the domestic labor market into foreign maritime trade.

The act further affirmed the *Bessie Dollar* decision by defining what was and what was not the United States as well as scaling up the U.S. imperial division of labor established by the 1902 exclusion law to a planetary level, well beyond the emerging U.S. imperial system. Section twenty-eight (a) of the act states that the United States, "when used in a geographical sense, means the states, the Territories of Alaska and Hawaii, the District of Columbia, Porto [*sic*] Rico, and the Virgin Islands."[56] The act, therefore, gave an explicit legislative definition of what was and could become incorporated into the domestic U.S. labor market, or metropole. Note that the law did not include the deck of an American-flagged ship in the definition of the United States. On the one hand, perhaps this is not surprising given that section twenty-eight (a) refers to the United States in a "geographical sense." However, on the other hand, when we view this clause in conjunction with section nineteen—which affirms the right of shipping companies to "employ alien seamen excluded from admission to the United States"—it becomes evident that U.S. ships were not considered part of the United States as defined by the Immigration Act.[57] Of course, the other territory of the U.S. imperial system not mentioned in the above definition was the Philippines, which, like the deck of an American-flagged ship, was not incorporated into the domestic U.S. labor market and was subsequently de-annexed in 1946. Additionally, the 1924 act absorbed the idea of geographical "barred zones" from the 1917 Immigration Act (expanding them to include Japan and the Philippines), whereby the people who populated those zones were deemed ineligible for U.S. citizenship and therefore excluded from admission to the United States.[58] These barred zones essentially covered all the "nonwhite" parts of the Eurasian landmass.[59]

By creating geographic "barred zones," the Immigration Act of 1924 projected an imperial/metropolitan divide—informed by organized labor's insistence on protection from any current and future U.S. imperial space—onto a global canvas. This global division of labor protected the areas defined as the "United States" from the potential labor competition of the people who lived in the barred zones. However, the act did not protect the foreign maritime trade because it did not consider ships in the foreign trade part of the United States. As had occurred twenty years prior, when organized labor led by the AFL protected its members by creating an imperial division of labor through the 1902 Exclusion Act, the labor space of U.S. merchant sailors in the foreign trade were on the wrong side of the dividing line. They again chose exclusion and lost.

The Open Shop, Industrial Unionism, and the Fall of the ISU

In the aftermath of the First World War, the ISU leadership faced the combined effects of a newly empowered and assertive shipping industry intent on imposing an open shop labor policy as well as an expanded and restless rank and file keen on challenging ISU orthodoxy. Indeed, the massive expansion of ISU members during the wartime maritime boom diluted even the small, tightly controlled, and ethnically homogenous SUP. These newer and younger members were far less attached to the ISU's craft union ideology. In just under a decade, between 1914 and 1922, a small organization of just thirteen thousand absorbed a broad coalition of one hundred thousand individuals into its ranks. These newer members were younger on average than the pre-existing membership. They were new to the industry and lacked the older guard's reverence and respect of the trade's mythical past. As Paul Scharrenberg would later explain, "[t]he membership had increased so fast that the new members didn't know what it was all about."[60] Atlantic union secretary George Bodine's belief (discussed in chapter 3) that the union leadership held outdated views concerning the necessary skills sailors required in the steamship age would have resonated with these new members. This was potentially problematic for the ISU leadership since they made the skill and traditions of the trade a central component of their identity as sailors and a cornerstone of their legislative strategy to insulate the maritime labor market. The changing structure of the ISU and SUP membership meant that it would be increasingly difficult for the leadership to maintain strict discipline and adherence to the principles of craft unionism. In the postwar labor environment, these tensions erupted into open conflict between the union leadership and the rank and file.

At the same time, the federal government's maritime labor policy began shifting back toward cheap labor while providing support for the private operators' open shop ambitions. The wartime decisions from the Commerce Department and Supreme Court ensured shipping companies easier access to cheap Chinese labor by giving them a lawful route around both the Exclusion Act and the Alien Contract Labor law. As a result, the state and U.S. shipping companies emerged from the war with all the tools necessary to break the union: a pipeline of cheap labor and the requisite corporatist institutions to neutralize the ISU's ability to disrupt the maritime labor process. Furuseth and the ISU responded to these challenges the only way they knew how: by doubling down on an exclusionary and hierarchical craft unionism. Needless to say, this tactic alienated the newly expanded membership who—though not necessarily Wobblies—sought greater cooperation and even integration with other maritime trades into a broader, more industrial style of unionism. The expansion of the ISU, combined with the shift in U.S. maritime labor policy back toward cheap labor, and Furuseth's response to it led to the downfall of the ISU and, with it, white American sailors' place within the U.S. imperial hierarchy.

In the summer of 1919, the U.S. government began shifting its maritime labor policy away from its wartime emphasis on highly paid, skilled, white American sailors back in the direction of cheap foreign labor. The U.S. Shipping Board (which still owned the vast majority of the U.S. merchant fleet at this point), with encouragement from the private operators, opposed two key demands from the Atlantic unions that evinced the Shipping Board's new policy direction away from skilled white American sailors. First, the shipping companies and the Shipping Board opposed a three-watch system at sea "because this would tend to increase the size of the crew at a time of great shortage of sailors."[61] Under the old two-watch system, ship captains divided watch duty into two twelve-hour shifts. A three-watch system divided the day into three eight-hour shifts, whereby three sailors covered a twenty-four-hour period instead of two with the two-watch system. Even though the war was over, the shipping boom and the increased demand for maritime labor continued.[62] Given that the labor shortage led to a surge in wages, the Shipping Board and private operators did not want to exacerbate the problem by agreeing to a policy that would create an even greater demand for maritime labor. Moreover, the two-watch system had the added benefit of creating a less attractive laboring environment for white Americans since a twelve-hour day was increasingly out of step with the prevailing norms to which skilled American workers had become accustomed. As the *Seamen's Journal* argued, "[t]he three-watch system at sea is the logical compliment of the eight-hour work day."[63] The sailors argued that the alternative two-watch system was detrimental to the "health and physical well-being of seamen."[64]

The other key measure was not about the more immediate necessity of reducing labor costs but the beginning of a longer-term strategy to weaken and ultimately break the sailors' unions. During the war, the Shipping Board and private operators officially recognized the unions by agreeing that at least 60 percent of all maritime jobs would go first to ISU members.[65] During the 1919 negotiations, the ISU wanted to maintain and increase this guarantee. At a joint industrial conference between the Shipping Board, private operators, and the ISU, Furuseth demanded that the ISU be given preferential hiring for all maritime jobs. However, the Shipping Board reversed its earlier policy of union preference, stating, "[i]t would be manifestly improper for the Shipping Board as a government agency to adopt a policy to give the members of the Seamen's Union or affiliated organizations preferential treatment with regard to the manning of vessels operated by or under the control of the Board."[66] After failing to reach an agreement, the unions and the private operators met separately, whereby the ISU offered a compromise. Instead of preferential hiring, the Atlantic unions proposed a "preference in employment for American citizens and then preference to union men."[67] The Shipping Board did not object to this compromise, but the private operators saw it as a Trojan horse of union preference and recognition. As the attorney for the American Steamship Association, Edwin H. Duff later told Congress, "the underlying purpose" of a preference for American citizens "was to try and force the steamship owner into recognizing the unions."[68] Furuseth, also present at the hearing, stated that he did not understand what the attorney meant by the "underlying purpose?"[69] Duff responded by saying, "[b]ecause the percentage of Americans was so small [on the Atlantic Coast] that it was tantamount to recognizing the unions."[70] With no agreement in sight, the Marine Firemen's Union voted to strike on July 8, 1919, with the remaining unions soon to follow.

Despite the seemingly hard line from the Shipping Board and the private operators, the strike was largely successful for the rank and file but less so for the union leadership. Among other things, the sailors won the initiation of a three-watch system, a $10 per month raise, and the right for union officials to have access "to all docks and ships controlled by the American Steamship Association and the U.S. Shipping Board."[71] However, they did not win preference for American citizens or union members.[72] This item was more of a problem for the ISU leadership than it was for the rank and file since it challenged the leadership's control over the hiring process. In the short term, the sailors won some important concessions, but in the long term the government and the shipping companies were eroding union control over the supply of seamen from their wartime heights.

The 1919 strike highlighted the emerging divisions between the ISU leadership and an increasingly assertive rank and file because both Furuseth and the union leadership were trying to avoid a strike.[73] In fact, the decision to strike mostly came from the rank and file. This is evident in the fact that a high percentage of seamen and cooks walked off the jobs immediately after the Firemen on July 8, but neither the Atlantic Seamen's Union nor the Cooks and Stewards Union actually sanctioned the strike until July 17.[74] The rank and file had seized the initiative from the union leadership.

The strike's success was not evidence of emerging union power but of external factors that worked in the union's favor. First, the continuation of the wartime maritime boom and the maritime labor shortage gave the unions the necessary leverage over the Shipping Board and the private operators to win concessions. After the sailors began walking off the job, between five hundred and eight hundred ships sat idle in ports up and down the Atlantic Coast, causing a major disruption to transatlantic trade.[75] Second, and perhaps more important, was the relative restraint exercised by the U.S. Shipping Board during the strike. Initially, the board ordered the Sea Service Bureau to man all vessels controlled by the Shipping Board in place of the striking ISU members, but then immediately rescinded the order.[76] The Shipping Board had all the necessary tools to break the union's hold on the hiring process if it decided to use them. Moreover, the shipping boom had to end sometime; the wartime demand for labor could not last indefinitely. By the next major strike in the summer of 1921, changes to U.S. maritime policy, as well as further internal fissures within the ISU and the end of the shipping boom in the fall of 1920, shifted the power dynamics decidedly away from the unions.

The internal dissent brewing within the sailors' unions was more than just a loss of faith in the leadership's ability to successfully lead strikes or negotiate with the private operators and the Shipping Board, but a deeper questioning of the ISU's strict craft union principles and tactics. In August 1920, the rank and file of the East Coast continued to assert their growing power when they voted to move the headquarters of the Atlantic unions from Boston to New York, where the vast majority of them lived and were shipped.[77] This move allowed the rank and file greater influence within the Atlantic branch because of the higher concentration of ISU members present in that city as opposed to Boston.[78] As a result, the average sailor had greater access to union votes and meetings. Whereas from Boston, it was far easier for the leadership to pack meeting halls with loyalists during crucial policy and leadership votes without fear of being outvoted by a sudden influx of rank-and-file attendees. This was also when some Atlantic Union members were helping organize the Oriental Seafarers Union in defiance of the ISU's and Atlantic district's constitution, which prohibited Asian sailors from membership or even affiliation.[79]

By 1921 the rank and file began challenging the craft-based organizational structure of the ISU. At the 1921 ISU convention, and in a move reminiscent of George Bodine back in 1912, the Marine Firemen of the Atlantic and Gulf Coast submitted a resolution calling for the "amalgamation of the Sailors, Firemen, Cooks and Stewards" into a single organization called "the Eastern and Gulf Sailors Association . . . under the International Seamen's Union of America."[80] The resolution's backers argued that such a move would "strengthen their position" and allow them to "barter successfully in the industrial field."[81] The resolution then called for a constitutional convention "whereby the amalgamation . . . may be effected."[82] Such a convention was necessary because the ISU and district constitutions operated under strict craft union principles and therefore forbade the amalgamation of the district craft unions.[83] Luckily for the ISU leadership, the resolution failed to carry. By attempting to change the constitution, the Atlantic firemen were trying to tear down a key pillar of the ISU's craft union organizational structure and ideology.

Unlike in 1912—when the Atlantic unions similarly tried to amalgamate—the rank-and-file rebellion against the leadership and its strict craft unionism was both deeper and broader because it had spread beyond the ethnically diverse Atlantic Coast to the Pacific, where both craft unionism and Furuseth's influence were far more entrenched. The first signs of an emerging rebellion were in January 1921, when J. Vance Thompson was elected editor of the *Seaman's Journal,* defeating long-time editor and ISU vice president Paul Scharrenberg by just forty-one votes.[84] This was a significant defeat for the leadership for two reasons. First, because the leadership-backed candidate and vice president of the national organization was defeated. Second, because Thompson was increasingly sympathetic to a growing sentiment among the rank and file for greater cooperation with other maritime workers, particularly longshoremen.[85] In July 1921, Thompson, in his new capacity as *Seamen's Journal* editor, published an op-ed arguing that the sailors "must seek close[r] affiliation with and more thorough understanding of the longshoreman."[86] Thompson added that "[t]he spirit of solidarity must be cultivated and fostered in all port and marine workers."[87] This, of course, went much further than the Atlantic Union's efforts to amalgamate the district unions within the ISU. Thompson was advocating for industrial amalgamation with maritime workers outside the sailing trades.

Beyond Furuseth's and the leadership's aversion to any deviation from strict craft union organizing principles and their belief in labor hierarchies, cooperation with the longshoremen was especially difficult for the ISU president to stomach. As Furuseth's biographer pointed out, he "felt a deep-seated distrust of all people on shore."[88] More than that, Furuseth subscribed to the idea that there was a limited amount of money shipping companies could spend on wages that had to be divided between "longshoremen, sailors, riggers, teamsters, and many others."[89] If sailors amalgamated with longshoremen or other maritime workers, it could hamstring their ability to push for the highest wages possible since they would have to consider the wages of the other groups as well. Moreover, among all the maritime workers, sailors were the least numerous. If they were to amalgamate with the other marine workers, Furuseth feared they would consistently outvote sailors within the organization.[90] Paul Scharrenberg echoed this fear years later and added that the itinerant nature of the maritime trade would further reinforce longshoreman control of any federation between the unions. He argued that it was a "fine idea, to have longshoremen in the union meeting. They're here all the time. And seamen, there at sea, and the longshoremen would make the rules and so forth."[91] Indeed, Furuseth and the union leadership often used this tactic to maintain their control over the rank and file. As a result, Thompson's election challenged both the leadership's control over the union and its strict commitment to craft unionism.

Meanwhile, the U.S. Shipping Board's increasingly hard line against the sailors' unions exacerbated the pre-existing divisions within the ISU. In response to a worldwide shipping slump that began in the fall of 1921, the board and the American Steamship Association announced a series of wage cuts aimed at sailors, firemen, cooks and stewards, and engineers.[92] Furthermore, the Shipping Board, which leased many of its ships to private operators, stated that any private firm sailing vessels owned by the board must impose similar wage cuts or risk losing their leases.[93] Furuseth and the ISU agreed to some cuts, given the state of the shipping economy, but demanded that the Shipping Board abolish the Sea Service Bureau, give employment preference to union men, and properly enforce the La Follette Seamen's Act.[94] On April 30, the Shipping Board head, Admiral William S. Benson, rejected these terms and announced that the wage cuts would take effect immediately. In response, the sailors voted to strike, though the Shipping Board and the private operators had already locked them out. To ensure a united front against the unions, the American Steamship Association announced that it would expel from the organization any firm that signed an agreement with the sailors.[95] More significantly, unlike in 1919, the Shipping Board finally pulled the trigger on using the Sea Service Bureau to continue manning its ships throughout the duration of the lockout/strike. With almost forty thousand sailors left unemployed from the shipping slump and the lockout, there was an ample supply of labor to keep the ships sailing.[96] As a result, the sailors' union had lost most of its leverage. Any leverage they did have was because the Marine Engineers Beneficent Association was refusing to work out of solidarity with the seamen.[97] When the Marine Engineers capitulated, the Atlantic unions were forced to end the strike, while the Pacific Coast sailors soldiered on.

The Pacific Coast sailors' decision to continue the strike was a direct rebuke by the rank and file to Furuseth and the spirit of craft unionism, leading to open conflict between the leadership and the membership over the union's organizing strategy. This all came to a head in early July 1921, when the steam schooner operators (which employed most of the Pacific Coast Sailors) "disregarded the open shop policy of the American Steamship Owners' Association and the Pacific American Steamship Association" and offered the SUP a new agreement with modest wage reductions.[98] Furuseth—who was never in favor of the strike in the first place—wired from Washington that the members should vote for acceptance considering it was likely the best offer they would get. After the capitulation of the engineers on the East Coast and the Atlantic sailors' return to work, Furuseth believed that the strike was rapidly weakening. However, the key sticking point for the rank and file was that the offer compelled sailors to work with nonunion longshoremen, who were also on strike.[99] Given Furuseth's enmity toward longshoremen, he did not see this as reason to reject the offer. After all, the sailors had agreed to this stipulation in previous strikes. But in 1921, according to Peter Gill, "the mutual support of seamen and longshoremen was" seen as "essential."[100] As a result, the membership overwhelmingly voted against Furuseth and rejected the offer 1,607 to 118.[101] At the same meeting, the members then threw their support behind an initiative that emerged from the SUP's Puget Sound branch to form an umbrella organization for all maritime workers, including longshoremen. This organization would become the Marine Transport Workers Federation of the Pacific. Following the Puget Sound branch, the San Francisco sailors adopted a resolution, almost unanimously, that authorized the formation of a committee of five to meet with local longshoremen to discuss joining the maritime federation.[102] Meanwhile, after the rejection of the schooner offer, the Shipowners Association opened an Employment Service Bureau modeled on the Shipping Board's Sea Service Bureau to break the union. Sensing disaster, Furuseth returned to San Francisco to end the strike.

However, Furuseth's efforts to end the strike would tear the union apart and feed the rank and file's desire for greater cooperation between sailors and other maritime workers. Upon his return from Washington, Furuseth called a meeting for July 29 in the San Francisco Civic Auditorium instead of the union hall. Furuseth then had his lieutenants scour "the city for sailors and ex-sailors loyal" to him so he could pack the crowd with supporters.[103] When he addressed the crowd, an angry and agitated Furuseth proceeded to attack Thompson and every other leader he believed had led the effort to reject the offer. According to Furuseth's biographer, the ISU president argued that the rejection of the offer was "engineered by the IWW in order to waste the SUP's funds on a useless struggle so that the Wobblies could take over what was left of the union."[104] Furuseth then whipped the crowd into such a frenzy that Thompson and other leaders who supported rejecting the schooner offer were lucky to get out of the meeting alive.[105] By the end of the meeting, the sailors had voted 1,272 to 481 in favor of ending the strike.[106]

Despite the leadership's apparent victory, the sentiment for greater cooperation among the rank and file did not go away and led to a clash between Furuseth and Thompson in the pages of the *Seamen's Journal.* Thompson, a key supporter of the Pacific maritime federation, argued for "greater solidarity among the port workers" and saw the federation of maritime workers as a necessary evolution for the sailors unions.[107] In another editorial, Thompson seemed to blame the current leadership's policies for the failure of the strike and urged the members to act, stating, "our weak spots have been brought to light, and an interested and observant membership must endeavor to remedy the situation."[108] The problem, according to Thompson, was that the leadership did not properly "understand our position" within the maritime industry, pointing out that "we are a mere unit on the great industrial field."[109] As a result, Thompson argued, "a more perfect solidarity as workers is a pressing necessity."[110] Furuseth countered Thompson by linking the Pacific Maritime Federation with the IWW, opining, "[t]he One Big Union crowd will tell us our form of organization is not good, or we should not have lost." However, Furuseth continued, "[a]sk where they have won? They cannot tell of any place."[111] He further pointed out that despite the amalgamation of the sailors, "the teamsters, the longshoremen, and the railroad men," the IWW had lost "in Holland, in France, in Sweden, [and] in Norway."[112] Indeed, Furuseth's efforts to link Thompson and the Marine Transport Workers Federation of the Pacific with the Wobblies was helped by the fact that the IWW's rival maritime union was called the Marine Transport Industrial Union No. 510, which sounded similar to the federation. In the article, Furuseth seems to amalgamate the two organizations and refers to the IWW as the International Transport Workers Federation. It, therefore, would not be difficult for readers to think they were the same organization. By this point, the ISU president increasingly saw any effort to stray from the union's craft union principles as evidence of an IWW plot.

Furuseth's ruthlessness when it came to the IWW is evidenced in his efforts to reach a new agreement with the shipping companies after the SUP voted to end the strike. In September 1921, Furuseth went to the shipowners to accept the original offer. However, the shipping companies balked, insisting that they could not sign any agreement with a union controlled by the "IWW."[113] In response, Furuseth told the shipowners that he could clear out the Wobblies (or who he believed were the Wobblies) within sixty days, telling them, "[i]f you will give us a chance we will go on board and point out the I.W.W. [members]."[114] The shipowners rejected this offer, however, and told Furuseth "we know who are I.W.W. better than you do."[115] Then, at a September 26 meeting of the SUP, Furuseth introduced a resolution accusing Thompson of using the *Seamen's Journal* to spread IWW propaganda. Again, Furuseth used the resolution to conflate the Marine Transport Workers Federation of the Pacific with the IWW's Marine Transport Industrial Union. The resolution read, "[t]he Seamen's Journal for some considerable time advocated the ideas of the IWW, the Marine Transport Workers Industrial Union No. 510, which is a section of the IWW, and of the One Big Union."[116] The resolution then stated that "the editor [of the *Seamen's Journal*], John Vance Thompson, be and is hereby instructed to cease all such propaganda in the Journal at once."[117] The resolution carried, and the union officially censured Thompson, though he remained as editor of the *Journal*. Unfortunately for Thompson and his followers, this was merely the beginning of Furuseth's and the ISU leadership's purge of "disloyal" members who advocated for industrial unionism.

Attempts to clear out who Furuseth believed were IWW supporters and their ideas from the SUP came to a head in November 1921 and marked the beginning of a mass exodus from the sailors' unions. In an October 31 meeting of the SUP, Furuseth charged Thompson with violating the September 26 resolution concerning IWW propaganda in the *Seamen's Journal.* In addition, Furuseth also charged Thompson with "being disloyal to the union and aiding the enemies of the Sailors Unions."[118] On November 14, Furuseth convened a disciplinary committee in a meeting packed with his supporters to hear the charges against Thompson. After Furuseth presented the charges, the disciplinary committee recommended expulsion and the members present—the majority of whom were Furuseth loyalists—voted to expel Thompson from the union.[119] Accounts vary on what exactly happened after the vote. According to the IWW, Thompson walked toward Furuseth and "threw his membership-book upon the desk" and "was followed by many other members who [also] threw their books in Furuseth's face."[120] The IWW then claimed that "shaking with fear, Furuseth drew a revolver from his pocket; though he did not have courage enough to raise it above the desk."[121] While there is likely some truth to this account, there is little evidence to corroborate it. Indeed, Peter Gill gives a detailed account of this meeting, but does not mention Thompson and his supporters throwing their union cards at Furuseth, nor does he mention that the ISU president was armed. What is known, however, is that the union expelled a further twenty-five members at the meeting and another thirty over the next few weeks.[122]

Yet despite Furuseth's vendetta, Thompson was hardly a Wobbly. In fact, he had worked undercover as an informant for the California Immigration and Housing Commission within the IWW in 1917 under the alias Joseph Richards.[123] Indeed, the IWW itself stated that while Thompson was a "progressive craft unionist" who "believe[s] in a union controlled by the rank and file," he "is not now, and never has been, connected with the I.W.W."[124] Moreover, Thompson supported the Marine Transport Workers Federation of the Pacific because he saw it as a middle way between the craft unionism of the SUP and the industrial radicalism of the IWW and believed that by supporting it, the SUP could discourage defections to the IWW.[125] This is what he told journalist George P. West, that "the Federation scheme was a concession for holding the men, for keeping them out of the I.W.W., for meeting the spirit of *inclusive* [emphasis added] brotherhood."[126] However, the nuances of Thompson's position were lost on Furuseth. For the ISU president, there was no middle ground. Furuseth saw any deviation from the ISU's strict craft union principles as advocating the ideology of the Wobblies. After these initial expulsions, members began deserting the ISU en masse.[127]

Did the rank and file's mass desertions from the ISU and the SUP mean that they all joined the IWW? Not exactly. Indeed, it is difficult to determine exactly who left the union, why they left, and where they went. Some no doubt left to join the Wobbly's Marine Transport Workers Industrial Union and others may have operated independently, finding work through the shipowner-controlled Employment Service Bureau. However, the available evidence suggests a significant proportion (though it is impossible to say how significant) likely left for the fledgling Marine Transport Workers Federation of the Pacific. First, Paul Scharrenberg maintained that the IWW's penetration of the SUP and the ISU was always exaggerated. He later stated that the Wobblies "never really got a hold[,] but they were a regular nuisance," pointing out that all they ever really did was "come into union meetings and harangue the crowd."[128] Additionally, George P. West—who interviewed both Furuseth and Thompson—believed about 10 percent of the membership were "flirting with the I.W.W.," but that this did not necessarily mean they shared the revolutionary radicalism of the IWW.[129] Moreover, Seattle branch agent Peter Gill later described the "sentiment for cooperation with the longshoremen" as the driving force behind the rank and file's actions during 1921 and 1922.[130] This suggests that a large proportion of the rank and file likely gravitated toward Thompson's middle of the road approach that eschewed the radicalism of the Wobblies but embraced a more industrial form of organization that rejected Furuseth's strict craft unionism. For these members, the Marine Transport Workers Federation of the Pacific would seem like their logical and ideal home. Beyond that, many sailors likely left the sailing trade for good now that the wartime shipping boom had ended.

However, what we can be certain of is that between late 1921 and 1923 the ISU lost about one hundred thousand members. In 1921 ISU membership peaked at around 115,000 members, and by 1923 that number had shrunk to its prewar level of thirteen thousand. The SUP fared a bit better, going from 6,500 members in 1921 to three thousand by 1923.[131] Indeed, while the SUP may have been the backbone of the ISU since its inception, they were always dwarfed by the East Coast's raw numbers. In addition, the wartime expansion disproportionately benefited the East Coast since it was the key supply line for men and material going to Europe. Again, it is impossible to say who stayed and who left. But based on the fact that the losses reflected (almost exactly) the wartime gains, it is not unreasonable to conclude that most of the members who stayed belonged to the old guard. These were members who joined before the wartime expansion and remained loyal to Furuseth and his rigid craft union ideology.

In any event, with Thompson and his allies out of the SUP, Furuseth used the 1922 ISU convention to close ranks and double down on his exclusionary craft unionism by further centralizing power and control within the ISU executive. Furuseth proposed a series of amendments to the ISU constitution, though two stand out in particular. One "authorized [the ISU] to step in and take charge of any district union that fails to abide by its own laws or that violate the constitution of the International Seamen's Union."[132] This allowed the ISU to take over the district unions if it determined they did something like organize Asian sailors or attempted to amalgamate with other marine workers. The other key change ensured that all organizers and educators in the field were under the supervision of the ISU, not the local districts.[133] Both measures passed with ease. Furthermore, the ISU took over the publication of the *Seamen's Journal* from the SUP and moved its offices from San Francisco to Washington, D.C.

Furuseth and the old guard's exclusionary craft unionists had won, but it cost them everything they had achieved since the First World War. They had successfully purged the ISU of the "IWW" and those sympathetic to a more industrial form of organization, but they lost one hundred thousand members in the process. Moreover, the combined efforts of the Shipping Board and the private operators' associations had succeeded in imposing an open shop labor policy on the U.S. shipping industry. The ISU would not recover until the mid-1930s. Finally, and most notably, the new constitution reaffirmed that ISU membership would be open only to those *eligible* for U.S. citizenship.[134] This was just another way of saying that ISU membership was open only to whites or those with European ancestry.

Of course, the final version of the 1924 Immigration Act demonstrated the short-sightedness of excluding anyone ineligible for U.S. citizenship from the ISU considering Furuseth was unable to bar excluded persons from employment on vessels bound for the United States. American and foreign shipping companies could continue bringing Chinese and any other sailors from the act's so-called barred zones into U.S. ports. By doubling down on racially exclusive craft unionism, Furuseth had inadvertently surrendered white American sailors' position within the emerging and ever-expanding U.S. imperial hierarchy. In this way, U.S.-flagged vessels existed more in the realm of the global barred zones than the U.S. domestic or metropolitan realm.

Conclusion

Boundaries matter. Whether real or imagined, they have material consequences in the lives of real people. For working people, the differences between the supposedly abstract concepts of foreign and domestic, or nation and empire, were far from abstract. For sailors, which side of the divide they labored under determined whether they worked under the protection of something as fundamental as the Thirteenth Amendment. Yet despite the concrete consequences of these boundaries, their existence was fluid. Their creation was part of a moving process shaped by the clashing interests of capital and labor. As a result, the relationship between nation and empire, or foreign and domestic, was fundamentally a labor question—a consequence of the collision and potential integration of disparate and uneven labor markets into an emerging U.S. imperial system. More significantly, it was the process through which the United States nation emerged, was defined, and redefined.

What lessons does the class struggle over America's borders offer broader working-class efforts to insulate uneven labor markets? The answer to this question lies in the divergent fortunes of the wider AFL-led craft union movement and the ISU specifically. Where the AFL succeeded in protecting its members from U.S. colonial and imperial labor markets, the ISU failed. Why did the ISU fail where the AFL succeeded? The key difference was that the ISU represented workers in an industry that was both transnational and operationally mobile, whereas broader U.S. industry was not. At least not yet. The transnational and operational mobility of U.S. shipping capital largely immunized the industry from both labor market insulation and government regulation. More than that, the ISU's exclusionary craft unionism, complete with racial prohibitions against nonwhites, helped ensure the continued existence of a cheaper alternative labor source. By embracing a politics of exclusion and aligning with empire in an industry that was mostly impervious to labor market insulation, the ISU was inadvertently complicit in the uneven segmentation of the global maritime labor market.

To deal with the potential disruption from U.S. imperial expansion on the domestic U.S. labor market, the craft union labor movement, led by the AFL and the ISU, resisted the effects of empire by aligning with it. Labor leaders resisted colonial-imperialism by advocating legislative polices that affirmed their commitment to white settler colonialism.[1] That is, organized labor sought to insulate its membership from the peoples and practices of America's newly acquired territory. To accomplish this, the craft union labor movement successfully fought to extend the Chinese Exclusion Act both through and around the United States imperial system in 1902. By securing their insulation and protection from specific parts of the U.S. imperial system, labor leaders were implicitly endorsing the concept of colonial-imperialism by insisting on a privileged and protected position within an incipient imperial hierarchy. As a result, immigration restriction emerged as organized labor's primary means of exercising influence over U.S. imperial expansion.[2] The broadest consequence of organized labor's alignment with empire was the emergence of a spatially defined and racially inflected imperial metropole around the North American (and later Hawaiian) territory of the U.S. imperial system.

After the successful extension of the exclusion law in 1902, the ISU and the AFL worked tirelessly to guarantee its proper enforcement and ensure that the metropolitan labor market remained protected from both U.S. colonial and imperial labor markets. Almost immediately after the law's passage, there was a growing lobby of anti-exclusionists who called for a relaxation of the law's enforcement or outright repeal. By 1905 opponents of exclusion forced the Roosevelt administration to move key aspects of the law's enforcement mechanism outside the U.S. metropole to consular officials abroad. A year later, the AFL and the ISU prevented the further erosion of the Exclusion Act's enforcement mechanism when they thwarted the passage of the Foster immigration bill. The Foster bill would have transferred these same enforcement mechanisms from U.S. consuls to the Chinese government. In 1908 labor leaders' agitation forced a reluctant Roosevelt to end Japanese immigration to the United States when he negotiated the Gentlemen's Agreement with the Japanese government—though he was able to keep the agreement out of Congress, where organized labor could exercise more influence. The next decade saw mass immigration to the United States come to a screeching halt as the world plunged itself into the cataclysm of the First World War. After the war, calls for an across-the-board reduction in immigration from all parts of the world reached fever pitch. With the passage of the 1924 Immigration Act, organized labor finally had succeeded in insulating the U.S. metropolitan labor market from colonial, imperial, and nearly all other foreign labor markets when Congress expanded the barred zones to include the Philippines and Japan.[3]

For sailors specifically, it was a much more complicated story replete with near-constant failure and reversals of fortune. From the mid-1890s, the SUP and the ISU relentlessly tried to insulate the maritime labor market from foreign competition. They failed to include U.S.-flagged vessels as part of the 1902 Exclusion Act extension. In 1907 their efforts to stop the use of Chinese crews on transpacific routes by expanding the Exclusion Act's coverage to the port of Honolulu failed when the Commerce Department almost immediately offered shipping companies a loophole that allowed them a way around the law. From 1894 onward, the ISU introduced multiple versions of what would become the La Follette Seamen's Act of 1915 in nearly every legislative session. Despite finally succeeding in 1915, the Commerce Department voided the act's principal means of insulating the maritime labor market in December of that year, a mere seven months after President Wilson signed the La Follette Act into law. Two years later, the U.S. Supreme Court removed the foreign maritime trade's last vestiges of the metropolitan labor market when it legalized the reshipment of Chinese crews in U.S. ports, declared the labor space of U.S.-flagged vessels in the foreign trade outside the domestic labor market, and ruled that sailors were not laborers. This decision broke with the Commerce Department's prevailing enforcement consensus in place since 1892 that understood the reshipment of Chinese sailors in U.S. ports as a violation of the Exclusion Act.[4] The ISU then tried to reverse these decisions by lobbying Congress to ban all sailors ineligible for U.S. citizenship from serving on American-flagged ships as part of the 1924 Immigration Act. This, too, failed. In the end, the 1924 Immigration Act reaffirmed the 1917 Supreme Court decision by providing a legislative definition of the U.S. metropole that set the limits of the domestic labor market at the water's edge of the continental United States.[5] The Immigration Act's definition of the U.S. metropole ensured that American-flagged vessels in the foreign trade remained an imperial formation that existed outside the domestic labor market and would therefore not be insulated from cheaper foreign and imperial labor markets. Where the AFL succeeded in protecting the overwhelming majority of its members, the ISU failed.

The key difference between white merchant sailors and the rest of the AFL's membership was that, operationally, broader U.S. industrial capital was not yet transnationally mobile, but shipping capital was. Aside from shipping firms, the only U.S. corporations that did operate transnationally were almost exclusively in the mineral or oil extraction business, since primary resources are indifferent to national and imperial boundaries.[6] Shipping capital's transnational and operational mobility allowed firms to crew their vessels in the world's cheapest possible labor markets. Broader U.S. industry, on the other hand, *could* recruit workers from cheaper labor markets, but only through a continuous pipeline of mass immigration to the U.S. metropole—workers were brought to the operational sites of U.S. industrial capital rather than U.S. industrial capital moving to their desired labor force. Yet as we have seen, this type of labor supply was vulnerable to nativist working-class organizing campaigns that painted mass immigration as an invasion of foreigners intent on destroying American culture, democracy, and standard of living. Once the pipeline of mass immigration was closed off, U.S. industrial firms had no choice but to rely on workers already present within the U.S. metropole. At best, U.S. firms could exploit the uneven labor markets within the United States, which they often did. As Jefferson Cowie demonstrated in his study of RCA, the company began its operations in the Northeast and relied on mostly southern and eastern European immigrants. Once these workers began an organizing drive in the 1930s, RCA turned to rural midwestern labor markets when it moved its operations to Indiana in 1940. When these workers became too unruly, RCA looked to the labor markets of the U.S. South when it relocated to Memphis, Tennessee, in the 1960s.[7]

Additionally, the transnationality of the foreign shipping trade meant that Congress was limited in its ability to regulate the industry since U.S. shipping firms were vulnerable to international competition in ways that the broader U.S. economy was not. This created a race to the bottom for wages within the global shipping industry. Even if Congress passed a law that forced American firms to hire only from high wage U.S. ports or applied the Chinese Exclusion Act to U.S.-flagged vessels, the transnational nature of the industry rendered the law nearly unenforceable. As the House Committee on Foreign affairs concluded in 1902, American shipping companies would simply switch their fleets' registry and flag their vessels under the British ensign to get around inconvenient U.S. legislation.[8] Moreover, preventing U.S. firms from using foreign registry would not solve the problem either, because it gave foreign shipping firms a competitive advantage over their American counterparts. Beyond this, even if it was possible for Congress to insulate the U.S shipping industry from foreign competition and thus decrease the incentive for U.S. firms to rely on cheaper foreign sailors, it would mean that American goods would be more expensive on the international market owing to higher shipping costs, and foreign goods would be more expensive in the United States for the same reason. This is why Pacific Mail Steamship Line director Maxwell Evarts argued that the extension of the Exclusion Act to American vessels was tantamount to a "tax on American commerce."[9]

The only time there was any real labor market insulation was during the First World War, when the major imperial powers withdrew their fleets from normal commerce. As chapter 4 demonstrates, the war temporarily affirmed Andrew Furuseth's argument that a reserve of well-trained citizen merchant sailors was necessary in a time of war. Additionally, the war pushed wages up to their highest levels and dramatically expanded both the U.S. merchant fleet and the ISU's membership. More than that, the circumstances of the war finally allowed white merchant sailors to reach their desired status as agents of U.S. empire. Everyone from the president to members of Congress and even shipping company executives praised the bravery, skill, and dedication of America's merchant sailors during the war.

However, the war represented a temporary reprieve from a downward spiral of status and material well-being for white American merchant sailors. Once the war ended, and the need for experienced and skilled American sailors quickly evaporated, the government supported the shipping companies' efforts to impose an open shop on the industry and destroy the sailors' unions once and for all. Yet even during the war, the courts and the executive were laying the groundwork for a return to cheap foreign labor on U.S. merchant ships. The Commerce Department removed the ISU's key mechanism for labor market insulation when it voided the La Follette Act's language clause in late 1915. In 1917 the Supreme Court unequivocally declared the foreign merchant trade outside the bounds of the U.S. labor market. It seemed that labor market insulation was possible only when both the government and shipping company executives allowed it.

The pattern was similar during and after the Second World War, twenty years later. While the unions may have recovered from the open shop era during the massive organizing campaigns of the 1930s, the shipping industry was still reeling from the effects of the Great Depression. However, the outbreak of war in 1939 and America's subsequent entry in 1941 led to a massive job boom and a surge in wages. Moreover, given America's two-front war against Germany and Japan, Pacific Coast sailors saw a much larger percentage of those job gains than they did twenty years earlier. Yet again, after the war ended, the gains began to evaporate. It was during the late 1940s and early 1950s when the modern Flag of Convenience system emerged. This system allowed shipping firms to flag their vessels in whatever national jurisdiction they pleased. Unsurprisingly, most firms chose registry in nations with little to no government regulation, which is why Panama and Liberia had long possessed the world's largest merchant fleets.[10] Given that the transnational reality of shipping capital neutralized the government's ability to effectively regulate the industry (except during national emergencies such as the two world wars) and thus insulate the U.S. maritime labor market, there effectively existed only one potential alternative strategy.

Rather than excluding sailors from low-wage foreign labor markets (specifically in China) from the union, the ISU leadership should have listened to their Atlantic affiliate in 1919 and directed its efforts toward expanding into those markets by organizing Chinese sailors and any other foreign sailors from cheaper labor markets. Unfortunately, Andrew Furuseth's and the ISU leadership's prejudice toward Chinese and other nonwhite sailors was far too powerful for the Oriental Seafarers Union organizers to overcome. Additionally, the ISU leadership's primary justification for insulating the maritime labor market from Chinese and foreign sailors was to build up and strengthen American naval power and reimagine white merchant sailors as agents rather than instruments of U.S. empire. The organization of Chinese and potentially other sailors from low-wage labor markets did not serve this goal. Indeed, Furuseth liked to point out that by relying on Chinese sailors, the U.S. merchant marine was training sailors for a future Chinese navy. This reflected the ISU's longer-term strategy of insulating the maritime labor market by amalgamating white merchant sailors with the national or imperial interest. The ISU leadership's alignment with empire had boxed them into a corner and left them little room to adapt to the changing dynamics in the postwar era.

The irony was that whatever the ISU's justification may have been for excluding Chinese and other nonwhite sailors from the union, it would succeed only in maintaining the continued existence of a cheap alternative source of labor for both the U.S. and global shipping industries. In refusing to admit Chinese (and others excluded from U.S. citizenship) into the union, Furuseth and the ISU allowed themselves to be outflanked by shipping capital. Without the protection of the ISU and the ability to share in the fruits of collective bargaining, Chinese and other excluded sailors would remain a cheap alternative for shipping capital. This was something that the organizers of the Oriental Seafarers Union understood all too well when they pointed out that by organizing Chinese sailors, they had finally deprived shipping companies of "their last pawns" against the sailors' unions.[11] Exclusion could never work in an industry that was largely impervious to labor market insulation. As a result, by refusing to organize Chinese and other excluded sailors, the ISU leadership was complicit in the segmentation of uneven maritime labor markets that shipping capital could easily exploit.

The failure of the ISU to insulate the maritime labor market through exclusion offers important lessons for organized labor in the era of globalized production. In the roughly one hundred years since Furuseth's and the ISU's campaign for maritime exclusion, U.S. manufacturing capital has become transnationally mobile. The shipping industry of the early twentieth century, therefore, was predictive of where broader capitalist trends were headed over the last one hundred years. Indeed, this is not the first time that the shipping industry has foreshadowed structural changes in the broader capitalist economy. As Marcus Rediker noted about the eighteenth-century shipping industry, the prevalence of wage labor within the merchant marine "symbolized the advancing structural transformation in relations between capital and labor."[12] Like shipping capital in the early twentieth century, the transnational mobility of manufacturing capital in the twenty-first century allowed multinational corporations access to a global labor market. And, just like shipping capital then and now, these firms sought out national jurisdictions with loose regulations and cheaper labor markets. For instance, by the 1970s, RCA's search for ever-cheaper sources of labor continued when the company relocated its operations from the U.S. South to the developing world when it set up shop in the Mexican state of Chihuahua.[13]

Modern working-class protest movements against globalized production cannot allow themselves to be outflanked by transnational capital—in the way the ISU was—by embracing the politics of anti-immigration and closed borders.[14] Workers need to think systemically about their place in the global economy to understand how their defensive actions within their specific national jurisdictions ripple throughout the broader system of transnational capitalism. Without a systemic understanding and approach to the problem of transnational production, working-class efforts to resist the effects of globalization could boomerang back on themselves. Closing borders and curtailing the international movement of people as a protest against the transnational mobility of manufacturing capital will succeed only in reinforcing and entrenching the segmentation of the global labor force into the uneven labor markets necessary for the global production process to flourish. With that in mind, workers should be wary of movements that view the loss of manufacturing jobs through the prism of national sovereignty.

One hundred years ago, labor leaders within the world's first transnationally mobile industry bet on an alignment with empire and privilege and lost. The transnational nature of the shipping industry made government regulation difficult and labor market insulation near impossible. As a result, every effort the ISU made to protect its members from the peoples and practices of the emerging U.S. empire either failed or were quickly reversed by Congress, the executive, or the courts. Despite a temporary period of prosperity and expansion during the First World War, the postwar open shop era decimated the ISU. When offered an alternative form of organization that sought bonds of solidarity beyond both the U.S. labor market and its narrow craft union organizational structure, the ISU doubled down on exclusionary craft unionism. However, in a transnationally mobile industry, the ISU's exclusionary tactics were ultimately self-defeating. At best, the psychological wages of whiteness—so relentlessly pursued by Furuseth and the ISU leadership—offered the ISU short-term gains at the expense of potentially long-term prosperity and solidarity.

Notes

Introduction

1. A barkentine is three-mast schooner.

2. The ISU was officially established in 1892 at a conference of regional seamen's union in Chicago. The organization was originally named the National Seaman's Union of America but became the International Seaman's Union of America in 1895.

3. *Robertson v. Baldwin*, 165 U.S. 283 (1897).

4. The Maritime Law of the Byzantine Empire.

5. *Robertson v. Baldwin*, 165, U.S. 283 (1897).

6. *Robertson v. Baldwin*, 165 U.S. 287 (1897).

7. *Robertson v. Baldwin*, 165 U.S. 277 (1897).

8. The Dred Scott case refers to the infamous 1857 Supreme Court case in which the Court, led by Chief Justice Roger Taney, held that slaveowners could bring their slaves into non-slave territory. Additionally, the Court held that African Americans were never intended to be citizens of the United States.

9. It should be noted that there was opposition to U.S. westward expansion in the Northeast. Powerful interests in that region feared that an expanding country would dilute the position they held within the nation.

10. Bartholomew H. Sparrow, *The Insular Cases and the Emergence of the American Empire* (Lawrence: University of Kansas Press, 2006), 4.

11. The insular cases were a series of Supreme Court cases beginning in 1901 and ending roughly around the early 1920s that attempt to define the relationship between the new American colonies and the United States. There is scholarly disagreement over the number of cases defined as part of the insular cases. In the strictest sense,

the cases number around seven or eight. Though Efren Rivera Ramos argues in Efren Rivera Ramos, *The Legal Construction of Identity: The Judicial and Social Legacy of American Colonialism in Puerto Rico* (Washington, D.C.: American Psychological Association, 2001) twenty-three cases and Bartholomew H. Sparrow in *Insular Cases* argues for a total of thirty-five cases. Though as Christine Duffy Burnette points out in an appendix to her work, Christine Duffy Burnette and Burke Marshall, eds., *Foreign in the Domestic: Puerto Rico, American Expansion, and the Constitution* (Durham, N.C.: Duke University Press, 2001) "there seems to be nearly universal consensus that the series culminates in *Balzac v. Puerto Rico* in 1922, and that *Downes v. Bidwell* is the single most important." For the insular cases, see Line-Noue Memea Kruse, *The Pacific Insular Case of American Samoa: Land Rights and Law in Unincorporated U.S. Territories* (New York: Palgrave, 2018); Gerald L. Newman and Tomiko Brown-Nargin, eds., *Reconsidering the Insular Cases: The Present and Future of American Empire* (Cambridge, Mass.: Harvard University Press, 2015); Sparrow, *Insular Cases*; Christina Duffy Burnette, "American Expansion and Territorial Deannexation," *University of Chicago Law Review* 72, no. 3 (Summer 2005): 797- 879; Christina Duffy Burnett and Burke Marshall, eds., *Foreign in a Domestic Sense: Puerto Rico, American Expansion, and the Constitution* (Durham, N.C.: Duke University Press, 2001); Ramos, *Legal Construction of Identity*; James E. Kerr, *The Insular Cases: The Role of the Judiciary in American Expansionism* (Port Washington, N.Y.: Kennikat Press, 1982).

12. See Julie Greene, "GAPE Presidential Address: Movable Empire: Labor, Migration, and U.S Global Power During the Gilded Age and Progressive Era," *Journal of the Gilded Age and Progressive Era* 15, no. 1 (2016): 4–20; Daniel E. Bender and Jana K. Lipman, "Through the Looking Glass: U.S. Empire Through the Lens of Labor History," in Daniel E. Bender and Jana K. Lipman, eds., *Making the Empire Work: Labor and United States Imperialism* (New York: New York University Press, 2015): 1–32; also Julie Greene, "The Wages of Empire: Capitalism, Expansion, and Working-Class Formation," in Bender and Lipman, eds., *Making the Empire Work*, 35–58; Jason Colby, *The Business of Empire: United Fruit, Race, and U.S. Expansion in Central America* (Ithaca, N.Y.: Cornell University Press, 2011); Greg Grandin, *Fordlandia: The Rise and Fall of Henry Ford's Forgotten Jungle City* (New York: Picador, 2010); Jefferson Cowie, *Capital Moves: RCA's Seventy Year Quest for Cheap Labor* (Ithaca, N.Y.: Cornell University Press, 1999); though Cowie's study is not framed as a study of U.S. empire or imperial expansion per se, but it does provide a case study of a U.S. corporation's exploitation and ongoing search for cheaper labor markets both within the United States nation and into countries that have an imperial relationship with the United States.

13. The idea of a privileged and protected segment of labor emerged out of nineteenth century Britain in what was referred to as a labor aristocracy, see Eric Hobsbawm, "Labour Aristocracy in Nineteenth Century Britain," in Eric Hobsbawm, *Labouring Men: Studies in the History of Labour* (London: Weidenfeld and Nicolson, 1964): 272–315; for the idea of the AFL and Craft Union movement in the United States as a labor aristocracy, see Stuart Bruce Kaufman, *Samuel Gompers and the Origins of the American Federation of Labor, 1848–1896* (London: Greenwood Press, 1973); Craig Phelan, *William*

Green: Biography of a Labor Leader (Albany: State University of New York Press, 1989); Julie Greene's *Pure and Simple Politics: The American Federation of Labor and Political Action, 1881–1917* (Cambridge, Mass.: Cambridge University Press, 1998), 10–11, points out that "By 1900, one could see in the United States a bifurcated working class, dominated by a minority of skilled workers, predominantly white native-born men, who made higher wages and exercised more power on the shop floor than did other workers." For an example of a labor aristocracy at the city level, see Michael Kazin's *Barons of Labor: The San Francisco Building Trades and Union Power in the Progressive Era* (Urbana: University of Illinois Press, 1987).

14. For work on the insular cases, see, Line-Noue Memea Kruse, *Pacific Insular Case*; Newman and Brown-Nargin, eds., *Reconsidering the Insular Cases*; Sparrow, *Insular Cases*; Burnette, "American Expansion and Territorial Deannexation," 797–879; Burnett and Marshall, eds., *Foreign in a Domestic Sense*; Kerr, *Insular Cases*.

15. *Downes v. Bidwell* 182 U.S. 244 (1901); for a discussion of *Downes v. Bidwell* and the doctrine of unincorporation, see Christina Duffy Burnett and Burke Marshall, "Between the Foreign and Domestic: The Doctrine of Unincorporation, Invented and Reinvented," in Burnett and Marshall, eds., *Foreign in a Domestic Sense*, 1–38.

16. For empire as labor systems, see Daniel E. Bender and Jana K. Lipman, "Introduction: Through the Looking Glass," in Bender and Lipman, eds., *Making the Empire Work*, 4.

17. Colby, *Business of Empire*; Grandin, *Fordlandia*; Julie Greene, *The Canal Builders: Making America's Empire at the Panama Canal* (New York: Penguin Press, 2009); Jana K. Lipman, *Guantanamo: A Working-Class History between Empire and Revolution* (Berkeley and Los Angeles: University of California Press, 2008); Harvey Neptune, *Caliban and the Yanks: Trinidad and the United States Occupation* (Chapel Hill: University of North Carolina Press, 2007); Aviva Chomsky, *West Indian Workers and the United Fruit Company in Costa Rica* (Baton Rouge: Louisiana State University Press, 1996).

18. Greene, "Wages of Empire," 36.

19. Ibid., 36.

20. Ibid.

21. Paul A. Kramer, "Power and Connection: Imperial Histories of the United States in the World," *American Historical Review* 116, no. 5 (2011): 1349.

22. Moon-Ho Jung recently reminded us that in conceiving of empire as an analytic concept or a relational process we should be careful not to make everything imperial. Doing so could have the unintended effect of rendering invisible both the U.S. empire and, more importantly, those who struggle against it. See Moon-Ho Jung, *Menace to Empire: Anti-Colonial Solidarities and the Transpacific Origins of the U.S. National Security State* (Oakland: University of California Press, 2022), 13 and 297.

23. Eric Wolfe, *Europe and the People Without History* (Berkeley: University of California Press, 1982), 3.

24. For imperial formations, see Ann Laura Stoler and Carole McGranahan, "Introduction: Reconfiguring the Imperial Terrains," in Ann Laura Stoler et al., *Imperial Formations* (Santa Fe, N.M.: School for Advanced Research Press, 2007), 8–9.

25. David Montgomery, "SHGAPE Distinguished Historian Address: Workers Movements in the United States Confront Imperialism: The Progressive Era Experience," *Journal of the Gilded Age and Progressive Era* 7, no. 1 (January 2008): 7–42.

26. For "imperial repertoires," see Frederick Cooper and Jane Burbank, *Empires in World History: Power and the Politics of Difference* (Princeton, N.J.: Princeton University Press, 2010), 3–8.

27. "Public Law 57–90 / Chapter 641, 57 Congress, Session 1, An Act: To prohibit the coming into and to regulate the residence within the United States, its Territories, and all territory under its jurisdiction, and the District of Columbia, of Chinese and persons of Chinese descent.," U.S. Statutes at Large 32, no. Main Section (1902): 176–77.

28. For the dual impetus of U.S. expansion, see Amy Kaplan, *The Anarchy of Empire in the Making of U.S. Culture* (Cambridge, Mass.: Harvard University Press, 2002), 15.

29. David Harvey's *The Enigma of Capital and the Crisis of Capitalism* (Oxford, U.K.: Oxford University Press, 2011) discusses how by the 1970s, capitalist interests, both inside and outside the United States, could not abide the limitations to accumulation that a powerful labor movement had placed upon it. Starting in the 1970s, capitalist interest began a sustained movement to transcend that barrier by neutralizing the power of labor unions. By the twenty-first century, according to Harvey, the labor problem had been solved with capital having access to a global labor market.

30. Beyond the most obvious example of Chinese exclusion and indigenous dispossession, Americans originally saw the West as a refuge for white Americans fleeing the racial antagonisms of the East. As a result, California considered banning African Americans from entering the state, whether slave or free. Oregon actually did ban the migration of African Americans in its constitution. See Tomas Almaguer, *Racial Fault Lines: The Historical Origins of White Supremacy in California* (Berkeley and Los Angeles: University of California Press, 1994).

31. Beth Lew-Williams, *"The Chinese Must Go": Violence, Exclusion, and the Making of the Alien in America* (Cambridge, Mass.: Harvard University Press, 2018), 170.

32. See Alexander Saxton, *The Indispensable Enemy: Labor and the Anti-Chinese Movement in California* (Berkeley and Los Angeles: University of California Press, 1971); Richard White, *It's Your Misfortune and None of My Own: A History of The American West* (Norman: University of Oklahoma Press, 1991).

33. Ronald Takaki, *Iron Cages: Race and Culture in 19th Century America* (New York: Oxford University Press, 2000), 236.

34. See Saxton, *Indispensable Enemy.*

35. Lew-Williams, *"The Chinese Must Go,"* 171.

36. See Alfred Thayer Mahan, *The Influence of Sea Power on History, 1660–1782,* 12th ed., (Boston: Little Brown, 1918). While Mahan's work deals with the role of naval power in the sixteenth and seventeenth centuries, he wrote the book to demonstrate the continuing importance of naval power and how the United States should become world class.

37. The Dingley Act of 1884 permitted U.S.-flagged vessels in the foreign trade to sign up crews anywhere in the world without having to reship them in the United States. This meant that shipping companies could bypass the labor market of U.S. ports. See "Chapter 121, 48 Congress, Session 1, An Act: To remove certain burdens

on the American merchant marine and encourage the American foreign carrying trade and for other purposes.," U.S. Statutes at Large 23, no. Main Section (1884): 53–60.

38. Alex Roland et al., *The Way of the Ship: America's Maritime History Reenvisioned, 1600–2000* (Hoboken, N.J.: John Wiley and Sons, 2008), 226.

39. For the difference between imperial and colonial subjects, see Carole McGranahan, "Empire Out of Bounds: Tibet in the Era of Decolonization," in Ann Laura Stoler et al., eds., *Imperial Formations*, 174.

40. For an examination of the Afro-Caribbean British subjects who helped build the Panama Canal, see Greene, *Canal Builders*.

41. Here I build the historian Justin Jackson's recent work on whiteness and the ISU; see Justin Jackson, "The Right Kind of Man: Flexible Capacity, Chinese Exclusion, and the Imperial Origins of Maritime Labor Reform in the United States, 1898–1905," *Labor: Studies in Working-Class History of the Americas* 10, no. 4 (Winter 2013): 39–60.

42. April Merleaux recently noted that any potential expansion of the domestic realm came with a strong desire to exclude nonwhites from "the boundaries of national belonging." See April Merleaux, *Sugar and Civilization: American Empire and the Cultural Politics of Sweetness* (Chapel Hill: University of North Carolina Press, 2015), 31.

43. See Lew-Williams, *"The Chinese Must Go,"* 170.

44. See Donna Gabaccia, *Foreign Relations: American Immigration in a Global Perspective* (Princeton, N.J.: Princeton University Press, 2012), 12–17.

45. *The Seamen's Act: Hearings on S.136, Day 7, Before the H. Comm. on the Merchant Marine and Fisheries*, 63rd Cong. 12 (1914) (statement of Robert Dollar, President of the Dollar Steamship Line).

46. Brian Rouleau, *White Sails Whitening Every Sea: Mariners and the Making of An American Maritime Empire* (Ithaca, N.Y.: Cornell University Press, 2014), 196; Alex Roland et al., *Way of the Ship*, 266.

47. Bruce Laurie, *Artisans into Workers: Labor in Nineteenth-Century America* (New York: Noonday Press, 1989), 184.

48. For the differences between whiteness on the Pacific and East coasts, see Almaguer, *Racial Fault Lines* and Linda Gordon, *The Great Arizona Orphan Abduction* (Cambridge, Mass.: Harvard University Press, 1999).

49. *A Bill to Abolish the Involuntary Servitude Imposed Upon Seamen in the Merchant Marine of the United States . . . : Hearing on H.R.23673, Day 1, Before the Subcomm. of Involuntary Servitude Imposed Upon Seamen of the S. Comm. on Commerce*, United States Senate, 62nd Cong., 56 (1912) (Statement of Andrew Furuseth, President of the International Seamen's Union of America).

50. Bruce Nelson, *Workers on the Waterfront: Seamen, Longshoreman, and Unionism in the 1930s* (Urbana: University of Illinois Press, 1988), 46.

51. See Mahan, *Influence of Sea Power*.

52. Joseph P. Goldberg, *The Maritime Story: A Study in Labor-Management Relations* (Cambridge, Mass.: Harvard University Press, 1959), 94.

53. See Elliot Young, *Alien Nation: Chinese Migration in the Americas from the Coolie Era Through World War II* (Chapel Hill: University of North Carolina Press, 2014), 8.

54. Tony Ballantyne, *Orientalism and Race: Aryanism in the British Empire* (Basingstoke, U.K.: Palgrave Press, 2002), 15.

55. For more on how societies or nations were made by their "colonial imperial projects," see Frederick Cooper and Ann Laura Stoler, "Between Metropole and Colony: Rethinking a Research Agenda," in Ann Laura Stoler and Frederick Cooper, eds., *Tensions of Empire: Colonial Cultures in Bourgeois World* (Berkeley and Los Angeles: University of California Press, 1997), 1–58.

56. Indeed, historian Charles Maier, in *One Within Borders: Territories of Power, Wealth, and Belonging Since 1500* (Cambridge, Mass.: Harvard University Press, 2016) recently argued that empires do not have borders. But as I argue in this book, that does not stop individuals or interest groups from trying to create, contest, and defend them.

57. There is a well-developed literature on the so-called exempted classes of the Chinese Exclusion Act: students, merchants, diplomats, and tourists. Each of these categories were presumed to be upper-class Chinese nationals. See Paul A. Kramer, "Imperial Openings: Civilization, Exemption, and the Geopolitics of Mobility in the History of Chinese Exclusion, 1868–1910," *Journal of the Gilded Age and Progressive Era* 14, no. 3 (2015): 317–47.

58. Stoler and Frederick Cooper, "Between Metropole and Colony," in Stoler and Cooper, eds., *Tensions of Empire,* 8.

59. For the role of the military as "white labor" in the empire, see Peter Way, "Black Service . . . White Money: The Peculiar Institution of Military Labor in the British Army During the Seven Years War, in *Workers Across the Americas: The Transnational Turn in Labor History,* ed. Leon Fink, with Eileen Boris, John French, Julie Greene, Joan Sangster, and Sheldon Stromquest, assoc. eds. (New York: Oxford University Press, 2011).

60. On the alignment between federalized immigration law and the domestic U.S. labor market, see Paul A. Kramer, "Embedding Capital: Political-Economic History, the United States, and the World," *Journal of the Gilded Age and Progressive Era* 15, no. 3 (2016): 344.

61. For the aberration thesis, see Samuel Bemis, *A Diplomatic History of the United States* (New York: H. Holt, 1936) and Samuel Bemis, "American Foreign Policy and the Blessings of Liberty," 1961 American Historical Association Presidential Address, http://www.historians.org/info/aha_history/sfbemis.htm; George F. Kennan, *American Diplomacy, 1900–1950* (Chicago: University of Chicago Press, 1951); Ernest May, *Imperial Democracy: The Emergence of America as Great Power* (Chicago: Imprint Publications, 1961), though for May it was more about how the United States had its great power status "thrust upon it." Historians Charles and Mary Beard were the notable exceptions to the aberration thesis, especially their work *The Rise of American Civilization* (New York: Macmillan, 1927). Taking a Marxian approach to the broad sweep of U.S. history, they argued that the United States was an empire from the very beginning.

62. Julie Greene, "Wages of Empire," 40; For the mid-twentieth-century revisionism of the Wisconsin School, see William Appleman Williams, *The Tragedy of American Diplomacy* (New York and Cleveland: World Publishing, 1959); William Appleman Williams, *The Contours of American History* (Cleveland: World Publishing, 1961); Walter LaFeber, *The New Empire: An Interpretation of American Expansion* (Ithaca, N.Y.: Cornell University Press, 1963); Thomas McKormick, *The China Market: America's Question for Informal Empire, 1893–1901* (Chicago, Quadrangle Books, 1967); For the 1980s

revisionism of the New Western Historians, see Sarah Deutsch, *No Separate Refuge: Culture, Class, and Gender on an Anglo-Hispanic Frontier in the American Southwest, 1880–1940* (New York: Oxford University Press, 1987); Patricia Nelson Limerick, *The Legacy of Conquest: The Unbroken Past of the American West* (New York: Norton, 1987); White, *It's Your Misfortune*; William Cronon, *Nature's Metropolis: Chicago and the Great West* (New York: W.W. Norton, 1991).

63. The notable exceptions were subjugated peoples within the boundaries of the continental United States, such as African Americans, Native Americans, and Californos from the 1848 annexation of Alto California.

64. Though as William Appleman Williams and, more recently, Paul A. Kramer pointed out, the term empire was frequently used by politicians and the public in the late eighteenth and early to mid-nineteenth centuries to define the nation and its expansion. See Williams, *Tragedy of American Diplomacy;* Williams, *Contours of American History;* see also Kramer, "Power and Connection," 1348–1391.

65. Upton Sinclair, *I, Candidate for Governor: And How I Got Licked* (Berkeley and Los Angeles: University of California Press, 1994 reprint), 109. The book was originally published in 1935.

66. In the Jacksonian period, white men achieved universal male suffrage but African American men and white women simultaneously lost the franchise. See Charles Sellers, *The Market Revolution: Jacksonian America, 1815–1946* (New York: Oxford University Press, 1991); Lee Benson, *The Concept of Jacksonian Democracy; New York, A Test Case* (Princeton, N.J.: Princeton University Press, 1961); Arthur M. Schlesinger, *The Age of Jackson* (Boston: Little, Brown, 1945).

67. Gavin Wright has argued that the southern labor market was a separate and isolated labor market from the North, and the rest of the world, though spatially it resided within what I am arguing is part of the United States metropole. It was a labor market that arguably had more in common with the Hawaiian system of contract labor or the labor regime of a merchant ship. See Gavin Wright, *Old South, New South: Revolutions in the Southern Economy Since the Civil War* (New York: Basic Books, 1986); for scholarship on U.S. expansion and immigration restriction, see Matthew Fry Jacobson, *Barbarian Virtues: The United States Encounter with Foreign People at Home and Abroad, 1876–1917* (New York: Hill and Wang, 2000); and Matthew Fry Jacobson, "Annexing the Other: The World's Peoples as Auxiliary Consumers and Imported Workers," in James T. Campbell et al., eds., *Race, Nation, and Empire in American History* (Chapel Hill: University of North Carolina Press, 2007), 103–29.

68. Alfred McCoy and Francisco A. Scarano recently argued that 1898 imperial expansion profoundly affected the United States and argued that the Spanish-American war was a crucible for everything that came after. See Alfred McCoy and Francisco A. Scarano, *Colonial Crucible: Empire in the Making of the Modern American State* (Madison: University of Wisconsin Press, 2009).

69. For how the Immigration Act of 1924 created a global racial hierarchy, see Mae Ngai, *Impossible Subjects: Illegal Aliens and the Making of Modern America* (Princeton, N.J.: Princeton University Press, 2004).

70. Geographer Neil Smith argued that the United States was the only power to aspire to planetary hegemony. See Neil Smith, *American Empire: Roosevelt's Geographer*

and the Prelude to Globalization (Berkeley and Los Angeles: University of California Press, 2003), xiii.

71. *Coast Seamen's Journal (CSJ),* November 23, 1898.

72. W. E. B. Du Bois, *Black Reconstruction: An Essay Toward a History of the Part Which Black Folk Played in the Attempt to Reconstruct Democracy in America, 1860–1880* (Philadelphia: Albert Saifeer, 1934), 700; see also David Reodiger, *The Wages of Whiteness: Race and the Making of the American Working Class* (London: Verso, 1991).

Chapter 1. "A Leak in the Ship of State"

1. See Erika Lee, *At America's Gates: Chinese Immigration During the Exclusion Era, 1882–1943* (Chapel Hill: University of North Carolina Press, 2003).

2. For literature on the California Exclusion campaign, see Alexander Saxton, *The Indispensable Enemy: Labor and the Anti-Chinese Movement in California* (Berkeley and Los Angeles: University of California Press, 1971); Alexander Saxton, *The Rise and Fall of the White Republic: Class Politics and Mass Culture in Nineteenth-Century America* (London and New York: Verso Press, 1990); Neil M. Shumsky, *The Evolution of Political Protest and the Workingmen's Party of California* (Columbus: Ohio State University Press, 1991); see Erika Lee, *At America's Gates: Chinese Immigration During the Exclusion Era, 1882–1943* (Chapel Hill: University of North Carolina Press, 2003); Kornel Chang, *Pacific Connections: The Making of the U.S.-Canadian Borderlands* (Berkeley and Los Angeles: University of California Press, 2012).

3. Despite this, ambitious "Anglo" U.S. settlers were often successful in dispossessing many former Mexican citizens, known as Californios, from their land over the next century.

4. Tomas Almaguer, *Racial Fault Lines: The Historical Origins of White Supremacy in California* (Berkley and Los Angeles: University of California Press, 1994), 130.

5. Ibid., 5.

6. Kornel Chang, *Pacific Connections: The Making of the U.S.–Canadian Borderlands* (Berkeley and Los Angeles: University of California Press, 2012), 12.

7. A lesser-known fact is that the Pacific Coast states all considered banning the immigration of African Americans to the state in their constitutions. Oregon was the only one that actually did it.

8. *Coast Seamen's Journal (CSJ),* November 23, 1898.

9. *Robertson v. Baldwin,* 165 U.S. 283 (1897).

10. David Montgomery, *Citizen Worker: The Experience of Workers in the United States with Democracy and the Free Market during the Nineteenth Century* (New Haven, Conn.: Yale University Press, 1993), 2 and 5.

11. Marcus Rediker, *Between the Devil and the Deep Blue Sea: Merchant Seamen, Pirates, and the Anglo-American Maritime World, 1700–1750* (Cambridge, U.K.: Cambridge University Press, 1987), 106.

12. Ibid., 103.

13. Hyman Weintraub, *Andrew Furuseth: Emancipator of the Seamen* (Berkeley and Los Angeles: University of California Press, 1959), 7.

14. Rediker, *Between the Devil,* 105 and 106.

15. Ibid.

16. *Sundry Bills Relating to the American Merchant Marine, Known as the "Maguire Bills:" Hearing on H.R. 5501 Before the H. Comm. on Merchant Marine and Fisheries*, 53rd Cong., 5 (1894) (Statement of Andrew Furuseth); For crimping and unfree practices of the maritime industry, see Rediker, *Between the Devil;* Peter Linebaugh and Marcus Rediker, *The Many-Headed Hydra: Sailors, Slaves, Commoners, and the Hidden History of the Revolutionary Atlantic* (Boston: Beacon Press, 2000); Alex Roland et al., *The Way of the Ship: America's Maritime History, Reenvisioned, 1600–2000* (Hoboken, N.J.: John Wiley & Sons, 2008); Leon Fink, *Sweatshops of the Sea: Merchant Seamen in the World's First Globalized Industry, From 1812 to the Present* (Chapel Hill: University of North Carolina Press, 2011).

17. *CSJ*, September 21, 1898. For an example of a padrone system, see Gunther Peck, *Reinventing Free Labor: Padrones and Immigrant Workers in the North American West, 1880–1930* (Cambridge, U.K.: Cambridge University Press, 2000).

18. Ibid.

19. Montgomery, *Citizen Worker*, 13; Rediker, *Between the Devil*, 77.

20. Joseph P. Goldberg, *The Maritime Story: A Study in Labor-Management Relations* (Cambridge, Mass.: Harvard University Press, 1958), 13–14.

21. Roland et al., *Way of the Ship*, 229; Fink, *Sweatshops of the Sea*, 56.

22. Goldberg, *Maritime Story*, 13–14.

23. Ibid., 13–14.

24. *CSJ*, November 23, 1887.

25. Ibid.

26. *Sundry Bills Relating to the American Merchant Marine, Known as the "Maguire Bills:" Hearing on H.R. 5501 Before the H. Comm. on Merchant Marine and Fisheries*, 53rd Cong., 5 (1894) (Statement of Andrew Furuseth).

27. Ibid.

28. Ibid.

29. "Chapter 29, 1 Congress, Session 2, An Act: For the government and regulation of seamen in the merchant service," U.S. Statutes at Large 1 (1790): 131–35; "Chapter 322, 42 Congress, Session 2, An Act: To authorize the appointment of shipping commissioners by the several circuit courts of the United States, to superintend the shipping and discharge of seamen engaged in merchant ships belonging to the United States, and for the further protection of seamen." U.S. Statutes at Large 17, no. Main Section (1872): 262–80.

30. "Chapter 29, 1 Congress, Session 2, An Act: For the government and regulation of seamen in the merchant service." U.S. Statutes at Large 1 (1790): 131–35.

31. *CSJ*, April 23, 1890.

32. A belaying pin is a metal or wooden device used on sailing ships to secure the rigging of sail lines.

33. *CSJ*, August 13, 1890.

34. *CSJ*, May 4, 1892.

35. Ibid.

36. *CSJ*, March 19, 1890; *CSJ*, January 28, 1890.

37. "Chapter 322, 42 Congress, Session 2, An Act: To authorize the appointment of shipping commissioners by the several circuit courts of the United States, to

superintend the shipping and discharge of seamen engaged in merchant ships belonging to the United States, and for the further protection of seamen." U.S. Statutes at Large 17, no. Main Section (1872): 262–80; Roland et al., *Way of the Ship,* 127.

38. "Chapter 322, 42 Congress, Session 2, An Act: To authorize the appointment of shipping commissioners by the several circuit courts of the United States, to superintend the shipping and discharge of seamen engaged in merchant ships belonging to the United States, and for the further protection of seamen." U.S. Statutes at Large 17, no. Main Section (1872): 262–80.

39. Peter B. Gill and Ottilie Markholt, "The Sailor's Union of the Pacific: 1885–1929," (unpublished manuscript, 1942) University of Washington Libraries, digital collection, 154–55.

40. "Chapter 121, 48 Congress, Session 1, An Act: To remove certain burdens on the American merchant marine and encourage the American foreign carrying trade and for other purposes." U.S. Statutes at Large 23, no. Main Section (1884): 53–60; Weintraub, *Andrew Furuseth,* 29.

41. "Chapter 421, 49 Congress, Session 1, An Act: To abolish certain fees for official services to American vessels, and to amend the laws relating to shipping commissioners, seamen, and owners of vessels, and for other purposes." U.S. Statutes at Large 24, no. Main Section (1886): 79–83.

42. "Chapter 322, 42 Congress, Session 2, An Act: To authorize the appointment of shipping commissioners by the several circuit courts of the United States, to superintend the shipping and discharge of seamen engaged in merchant ships belonging to the United States, and for the further protection of seamen." U.S. Statutes at Large 17, no. Main Section (1872): 262–80.

43. Weintraub, *Andrew Furuseth,* 29.

44. "Chapter 801, 51 Congress, Session 1, An Act to Amend the Laws Relative to Shipping Commissioners," U.S. Statutes at Large 26, no Main Section (1890): 320.

45. Paul Scharrenberg, "Paul Scharrenberg: Reminiscences." Interview by Corinne Gilb in 1954. Oral History Center, Bancroft Library, University of California, Berkeley, 1954, p. 10.

46. Ibid., 5.

47. Ibid., 1.

48. Ibid., 12.

49. Weintraub, *Andrew Furuseth,* 28.

50. Scharrenberg, "Paul Scharrenberg: Reminiscences," 11.

51. George P. West, "Andrew Furuseth and the Radicals," *The Survey,* November 5, 1921, p. 207.

52. Carl Lynch, Speech to the Furuseth Club of New York, Thursday March 12, 1946, quoted in *Congressional Record,* 79th Cong., 2nd Sess., XCII, part 10, p A1360-61; Weintraub, *Andrew Furuseth,* 1.

53. Lynch, Speech to the Furuseth Club, March 12, 1946; Weintraub, *Andrew Furuseth,* 1.

54. Gill and Markholt, "Sailor's Union of the Pacific," 48.

55. Ibid.

56. West, "Andrew Furuseth and the Radicals," 207.

57. Roger Daniels, *The Politics of Prejudice: The Anti-Japanese Movement in California and the Struggle for Japanese Exclusion* (New York: Antheneum, 1972), 19.

58. Weintraub, *Andrew Furuseth*, 30.

59. Ibid.

60. Gill and Markholt, "Sailor's Union of the Pacific," 206.

61. Weintraub, *Andrew Furuseth*, 32.

62. *New York Times*, October 4, 1889.

63. Gill and Markholt, "Sailor's Union of the Pacific," 206.

64. Weintraub, *Andrew Furuseth*, 28.

65. *CSJ*, September 26, 1894.

66. "Chapter 97, 53 Congress, Session 3, An Act: To amend an act entitled 'An Act to amend the laws relative to shipping commissioners,' approved August nineteenth, eighteen hundred and ninety, and for other purposes." U.S. Statutes at Large 28 (1895): 667–68.

67. *CSJ*, October 31, 1894.

68. *CSJ*, March 20, 1895.

69. "Chapter 28, 55 Congress, Session 3, "An Act: To amend the laws relating to American seamen, for the protection of such seamen, and to promote commerce." U.S. Statutes at Large 30, no. Main Section (1898): 755–64; Goldberg, *Maritime Story*, 22.

70. This, of course, was a point of dispute between the sailors' unions and shipping companies. The union, unsurprisingly, maintained that steam did not render sailing skills obsolete, whereas the shipping companies argued it did.

71. "Chapter 121, 48 Congress, Session 1, An Act: To remove certain burdens on the American merchant marine and encourage the American foreign carrying trade and for other purposes." U.S. Statutes at Large 23, no. Main Section (1884): 53–60.

72. Goldberg, *Maritime Story*, 11.

73. Roland et al., *Way of the Ship*, 226.

74. *The Chinese Exclusion Act of 1902: Hearings on S. Bill 2960, Day 5, Before the S. Comm. on Immigration*, 57th Cong., 245 (1902) (Statement of Andrew Furuseth, President of the International Seamen's Union of America).

75. I take the idea of the ship as an economic institution of empire from Ann Stoler and Frederick Cooper's 1997 essay "Between Metropole and Colony: Rethinking a Research Agenda," in Ann Stoler and Frederick Cooper, eds., *Tensions of Empire: Colonial Cultures in Bourgeois World* (Berkeley and Los Angeles: University of California Press, 1997) 1–58, in which they suggest that a fruitful way to study empire was to focus on "sites of conflict" in specific "economic institutions of a colony." A ship may not be a colony, but it exists under an imperial framework that fuses private industry and the coercive power of the state into a singular authority.

76. *CSJ*, December 9, 1891.

77. *CSJ*, July 27, 1892.

78. Ibid.; "Chapter 322, 42 Congress, Session 2, An Act: To authorize the appointment of shipping commissioners by the several circuit courts of the United States, to superintend the shipping and discharge of seamen engaged in merchant ships belonging to the United States, and for the further protection of seamen." U.S. Statutes at Large 17, no. Main Section (1872): 262–80.

79. *CSJ*, July 27, 1892.

80. *CSJ*, August 3, 1892.

81. *The Chinese Exclusion Act of 1902: Hearings on S. Bill 2960, Day 5, Before the S. Comm. On Immigration*, 57th Cong., 246 (1902) (Statement of Andrew Furuseth, President of the International Seamen's Union of America).

82. Ravi Ahuja's article, "Mobility and Containment: The Voyage of South Asian Seamen, c. 1900–1960," *International Review of Social History* 51, no. S14 (2006): 11–141, talks about how immigration law had affected the shore leave of sailors.

83. In *The People v. Hall* 4 Cal. 499 (1854), the California Supreme Court ruled that a white man could not be found guilty based on Chinese testimony; for the ability of Chinese Americans to testify and give evidence in U.S. courts, see Gabriel J. Chin, "A Chinaman's Chance in Court: Asia Pacific Americans and Racial Rules of Evidence," *University of California Irvine Law Review*, 3, no. 4 (December 2013): 967; Alexander Saxton, *The Rise and Fall of the White Republic: Class Politics and Mass Culture in Nineteenth-Century* America (New York: Verso, 1990), 217.

84. The 1844 Treaty of Wangxia between the United States and China stated that "citizens of the United States who may commit any crime in China shall be subject to be tried and punished by the Consul or other public functionary of the United States thereto authorized according to the laws of the United States." See Par Kristoffer Cassel, *Grounds of Judgment: Extraterritoriality and Imperial Power in Nineteenth-Century China and Japan* (Oxford, U.K.: Oxford University Press, 2012), 53.

85. *CSJ*, June 15, 1898.

86. *CSJ*, July 13, 1898; *CSJ*, August 3, 1898.

87. *CSJ*, July 13, 1898.

88. Ibid.

89. Ibid.

90. *CSJ*, July 27, 1892. The SUP points out that the Pacific Mail Steamship Company was using Chinese crews while also receiving federal mail subsidies.

91. *CSJ*, August 3, 1898.

92. Letter from the Sailor's Union of the Pacific to President William McKinley, August 5, 1898, quoted in *CSJ*, August 31, 1898.

93. Letter from Assistant Secretary of War Meiklejohn to Andrew Furuseth, August 29, 1898, quoted in *CSJ*, August 31, 1898.

94. For the China market thesis of Hawaiian and Philippine annexation, see Matthew Fry Jacobson, "Annexing the Other: the World's Peoples as Auxiliary Consumers and Imported Workers: 1876–1917," in James T. Campbell, Matthew Pratt Guterl, and Robert G. Lee, ed., *Race Nation and Empire in American History* (Chapel Hill: University of North Carolina Press, 2007), 103–30; Matthew Fry Jacobson, *Barbarian Virtues: The United States Encounter with Foreign People at Home and Abroad, 1876–1917* (New York: Hill and Wang, 2000); Thomas J. McCormick, *China Market: America's Quest for Informal Empire, 1893–1901* (Chicago: Quadrangle Books, 1967).

95. Edgar Wickberg, *The Chinese in Philippine Life, 1850–1898* (London: Yale University Press, 1965), 3.

96. For the Chinese community in the Philippines, see Wong Kwonk-Chu, *The Chinese in the Philippine Economy, 1898–1941* (Manila: Ateneo de Manila University Press, 1999); Daniel Chirot and Anthony Reid, eds., *Essential Outsiders: Chinese and Jews in the*

Modern Transformation of Southeast Asia and Central Europe (Seattle: University of Washington Press, 1997); Wickberg, *Chinese in Philippine Life*.

97. *The Chinese Exclusion Act of 1902: Hearings on S. Bill 2960, Day 5, Before the S. Comm. On Immigration*, 57th Cong., 490 (1902) (Statement of William Howard Taft, Governor of the Philippine Commission).

98. *CSJ*, November 3, 1897.

99. *CSJ*, December 15, 1897.

100. P. J. McGuire, "Nashville's Great Convention," *American Federationist*, January 1898, 256.

101. *CSJ*, November 3, 1897. For literature on the anti-Chinese movement, see Alexander Saxton, *The Indispensable Enemy: Labor and the Anti-Chinese Movement in California* (Berkeley and Los Angeles: University of California Press, 1971); Alexander Saxton, *The Rise and Fall of the White Republic: Class Politics and Mass Culture in Nineteenth Century America* (London and New York: Verso Press, 1990); Neil M. Shumsky, *The Evolution of Political Protest and the Workingmen's Party of California* (Columbus: Ohio State University Press, 1991); See Erika Lee, *At America's Gates: Chinese Immigration During the Exclusion Era, 1882–1943* (Chapel Hill: University of North Carolina Press, 2003); Kornel Chang, *Pacific Connections: The Making of the U.S.-Canadian Borderlands* (Berkeley and Los Angeles: University of California Press, 2012); for the latest work on the nineteenth-century anti-Chinese movement, see Beth Lew-Williams, *"The Chinese Must Go": Violence, Exclusion, and the Making of the Alien in America* (Cambridge, Mass.: Harvard University Press, 2018).

102. For the broadest distillation of the AFL's attitude toward Chinese workers, see U.S. Senate, Committee on Immigration, "Some Reasons for Chinese Exclusion: Meat V. Rice: American Manhood Against Asiatic Coolieism: Which Shall Survive, by the American Federation of Labor, (S. Doc. 137) (Government Printing Office, 1902).

103. *CSJ*, November 23, 1898.

104. *CSJ*, November 16, 1898.

105. Samuel Gompers, "The Future Foreign Policy of the United States," *American Federationist*, September 1898, 138.

106. Indeed, the AFL's view of Hawai'i's and the Philippines' labor system is well known. The Article Meat Versus Rice, U.S. Senate, Committee on Immigration, "Some Reasons for Chinese Exclusion: Meat V. Rice: American Manhood Against Asiatic Coolieism: Which Shall Survive, by the American Federation of Labor (S. Doc. 137) (Government Printing Office, 1902).

107. *CSJ*, November 3, 1897.

108. Gompers, "The Future Foreign Policy of the United States," 138.

109. *CSJ*, November 3, 1897.

110. *CSJ*, December 8, 1897.

111. Aims McGuinness, *The Path of Empire: Panama and the California Gold Rush* (Ithaca, N.Y. and London: Cornell University Press, 2008), 7.

112. *CSJ*, December 8, 1897.

113. *CSJ*, July 13, 1898.

114. *CSJ*, November 3, 1897.

115. Gompers, "The Future Foreign Policy of the United States," 139.

116. Ibid.

117. Ibid.

118. *CSJ*, December 15, 1897.

119. Ibid.

120. *CSJ*, December 8, 1897.

121. Ibid.

122. Arif Dirlik, "Introduction: Pacific Contradictions," in Arif Dirlik, ed, *What is in a Rim: Critical Perspectives on the Pacific Region Idea* (Lanham, Md.: Rowman & Littlefield, 1998), 4.

123. *CSJ*, December 8, 1897; the "Leper Settlement" referred to the Hawaiian Island of Molokai, which had served as a leper colony since 1866.

124. Mai Ngai, "Trouble with the Rand: The Chinese Question in South Africa and the Apogee of White Settlerism," *International Labor and Working Class History* 91 (Spring 2017): 73; see also Adam McKeown, *Melancholy Order: Asian Immigration and the Globalization of Borders* (New York: Columbia University Press, 2008); Marilyn Lake and Henry Reynolds, *Drawing the Global Color Line: White Men's Countries and the International Challenge of Racial Equality* (Cambridge, U.K.: Cambridge University Press, 2008); Erik Olssen, "The New Zealand Labour Movement and Race," in Marcel van der Linden and Jan Lucassen et al., eds., *Racism and the Labour Market* (Berne: Peter Lang, 1995), 373–91; Raymond Markey, "Race and Organized Labour in a White Settler Society: The Australian Case, 1850–1901," in van der Linden and Lucassen et al., eds., *Racism and the Labour Market*; Robert A. Huttenback, *Empire and Racism: White Settlers and Colored Immigrants in the British Self-governing Colonies, 1830–1910* (Ithaca, N.Y.: Cornell University Press, 1976).

125. See Elliott Young, *Alien Nation: Chinese Migration in the Americas from the Coolie Era Through World War II* (Chapel Hill: University of North Carolina Press, 2014), 8.

126. See Eric Foner, chapter 4, "Abolitionism and the Labor Movement in Ante-Bellum America," in Eric Foner, ed., *The Politics and Ideology of the American Civil War* (New York: Oxford University Press, 1980), 57- 76; and Eric Foner, "Racial Attitudes of the New York Free Soilers," in Foner, *Politics and Ideology*, 70, 74, 80, and 82.

127. David M. Potter, *The Impending Crisis, 1848–1861* (New York: Harper & Row, 1976), 286 and 293; for a fuller discussion of Dred Scott and its significance, see all of chapter 11, "Dred Scott and the Law of the Land," 267–93.

128. Abraham Lincoln, "Letter to George Robinson, August 15, 1855," quoted in Bruce Levine, *Half Slave Half Free: The Roots of the Civil War* (New York: Hill and Wang, 1992), xi.

129. *CSJ*, January 12, 1898.

130. Weintraub, *Andrew Furuseth*, 35.

131. *Robertson v. Baldwin*, 165 U.S. 283 (1897).

132. "Chapter 339, 56 Congress, Session 1, An Act: To provide a government for the Territory of Hawaii," U.S. Statutes at Large 31, no. Main Section (1900): 141–62; Andrew Furuseth et al., Report of the Legislative Committee of the A.F. of L., *American Federationist*, July 1900, 194.

133. *CSJ*, November 23, 1898.

134. *Robertson v. Baldwin*, 165 U.S. 302 (1897); John C. Appel, "American Labor and the Annexation of Hawaii: A Study in Logic and Economic Interest," *Pacific Historical Review* 23, no. 1 (February 1954): 13.

135. *CSJ*, February 8, 1899.

136. Hawaiian leaders studied the Mississippi Constitutional Convention of 1891 to learn how to keep a subject labor force under firm control. See Eric T. Love, *Race over Empire: Racism and US Imperialism, 1865–1900* (Chapel Hill: University of North Carolina Press, 2004), 116. William Adam Russ, *The Hawaiian Revolution (1893–94)* (Selinsgrove, Pa.: Susquehanna University Press, 1959); *CSJ*, November 1, 1899.

137. 31 Cong. Rec. 6533 (1898) (statement of Sen. Tillman); *CSJ*, July 20, 1898; historian John C. Appel explored the *CSJ*'s reaction to Tillman's comments in Appel, "American Labor and the Annexation of Hawaii," 1–18. Appel also notes the SUP fear that the *Arago* precedent could be used to bring contract labor into the United States.

138. C. Vann Woodward, *Origins of the New South* (Baton Rouge: Louisiana State University Press, 1951), 325.

139. *CSJ*, November 1, 1899.

140. Ibid.

141. Ibid.

142. *CSJ*, July 20, 1898.

143. "Chapter 801, 51 Congress, Session 1, An Act to Amend the Laws Relative to Shipping Commissioners," U.S. Statutes at Large 26, no Main Section (1890): 320; "Chapter 322, 42 Congress, Session 2, An Act: To authorize the appointment of shipping commissioners by the several circuit courts of the United States, to superintend the shipping and discharge of seamen engaged in merchant ships belonging to the United States, and for the further protection of seamen," U.S. Statutes at Large 17, no. Main Section (1872): 262–80.

144. "Chapter 97, 53 Congress, Session 3, An Act: To amend an act entitled 'An Act to amend the laws relative to shipping commissioners,' approved August nineteenth, eighteen hundred and ninety, and for other purposes." U.S. Statutes at Large 28 (1895): 667–68; *Robertson v. Baldwin*, 165 U.S. (1897).

145. *CSJ*, May 15, 1900.

146. "Section 101" of the *Organic Act of the Territory of Hawaii (as amended)* (Honolulu: Bulletin Publishing, 1911), 70.

Chapter 2. Does Exclusion Follow the Flag?

1. The phrase "Making the Empire Work" is from the title of Daniel E. Bender's and Jana Lipman's *Making the Empire Work: Labor and United States Imperialism* (New York: New York University Press, 2015).

2. For an illustration of imperial formations, see Ann Laura Stoler and Carole McGranahan, "Introduction: Reconfiguring the Imperial Terrains," in Ann Laura Stoler et al., *Imperial Formations* (Santa Fe, N.M.: School for Advanced Research Press, 2007), 8–9.

3. The Organic Act of 1900 applied the Exclusion Act to the territory of Hawai'i.

4. For "imperial repertoires," see Frederick Cooper and Jane Burbank, *Empires in World History: Power and the Politics of Difference* (Princeton, N.J.: Princeton University Press, 2010), 3–8.

5. *The Chinese Exclusion Act of 1902: Hearings Senate Bill 2690, Day 6, Before the S. Comm. on Immigration,* 57th Cong., 269 (1902) (Statement of Samuel Gompers, President of the American Federation of Labor).

6. H.R. Doc. 57–562, at 2 (1902).

7. Andrew Furuseth and Thomas F. Tracy, "The New Chinese Exclusion Law," *American Federationist,* June 1902, 278.

8. Ibid.

9. Ibid.

10. Ibid.

11. See Thomas McCormick, *China Market: America's Quest for Informal Empire, 1893–1901* (Chicago: Quadrangle Books, 1967), 107. For the idea of the Philippines as a stepping stone to China, see James Lorence, "Organized Business and the Myth of the China Market: The American Asiatic Association, 1898–1937, *Transactions in the American Philosophical Society,* 71, no. 4 (1981): 19; and Matthew Frye Jacobson, "Annexing the Other: the World's Peoples as Auxiliary Consumers and Imported Workers, 1876–1917," in James Campbell et al., eds., *Race, Nation, & Empire in American History* (Chapel Hill: University of North Carolina Press, 2007), 109.

12. John Foord told the committee the delegation that traveled with him included: Mr. Ellison A. Smyth, of Pelzer and Belton Mills; Mr. W. A. Courtenay, of the Courtenay Manufacturing Company; Mr. John B. Cleveland, of the Whitney Manufacturing Company; Mr. J. H. Montgomery, of the Pacolet and Spartan Mills; Mr. John C. Cary, of the Lockhart Mills; Mr. T. J. Hickman, of the Graniteville Mills; They represented, according to Foord, around thirty thousand of the "entire mill hands in South Carolina." From New England, "representing the cotton-mill industry of that part of the country": Mr. Theophilus Parsons from the Lyman Mills, at Holyoke, Mass; Mr. P. Y. De Normandie, of the Laconia and Pepperell Mills, of Maine; Mr. Charles S. Hamlin, representing the Boston Merchants' Association and Chamber of Commerce. Also with him was John T. Nichols of Minot, of New York, selling agents for the produce of southern and New England Mills; Mr. Silas D. Webb, of the China and Japan Trading Company, of New York and China; and Mr. Clarence Cary, representing the American China Development Company, which is constructing a railroad from Hankow to Canton.

13. *The Chinese Exclusion Act of 1902: Hearings on Senate Bill 2960, Day 1, Before the S. Comm. on Immigration,* 57th Cong. 10 (1902) (Statement of John Foord of the American Asiatic Association and the American Association of China).

14. Ibid.

15. Ibid., 11.

16. Ibid.

17. *New York Times,* February 9, 1902.

18. *The Chinese Exclusion Act of 1902: Bill 2960, Day 5, Before Comm. on Immigration,* 57th Cong. 243 (1902) (Statement of Andrew Furuseth, President of the International Seamen's Union of America).

19. *CSJ,* February 12, 1902.

20. *The Chinese Exclusion Act of 1902: Hearings on Senate Bill 2960, Day 8, Before the S. Comm. on Immigration,* 57th Cong. 359 (1902) (Statement by Maxwell Evarts, Director of the Pacific Mail Steamship Company).

21. Furuseth and Tracy, "The New Chinese Exclusion Law," 286; James Lorence, "Organized Business and the Myth of the China Market: The American Asiatic Association, 1898–1937, *Transactions in the American Philosophical Society* 71, no. 4 (1981): 13.

22. Furuseth and Tracy, "The New Chinese Exclusion Law," 283.

23. I say mostly free because the sharecropping system of the southern states was hardly free labor. Although, despite the South's presence within the United States nation, southern planters ensured the South's labor market was largely isolated from the rest of the country, which, in many ways, constituted a separate market. For work on the South as an isolated labor market, see Gavin Wright, *Old South, New South: Revolutions in the Southern Economy Since the Civil War* (Baton Rouge: Louisiana State University Press, 1997).

24. *The Chinese Exclusion Act of 1902: Hearings on Senate Bill 2960, Day 9, Before the S. Comm. on Immigration,* 57th Cong. 382 (1902) (Statement of John R. Thurston, Representative of U.S. Business Interests in the Philippines and China).

25. *The Chinese Exclusion Act of 1902: Hearings on Senate Bill 2960, Day 8, Before the S. Comm. on Immigration,* 57th Cong. 359 (1902) (Statement by Maxwell Evarts, Director of Pacific Mail Steamship Company).

26. *The Chinese Exclusion Act of 1902: Hearings Senate Bill 2960, Day5, Before the S. Comm. on Immigration,* 57th Cong. 246 (Feb. 4, 1902) (Statement of Andrew Furuseth, President of the International Seamen's Union of America). Although Furuseth does admit that engineers had to be American citizens, and thus usually white, this still conforms to the racialized division of labor emerging on the high seas.

27. *The Chinese Exclusion Act of 1902: Hearings Senate Bill 2960, Day 10, Before the S. Comm. on Immigration,* 57th Cong. 491 (1902) (Statement of William Howard Taft, Governor of The Philippine Commission).

28. *The Chinese Exclusion Act of 1902: Hearings Senate Bill 2960, Day 9, Before the S. Comm. on Immigration,* 57th Cong. 364 (1902) (Statement of William Brownell Seabury, Ships Captain of Pacific Mail Steamship Company).

29. Ibid.

30. *The Chinese Exclusion Act of 1902: Hearings Senate Bill 2960, Day 1, Before the S. Comm. on Immigration,* 57th Cong. 26 (1902) (Statement of Maxwell Evarts, Director of Pacific Mail Steamship Line).

31. Committee on Foreign Affairs, Chinese Exclusion Act of 1902, H.R. Rep. No. 57–1231, Views of the Majority (1902), 2.

32. Ibid.

33. For the capitalist drive into the Pacific see McCormick, *China Market: America's Quest for Informal Empire, 1893–1901* (Chicago: Quadrangle Books, 1967); Walter Lafeber, *The New Empire: An Interpretation of American Expansion, 1860–1898* (Ithaca, N.Y.: Cornell University Press, 1963); William Applemann Williams, *The Tragedy of American Diplomacy* (New York: Delta Books, 1959).

34. Roland et al., *Way of the Ship*, 227.

35. For the Australian and New Zealand sailors' unions anti-Chinese agitation, see Erik Olssen, "The New Zealand Labour Movement and Race," in Marcel van der Linden and Jan Lucassen et al., eds., *Racism and the Labour Market* (Berne: Peter Lang, 1995), 373–91; Raymond Markey, "Race and Organized Labour in a White Settler

Society: The Australian Case, 1850–1901," in Marcel van der Linden Jan Lucassen et al., eds., *Racism and the Labour Market* (Berne: Peter Lang, 1995); Robert A. Huttenback, *Empire and Racism: White Settlers and Colored Immigrants in the British Self-Governing Colonies, 1830–1910* (Ithaca, N.Y.: Cornell University Press, 1976).

36. See Jackson, "The Right Kind of Man," 39–60.

37. Gill and Markholt, "Sailors Union of the Pacific," 11.

38. *CSJ*, December 24, 1902; Jeremiah Jenks, *Report on Certain Economic Questions in the English and Dutch Colonies in the Orient* (Washington, D.C.: Government Printing Office, 1902), 159.

39. Ibid.

40. *CSJ*, December 24, 1902; Jeremiah Jenks, *Report on Certain Economic Questions in the English and Dutch Colonies in the Orient* (Washington, D.C.: Government Printing Office, 1902), 159.

41. *CSJ*, December 24, 1902.

42. Ibid.

43. Ibid.

44. Gompers, "The Future Foreign Policy of the United States," 138; *CSJ*, November 16, 1898.

45. Clark L. Alejandrino, *The History of the 1902 Chinese Exclusion Act: American Colonial Transmission and Deterioration of Filipino-Chinese Relations* (Manila: Kaisa Para Sa Kaunlaran, 2003), 39.

46. *CSJ*, December 24, 1902; Jeremiah Jenks, *Report on Certain Economic Questions in the English and Dutch Colonies in the Orient*, 157.

47. Paul Kramer recently reframed restriction in light of the exempted classes as more of a filter than a wall. See Paul A. Kramer, "Imperial Openings: Civilization, Exemption, and the Geopolitics of Mobility in the History of Chinese Exclusion," *Journal of the Gilded Age and Progressive Era* 14, no. 3 (2015): 319.

48. Ibid., 326.

49. Ibid., 333.

50. Report of the Secretary of Commerce and Labor, Annual Report 1907, H.R. Rep. No. 60–7 (1907), p. 16.

51. Ibid., 17.

52. Ibid.

53. For more on the tension between the Executive Branch and Congress concerning Chinese restriction specifically, and immigration policy generally, see Donna Gabaccia, *Foreign Relations: American Immigration in a Global Perspective* (Princeton, N.J.: Princeton University Press, 2012), 12–17.

54. For work on the humiliating searches and interrogations U.S. officials subjected Chinese immigrants, exempted classes or not, see Erika Lee, *At America's Gates: Chinese Immigration During the Exclusion Era, 1882–1943* (Chapel Hill: University of North Carolina Press, 2003).

55. *CSJ*, June 28, 1905.

56. Ibid.

57. Ibid.

58. Kramer, "Imperial Openings," 337.

59. *CSJ*, June 28, 1905; Kramer "Imperial Openings," 337.

60. *CSJ*, September 6, 1905.

61. *Hearings on H.R. 12973, Day 4, Before the H. Comm. on Foreign Affairs*, 59th Cong. 150 (1906) (Statement of Samuel Gompers, President, American Federation of Labor).

62. Ibid.

63. *CSJ*, June 28, 1905.

64. *CSJ*, August 3, 1898.

65. *CSJ*, June 18, 1902.

66. Samuel Gompers and Herman Gutstadt, "Some Reasons for Chinese Exclusion Meat v. Rice: American Manhood Against Asiatic Coolism, Which Will Survive?" Comm. on Immigration, S. Doc. No. 137, at 45 (1902).

67. *CSJ*, June 28, 1905.

68. Kramer, "Imperial Openings," 326.

69. The SUP's shift in strategy to a more totalizing racialization is consistent with the broader pattern and evolution of anti-Chinese sentiment in Pacific Rim settler colonies. See Olssen, "The New Zealand Labour Movement and Race," 381.

70. *CSJ*, June 28, 1905.

71. *Hearings on H.R. 12973, Day 4, Before the H. Comm. on Foreign Affairs*, 59th Cong. 167 (1906) (Statement of Andrew Furuseth, Vice President of the Japanese and Korean Exclusion League).

72. *CSJ*, June 28, 1905.

73. *CSJ*, August 9, 1905.

74. *CSJ*, February 14, 1906.

75. A Bill To Prohibit the Coming of Chinese Laborers into the United States and Other Purposes, H.R. 12973, 59th Cong. (1906); *CSJ*, February 21, 1906.

76. Theodore Roosevelt, State of the Union Message, December 5, 1905, The American Presidency Project, https://presidency.ucsb.edu/documents/fifth-annual-message-4 (accessed September 6, 2016).

77. *Hearings on H.R. 12973, Day 4, Before the H. Comm. on Foreign Affairs*, 59th Cong. 149 (1906) (Statement of Samuel Gompers, President American Federation of Labor).

78. Ibid.

79. Lew-Williams, *"The Chinese Must Go,"* 171.

80. A Bill to Prohibit the Coming of Chinese Laborers into the United States and Other Purposes, H.R. 12973, 59th Cong. (1906); *CSJ*, February 21, 1906; Kramer, "Imperial Openings," 338.

81. *CSJ*, February 14, 1906.

82. Ibid.

83. *CSJ*, February 21, 1906.

84. Eiichiro Azuma, *Between Two Empires: Race, History, and Transnationalism in Japanese America* (New York: Oxford University Press, 2005), 29.

85. *CSJ*, May 10, 1905.

86. *CSJ*, March 1, 1905.

87. Roger Daniels, *The Politics of Prejudice: The Anti-Japanese Movement in California and the Struggle for Japanese Exclusion* (New York: Atheneum, 1973), 21.

88. September 20, 1908, "Proceedings of the Asiatic Exclusion League," p. 295. Asiatic Exclusion League Records, larc.ms.0145, Labor Archives and Research Center, San Francisco State University.

89. William Michael Morgan, "The Anti-Japanese Origins of the Hawaiian Annexation Treaty of 1897," *Diplomatic History* 6, no. 4 (1982), 25.

90. *CSJ*, March 1, 1905.

91. *CSJ*, January 3, 1906.

92. Ibid.

93. Ibid.

94. Ibid.

95. *CSJ*, October 26, 1904.

96. *CSJ*, January 29, 1908.

97. This fear was, of course, taken to its logical conclusion during the Second World War when thousands of Japanese Americans, many of them citizens, were forced into internment camps for the duration of the war.

98. Frank McGowan, "Address of the Honorable Frank McGowan," August 26, 1906, in "Proceedings of the Asiatic Exclusion League," p. 24. Asiatic Exclusion League Records, larc.ms.0145, Labor Archives and Research Center, San Francisco State University.

99. *CSJ*, November 14, 1906.

100. *CSJ*, April 30, 1906.

101. *CSJ*, December 27, 1905.

102. Ibid.

103. *CSJ*, November 14, 1906.

104. *CSJ*, December 27, 1905.

105. *CSJ*, May 16, 1906.

106. Marc Anthony, "Speech to the Asiatic Exclusion League," December 20, 1908, in "Proceedings of the Asiatic Exclusion League," p. 348. Asiatic Exclusion League Records, larc.ms.0145, Labor Archives and Research Center, San Francisco State University.

107. *CSJ*, January 38, 1908.

108. "Asiatic Immigration: The Industrial Menace," May 10, 1908, in "Proceedings of the Asiatic Exclusion League," p. 232. Asiatic Exclusion League Records, larc.ms.0145, Labor Archives and Research Center, San Francisco State University.

109. "Land Occupation and Operation by Asiatics," August 15, 1909, in "Proceedings of the Asiatic Exclusion League," p. 447. Asiatic Exclusion League Records, larc.ms.0145, Labor Archives and Research Center, San Francisco State University.

110. Ibid., 447.

111. Mae Ngai, *Impossible Subjects: Illegal Aliens and the Making of Modern America* (Princeton, N.J.: Princeton University Press, 2004), 39.

112. Ibid.

113. *CSJ*, February 27, 1907; *CSJ*, February 23, 1907; *CSJ*, May 8, 1907.

114. John R. Commons, *Race and Immigrants in America* (New York: Augustus M. Kelley, 1907), 102; *CSJ*, February 23, 1907.

115. *CSJ*, February 26, 1908.

116. William Temple, "Japan vs. United States," "Fifth Annual Meeting of the Asiatic Exclusion League," May 15, 1910, p. 13, in *Proceedings of the Asiatic Exclusion League, 1907–1913* (New York: Arno Press, 1977).

Chapter 3. Riding the Waves of Empire

1. Alex Roland et al., *The Way of the Ship: America's Maritime History Reenvisioned, 1600–2000* (Hoboken, N.J.: John Wiley & Sons 2008), 266.

2. Joseph P. Goldberg, *The Maritime Story: A Study in Labor-Management Relations* (Cambridge, Mass.: Harvard University Press, 1958), 4.

3. This trend began in 1907–1908 when President Roosevelt signed the Gentlemen's Agreement with Japan, in which the Japanese government agreed not to issue passports for its citizens to travel to the United States in exchange for Japanese students not being barred from attending public schools. The 1917 Immigration Act (barred Zone Act) barred individuals from geographic territory rather than explicitly focusing on race, even though the effect was largely the same. This trend culminated in the 1924 Immigration Act, which consolidated most of the restrictionist legislation up to that point. This law expanded the barred zones of the 1917 act and focused instead on quotas based on a nationalities population in America in 1890.

4. Marcus Rediker, *Between the Devil and the Deep Blue Sea: Merchant Seamen, Pirates, and the Anglo-American Maritime World, 1700–1750* (Cambridge, U.K.: Cambridge University Press, 1987), 105 and 106.

5. Committee on Foreign Affairs, Chinese Exclusion Act of 1902, H.R. Rep. No. 57–1231, Views of the Majority (1902), 2.

6. The modern flag of convenience system allows shipping companies to flag or register their vessels in whatever national registry that best suits them. This is why states like Panama and Liberia technically have the largest merchant fleets in the world in 2006. For work on flag of convenience, see Nathan Lillie, *Global Union for Global Workers: Collective Bargaining and Regulatory Politics in Maritime Shipping* (New York: Routledge, 2006); Nathan Lillie, "Collective Bargaining on the Flag of Convenience Shipping," *British Journal of Industrial Relations* 42 (March 2004): 153–79.

7. *The Seamen's Act: Hearings on S.136, Day 7, Before the H. Comm. on the Merchant Marine and Fisheries*, 63rd Cong. 12 (1914) (statement ofRobert Dollar, President of the Dollar Steamship Line).

8. Committee on Foreign Affairs, Chinese Exclusion Act of 1902, H.R. Rep. No. 57–1231, Views of the Majority (1902), 2.

9. For work on "Lascars" in the British merchant marine, see Jonathan Hyslop "Steamship Empire: Asian, African, and British Sailors in the Merchant Marine, c. 1880–1945," *Journal of Asian and African Studies* 44, no., 1 (2009): 69–95; Michael H. Fisher, "Working Across the Seas: Indian Maritime Labourers in India, Britain, and in Between," *International Review of Social History* 51, no. S14 (2006): 21–45; Ravi Ahuja, "Mobility and Containment: The Voyage of South Asian Seamen, c. 1900–1960," *International Review of Social History* 51, no. S14 (2006):11–141; Goplan Balachandran, "Conflicts in the International Maritime Labour Market: British and Indian Seamen, Employers, and the State, 1890–1939," *Indian Economic and Social History Review* 39, no. 1 (2002): 71–100.

10. As chapter 2 demonstrated, after the successful passage of the 1902 exclusion law, anti-exclusion forces, and their allies in both the White House and Congress, were constantly trying to water down the enforcement mechanism of the act. Some attempts, like the Foster bill of 1906, led the SUP to refer to the bill as a virtual repeal of the Exclusion Act, if it passed. Luckily for organized labor, the Foster bill was unsuccessful. See chapter 2 for further examples.

11. *The Seamen's Act: Hearings on S.136, Day 10, Before the H. Comm. on the Merchant Marine and Fisheries* 63rd Cong. 227 (1914) (Statement of Andrew Furuseth, President of International Sailors Union of America).

12. It should be noted that trade between Atlantic and Pacific ports was not included in the domestic trade.

13. "Chapter 28, 55 Congress, Session 3, An Act: To amend the laws relating to American seamen, for the protection of such seamen, and to promote commerce," U.S. Statutes at Large 30, no. Main Section (1898), 755–64.

14. Rene De La Pedraja, *The Rise and Decline of the American Merchant Shipping in the Twentieth Century* (New York: Twayne Publishers, 1992), 23.

15. Letter from Andree Furuseth to Commerce Secretary Oscar Strauss, June 10, 1907, quoted in *Coast Seamen's Journal,* July 17, 1907.

16. Charles Earl Commerce Department Solicitor to Commerce Secretary Oscar Strauss, June 10, 1907, quoted in *CSJ,* July 17, 1907.

17. Ibid.

18. Ibid.

19. Ibid.

20. Ibid.

21. *CSJ,* July 17, 1907.

22. Letter from Andrew Furuseth and SUP Attorney H. Hutton to Commerce Secretary Oscar Strauss, July 31, 1907, quoted in *CSJ,* October 16, 1907.

23. Ibid.

24. *CSJ,* November 23, 1898.

25. Letter from Commerce Secretary Oscar Strauss to Andrew Furuseth, secretary, Sailor's Union of the Pacific, September 24, 1907, quoted in *CSJ,* October 16, 1907; it is also significant to note that Strauss is indirectly calling the hiring of cheap foreign labor a privilege.

26. Ibid.

27. Ibid.

28. Ibid.

29. Ibid.

30. Ibid.

31. Ibid.

32. Ibid.

33. *CSJ,* October 16, 1907.

34. Ibid.

35. Ibid.

36. *CSJ,* July 17, 1907.

37. The bill and eventual law went well beyond setting standards of skill and training for sailors; it also prescribed equipment-based standards such as the number of lifeboats required, though it is the skill requirements that dealt with the protection and insulation of the maritime labor market.

38. Historian Bruce Laurie argued that "trade agreements insulated labor markets and preserved laboring traditions by specifying training requirements or recruitment rights and carefully fixing work rules." See Bruce Laurie, *Artisans into Workers: Labor in Nineteenth-Century America* (New York: Noonday Press, 1989), 184.

39. On the differences between West Coast and East Coast race thinking, see Linda Gordon, *The Great Arizona Orphan Abduction* (Cambridge, Mass.: Harvard University Press, 1999); see also Tomas Almaguer, *Racial Fault Lines: The Historical Origin of White Supremacy* (Berkeley: University of California Press, 1994).

40. *The Seamen's Act: Hearings on S.136, Day 7, Before the H. Comm. on the Merchant Marine and Fisheries* 63rd Cong. 33 (1914) (Statement ofRobert Dollar, President of the Dollar Steamship Line); Robert Dollar provided a unique perspective because he began his life as a sailor and eventually founded his own steamship company that would become known as the Dollar Steamship Line.

41. *CSJ*, June 4, 1902.

42. *CSJ*, April 13, 1904.

43. Lisa Lowe, *Immigrant Acts: Asian American Cultural Politics (*Durham, N.C. and London: Duke University Press, 1996), 11.

44. Ibid., 11.

45. Samuel Gompers and Herman Gutstadt, "Some Reasons for Chinese Exclusion Meat v. Rice: American Manhood Against Asiatic Coolism, Which Will Survive?" Comm. on Immigration, S. Doc. No. 57–137, at 45 (1902).

46. Peter Cole, *Wobblies on the Waterfront: Interracial Unionism in Progressive-Era Philadelphia* (Urbana and Chicago: University of Illinois Press, 2007), 67.

47. "Resolution No. 11" in *Proceedings of the Sixteenth Annual Convention of the International Seamen's Union of America,* Baltimore, Md., December 6, 1911, p. 120.

48. The La Follette Act would apply to all vessels destined for U.S. ports regardless of national registry; Bieito Alonso, "Spanish Anarchists and Maritime Workers in the IWW," trans. Kevin Antonio Aguilar, in Peter Cole, ed. et al., *Wobblies of the World: A Global History of the IWW* (London: Pluto Press, 2017), 96.

49. "Resolution No. 11" in *Proceedings of the Sixteenth Annual Convention of the International Seamen's Union of America,* Baltimore, Md., December 6, 1911, p. 120.

50. *Hearings on H.R. 11372, Day 1, Before the H. Comm. on Merchant Marine and Fisheries* 62nd Cong. 9 (1911) (Preliminary Statement of Andrew Furuseth); *CSJ*, February 7, 1912.

51. *Hearings on H.R. 11372, Day 3, Before the H. Comm. on Merchant Marine and Fisheries* 62nd Cong. 196 (1912) (Statement of George Bodine, Secretary of the Atlantic Seamen's Union).

52. Ibid.

53. Ibid.

54. Ibid.

55. Ibid., 199.

56. Ibid.

57. "Chapter 153, 63 Congress, Session 3, An Act: To promote the welfare of American seamen in the merchant marine of the United States; to abolish arrest and imprisonment as a penalty for desertion and to secure the abrogation of treaty provisions in relation thereto; and to promote safety at sea," U.S. Statutes at Large 38, no. Main Section (1915): 1164–1185.

58. *Hearings on H.R. 11372, Day 3, Before the H. Comm. on Merchant Marine and Fisheries,* 62nd Cong. 200 (1912) (Statement of George Bodine, Secretary of the Atlantic Seamen's Union).

59. Ibid., 201.

60. Ibid.

61. Ibid.

62. Ibid.

63. *The Seamen's Act: Hearings on S.136, Day 7, Before the H. Comm. on the Merchant Marine and Fisheries* 63rd Cong. 33 (1914) (Statement of Robert Dollar, President of the Dollar Steamship Line).

64. Weintraub, *Andrew Furuseth,* 104.

65. Though not explicitly stated, it is likely that "Anglo-Saxon" meant non-Spanish rather than people of English descent.

66. Weintraub, *Andrew Furuseth,* 103.

67. Ibid.

68. Ibid.,104.

69. Ibid.,105.

70. Ibid.

71. Ibid.

72. Ibid., 79 and 80.

73. *CSJ,* February 22, 1922.

74. Ibid.

75. Ibid.

76. For the West Coast encounter with race and how it differed from the East, see Almaguer, *Racial Fault Lines,* and Gordon, *Great Arizona Orphan Abduction.*

77. P. F. Brissenden, "A Report on the I.W.W. in California," August 1914, United States Commission on Industrial Relations Papers, State Historical Society of Wisconsin, quoted in Bruce Nelson, "J. Vance Thompson, the Industrial Workers of the World, and the Mood of Syndicalism, 1914–1921," *Labor's Heritage* 2, no. 4 (1990): 60.

78. Fink, *Sweatshops of the Sea,* 95.

79. Goldberg, *Maritime Story, 65.*

80. Letter from Andrew Furuseth to Commerce Secretary William C. Redfield, September 13, 1913, quoted in *CSJ,* November 5, 1913.

81. Letter from Andrew Furuseth and Patrick Flynn to the Members of the Committee on Merchant Marine and Fisheries, April 5, 1912, quoted in *The Seamen's Act: Hearings on S.136, Day 11, Before the H. Comm. on the Merchant Marine and Fisheries,* 63rd Cong. 327 (1914) (Statement of Andrew Furuseth, President of International Sailors Union of America).

82. Ibid.

83. Ibid.
84. Ibid.
85. Ibid.
86. Ibid.
87. Ibid.
88. Julie Greene, *Pure and Simple Politics: The American Federation of Labor and Political Actin, 1881–1917* (Cambridge, Mass.: Cambridge University Press, 1998), 36 and 47.
89. *CSJ*, August 3, 1898.
90. *The Seamen's Act: Hearings on S.136, Day 10, Before the H. Comm. on the Merchant Marine and Fisheries*, 63rd Cong. 233 (1914) (Statement of Andrew Furuseth, President of International Sailors Union of America).
91. Ibid., 184.
92. *CSJ*, April 15, 1914.
93. *The Seamen's Act: Hearings on S.136, Day 11, Before the H. Comm. on the Merchant Marine and Fisheries*, 63rd Cong. 277 (1914) (Statement of Andrew Furuseth, President of International Sailors Union of America).
94. Ibid.
95. *The Seamen's Act: Hearings on S.136, Day 7, Before the H. Comm. on the Merchant Marine and Fisheries*, 63rd Cong. 23 (1914) (Statement of Robert Dollar, President of the Dollar Steamship Line).
96. Ibid., 7.
97. For the popular image of the sailor in America and the wider Anglo-American world, see Leon Fink, *Sweatshops at Sea*, 35–63.
98. *CSJ*, June 28, 1905.
99. *CSJ*, December 11, 1912.
100. *The Seamen's Act: Hearings on S.136, Day 10, Before the H. Comm. on the Merchant Marine and Fisheries*, 63rd Cong. 233 (1914) (Statement of Andrew Furuseth, President of International Sailors Union of America).
101. *CSJ*, September 24, 1913.
102. *CSJ*, August 27, 1913.
103. *CSJ*, August 3, 1898.
104. *CSJ*, February 4, 1914.
105. *The Seamen's Act: Hearings on S.136, Day 10, Before the H. Comm. on the Merchant Marine and Fisheries*, 63rd Cong. 227 (1914) (Statement of Andrew Furuseth, President of International Sailors Union of America).
106. "Chapter 153, 63 Congress, Session 3, An Act: To promote the welfare of American seamen in the merchant marine of the United States; to abolish arrest and imprisonment as a penalty for desertion and to secure the abrogation of treaty provisions in relation thereto; and to promote safety at sea," U.S. Statutes at Large 38, no. Main Section (1915): 1164–85.
107. Ibid.
108. Ibid.
109. *CSJ*, November 19, 1913.
110. "Chapter 153, 63 Congress, Session 3, An Act: To promote the welfare of American seamen in the merchant marine of the United States; to abolish arrest and imprisonment

as a penalty for desertion and to secure the abrogation of treaty provisions in relation thereto; and to promote safety at sea," U.S. Statutes at Large 38, no. Main Section (1915): 1164–85; also, note that the act does not say English here, just that the crew must be able to understand the language or orders of the offices, whatever language that may be.

111. Jerold S. Aurbach, "Progressives at Sea: The La Follette Seamen's Act of 1915," *Labor History* 2, no. 3 (1961): 355.

112. More generally, historian David Roediger noted this connection thirty years ago in his work *The Wages of Whiteness* (New York: Verso, 1991), where he argued that in the nineteenth century, the term "worker" became associated with whiteness. For other works on the connection between whiteness, race, work, and labor, see Julie Greene, *The Canal Builders: Making America's Empire at the Panama Canal* (New York: Penguin Press, 2009); David Roediger, *Working Toward Whiteness: How America's Immigrants Became White* (New York: Basic Books, 2005); Thomas A. Guglielmo, *White on Arrival: Italians, Race, Color and Power in Chicago, 1890–1945* (New York: Oxford University Press, 2003); Evelyn Nakano Glenn, *Unequal Freedom: How Race and Gender Shaped American Citizenship and Labor* (Cambridge, Mass.: Harvard University Press, 2002); Michelle Bratton, *The Politics of Whiteness: Race Workers, and Culture in the Modern South* (Princeton, N.J.: Princeton University Press, 2001); Eric Arnesen, "Whiteness of and in the Historians' Imagination," *International Labor and Working Class History*, no. 60 (Fall 2001): 3–32; Neil Foley, *The White Scourge: Mexicans, Blacks, and Poor Whites in Texas Cotton Culture* (Berkeley: University of California Press, 1997); Rick Halpern, *Down on the Killing Floor: Black and White Workers in Chicago's Packinghouse, 1904–1954* (Urbana and Chicago: University of Illinois Press, 1997); Matthew Fry Jacobson, *Whiteness of a Different Color: European Immigrants and the Alchemy of Race* (Cambridge, Mass.: Harvard University Press, 1998); Noel Ignatiev, *How the Irish Became White* (New York: Routledge, 1995); Barbara Jeanne Fields, "Ideology and Race in American History," in J. Morgan Kousser and James M. McPherson eds., *Region, Race, and Reconstruction: Essays in Honor of C. Vann Woodward* (New York: Oxford University Press, 1982).

113. *An Bill to Abolish the Involuntary Servitude Imposed Upon Seamen in the Merchant Marine of the United States . . . : Hearing on H.R.23673, Day 1, Before the Subcomm. of Involuntary Servitude Imposed Upon Seamen of the S. Comm. on Commerce*, 62nd Cong., 56 (1912) (Statement of Andrew Furuseth, President of International Seamen's Union of America).

114. Goldberg, *Maritime Story*, 59.

115. *The Seamen's Act: Hearings on S.136, Day 7, Before the H. Comm. on the Merchant Marine and Fisheries*, 63rd Cong. 7 (1914) (statement of Robert Dollar, President of the Dollar Steamship Line).

116. Aurbach, "Progressives at Sea," 351.

117. However, the act gave foreign firms a two-year grace period.

118. Marcus Rediker uses this phrase in his *Between the Devil and the Deep Blue Sea: Merchant Seamen, Pirates, and the Anglo-American Maritime World, 1700–1750* (Cambridge, U.K.: Cambridge University Press, 1987),105 and 106.

119. "Chapter 28, 55 Congress, Session 3, An Act: To amend the laws relating to American seamen, for the protection of such seamen, and to promote commerce," U.S. Statutes at Large 30, no. Main Section (1898), 755–64.

120. Fink, *Sweatshops at Sea*, 101.

121. Ibid.

122. "Chapter 153, 63 Congress, Session 3, An Act: To promote the welfare of American seamen in the merchant marine of the United States; to abolish arrest and imprisonment as a penalty for desertion and to secure the abrogation of treaty provisions in relation thereto; and to promote safety at sea," U.S. Statutes at Large 38, no. Main Section (1915), 1164–85.

123. Letter from ISU President Andrew Furuseth and ISU Vice President Patrick Flynn to President Woodrow Wilson, March 25, 1912, quoted in *The Seamen's Act: Hearings on S.136, Day 11, Before the H. Comm. on the Merchant Marine and Fisheries*, 63rd Cong. 326 (1914) (Statement of Andrew Furuseth, President of International Seamen's Union of America).

124. *The Seamen's Act: Hearings on S.136, Day 7, Before the H. Comm. on the Merchant Marine and Fisheries*, 63rd Cong. 25 (1914) (Statement of Robert Dollar, President of the Dollar Steamship Line).

125. *The Seamen's Act: Hearings on S.136, Day 10, Before the H. Comm. on the Merchant Marine and Fisheries*, 63rd Cong. 220 (1914) (Statement of Andrew Furuseth, President of International Sailors Union of America).

126. Leo Panitch and Sam Gindin, *The Making of Global Capitalism: The Political Economy of the American Empire* (London and Brooklyn, N.Y.: Verso, 2012), 28.

127. Fink, *Sweatshops of the Seas*, 100.

128. Robert F. Hannigan, *The New World Power: American Foreign Policy, 1898–1917* (Philadelphia: University of Pennsylvania Press, 2002), 99.

129. For the Open-Door Policy, see Gregory Moore, *Defining and Defending the Open Door Policy: Theodore Roosevelt and China, 1901–1909* (New York: Lexington Books, 2015).

130. William Appleman Williams, *The Tragedy of American Diplomacy* (New York: The World, 1959), 37; More generally and more recently, the late geographer Neil Smith argued in his work *American Empire: Roosevelt's Geographer and the Prelude to Globalization* (Berkeley: University of California Press, 2003), 19, that "The emerging American Empire defined its power in the first place through the more abstract geography of the world market rather than through direct political control of territory."

131. Copy of a letter the ISU and the SUP encouraged their members to send their respective congressmen and senators, printed in the *Coast Seamen's Journal*, February 11, 1914.

132. Aurbach, "Progressives at Sea," 347. For a more recent study on how the sailors unions used "innocuous issues of skill, language" and so forth to drive Asian sailors from the U.S. merchant marine see, Justin F. Jackson, "The Right Kind of Man: Flexible Capacity, Chinese Exclusion, and the Imperial Origins of Maritime Labor Reform in the United States, 1898–1905," *Labor: Studies in Working-Class History of the Americas*, 10, no. 4 (Winter 2013): 39–60.

133. Aurbach, "Progressives at Sea," 356.

134. 50 Cong. Rec. 5715 (1913) (statement of Sen. La Follette).

135. 50 Cong. Rec. 5779 (1913) (statement of Sen. La Follette).

136. Robert M. La Follette, "Andrew Furuseth and His Great Work," *La Follette's Magazine*, April 1915, p. 2; see also, Aurbach, "Progressives at Sea," 356.

137. La Follette, "Andrew Furuseth," April 1915, p. 2; see also, Aurbach, "Progressives at Sea," 356.

138. According to historian Jerold Aurbach, Senators Duncan Fletcher (D-FL), James K. Vardaman (D-MS), and James Sharp Williams (D-MS), and in the House, Representatives Joshua Alexander (D-MI) and Rufus Hardy (D-TX), played key roles in helping get the La Follette Act passed.

139. 50 Cong. Rec. 5749 (1913) (statement of Sen. Fletcher); see also, Auerbach, "Progressives at Sea," 356.

140. Marilyn Lake, *Progressive New World: How Settler Colonialism and Transpacific Exchange Shaped American Reform* (Cambridge, Mass.: Harvard University Press, 2019), 5.

141. *CSJ*, July 14, 1915; see also Aurbach, "Progressives at Sea," 356.

142. *Robertson v. Baldwin*, 165 U.S. (1897); the White Act did not end the criminalization for desertion for Americans on U.S. vessels in foreign ports, only in U.S. ones.

143. *The Seamen's Act: Hearings on S.136, Day 10, Before the H. Comm. on the Merchant Marine and Fisheries*, 63rd Cong. 218 (1914) (Statement of Andrew Furuseth, President of International Sailors Union of America).

144. *CSJ*, September 7, 1898.

145. "Chapter 153, 63 Congress, Session 3, An Act: To promote the welfare of American seamen in the merchant marine of the United States; to abolish arrest and imprisonment as a penalty for desertion and to secure the abrogation of treaty provisions in relation thereto; and to promote safety at sea," U.S. Statutes at Large 38, no. Main Section (1915): 1164–85.

146. Though the Chinese imperial government was technically in charge of Shanghai, the treaty rights of the major imperial powers gave them virtual control over the city. See Eileen P. Scully, "Taking the Low Road to Sino-American Relations: Open Door Expansionists and the Two China Markets," *Journal of American History* 82, no. 1 (June 1995): 63.

147. *The Seamen's Act: Hearings on S.136, Day 10, Before the H. Comm. on the Merchant Marine and Fisheries*, 63rd Cong. 227 (1914) (Statement of Andrew Furuseth, President of International Sailors Union of America).

148. Marilyn Lake and Henry Reynolds, *Drawing the Global Colour Line: White Men's Countries and the International Challenge of Racial Equality* (Cambridge, U.K.: Cambridge University Press, 2008).

149. Ibid.

150. *The Seamen's Act: Hearings on S.136, Day 10, Before the H. Comm. on the Merchant Marine and Fisheries*, 63rd Cong. 198 (1914) (Statement of Andrew Furuseth, President of International Sailors Union of America).

Chapter 4. Agents of Empire

1. Jon Sumida, "Alfred Thayer Mahan, Geopolitician," *Journal of Strategic Studies* 2–3, no. 22 (June 1999): 39. For the influence of Mahan on U.S. cultural underpinnings of the 1890s and Spanish-American War, see Kristin Hoganson, *Fighting For American Manhood: How Gender Politics Provoked the Spanish-American and Philippine-American Wars* (New Haven, Conn. and London: Yale University Press, 1998), 10.

2. Historian Justin Jackson pointed out that to Furuseth, the ISU, and their allies, "the merchant mariner and his labor constituted the basic unit of a nation's overall

maritime strength," see Justin Jackson, "The Right Kind of Man: Flexible Capacity, Chinese Exclusion, and the Imperial Origins of Maritime Labor Reform in the United States, 1898–1905," *Labor: Studies in Working-Class History of the Americas* 10, no. 4 (Winter 2013): 41.

3. K. Jack Bauer, *A Maritime History of the United States: The Role of America's Seas and Waterways* (Columbia: University of South Carolina Press, 1988), 298.

4. Joseph P. Goldberg, *The Maritime Story: A Study in Labor-Management Relations* (Cambridge, Mass.: Harvard University Press, 1959), 94.

5. Peter Way, "Black Service . . . White Money: The Peculiar Institution of Military Labor in the British Army During the Seven Years War," in *Workers Across the Americas: The Transnational Turn in Labor History*, ed. Leon Fink, with Eileen Boris, John French, Julie Greene, Joan Sangster, and Sheldon Stromquest, associate editors (New York: Oxford University Press, 2011), 74.

6. Ibid.

7. Ibid.

8. *Robertson v. Baldwin*, 165 U.S. (1897); Joseph P. Goldberg, *The Maritime Story: A Study in Labor-Management Relations* (Cambridge, Mass.: Harvard University Press, 1958), 10 and 11.

9. Alfred Thayer Mahan, *The Influence of Sea Power on History, Present and Future* (Boston: Little, Brown, 1917); while Mahan's work deals with naval power in the sixteenth and seventeenth centuries, he wrote the book to demonstrate the continuing importance of naval power and how the United States should become world class.

10. Way, "Black Service," 74.

11. Verity G. McInnis demonstrated how the wives of army officers were able to leverage their access to an institution of empire in the imperial army to carve out a role for themselves that allowed them to become "indirect agents of empire." See Verity G. McInnis, "Indirect Agents of Empire: Army Officers' Wives in British India and the American West, 1830–1875," *Pacific Historical Review* 83 no. 3 (August 2014): 378–409.

12. *The Chinese Exclusion Act of 1902: Hearings on S. Bill 2960, Day 5, Before the S. Comm. On Immigration*, 57th Cong. 253 (1902) (Statement of Andrew Furuseth, President of the International Seamen's Union of America).

13. Ibid.

14. Ibid.

15. Ibid.

16. *CSJ*, August 31, 1898.

17. Ibid.

18. Letter from the Sailor's Union of the Pacific to President William McKinley, August 5, 1898, quoted in *CSJ*, August 31, 1898; On the "feminization" of Chinese men in the United States, see Lisa Lowe, *Immigrant Acts: Asian American Cultural Politics* (Durham, N.C. and London: Duke University Press, 1996), 11.

19. *The Chinese Exclusion Act of 1902: Hearings on S. Bill 2960, Day 5, Before the S. Comm. On Immigration*, 57th Cong. 248 (1902) (Statement of Andrew Furuseth, President of the International Seamen's Union of America).

20. *CSJ*, March 5, 1902.

21. *The Seamen's Act: Hearings on S.136, Day 10, Before the H. Comm. on the Merchant Marine and Fisheries,* 63rd Cong. 230 (1914) (Statement of Andrew Furuseth, President of International Seamen's Union of America).

22. Ibid., 228.

23. *CSJ,* July 14, 1915.

24. *An Bill to Abolish the Involuntary Servitude Imposed Upon Seamen in the Merchant Marine of the United States. . . . : Hearing on H.R.23673, Day 1, Before the Subcomm. of Involuntary Servitude Imposed Upon Seamen of the S. Comm. on Commerce,* 62nd Cong. 56 (1912) (Statement of Andrew Furuseth, President of the International Seamen's Union of America).

25. For a detailed description of how the La Follette Act accomplished all this, see chapter 3 of this volume.

26. For the U.S. imperial quest for markets, see William Appleman Williams, *The Tragedy of American Diplomacy* (Cleveland and New York: World Publishing, 1959) and Thomas McCormick, *China Market: America's Quest for Informal Empire, 1893–1901* (Chicago: Quadrangle Books, 1967); for the U.S. search for cheap labor, see Daniel E. Bender and Jana K. Lipman, *Making the Empire Work: Labor and United States Imperialism* (New York: New York University Press, 2015); for more specific examples of U.S. imperial projects' search for cheap labor, see Julie Greene, *The Canal Builders: Making America's Empire at the Panama Canal* (New York: Penguin Press, 2009); Greg Grandin, *Fordlandia: The Rise and Fall of Henry Ford's Forgotten Jungle City* (New York: Metropolitan Books, 2009); Jefferson Cowie, *Capital Moves: RCA's Seventy Year Quest for Cheap Labor* (Ithaca, N.Y.: Cornell University Press, 1999).

27. *CSJ,* February 3, 1915.

28. Ibid.

29. Rene De La Pedraja, *The Rise and Decline of U.S. Merchant Shipping in the Twentieth Century* (New York: Twayne Publishers, 1992), 47.

30. Bruce L. Felknor, ed., *The U.S. Merchant Marine at War, 1775–1945* (Annapolis, Md.: Naval Institute Press, 1998), 106.

31. Fink, *Sweatshops at Sea,* 34.

32. See Jeffrey J. Stafford, *Wilsonian Maritime Diplomacy, 1913–1921* (New Brunswick, N.J.: Rutgers University Press, 1978), 36.

33. "Chapter 451, 64 Congress, Session 1, An Act: To establish a United States Shipping Board for the purpose of encouraging, developing, and creating a naval auxiliary and naval reserve and a merchant marine to meet the requirements of the commerce of the United States with its Territories and possessions and with foreign countries; to regulate carriers by water engaged in the foreign and interstate commerce of the United States; and for other purposes," U.S. Statutes at Large 39, no. Main Section (1916): 728–39.

34. Ibid.; See also Clinton H. Whitehurst Jr., "Rules of the Game," in Clinton H. Whitehurst Jr., ed., *The U.S. Merchant Marine: In Search of an Enduring Policy* (Annapolis, Md.: Naval Institute Press, 1984), 33

35. Bauer, *Maritime History of the United States,* 298; *CSJ,* December 27, 1916, "Chapter 451, 64 Congress, Session 1, An Act: To establish a United States Shipping Board for the purpose of encouraging, developing, and creating a naval auxiliary and naval reserve and a merchant marine to meet the requirements of the commerce of the United States with its Territories and possessions and with foreign countries; to

regulate carriers by water engaged in the foreign and interstate commerce of the United States; and for other purposes," U.S. Statutes at Large 39, no. Main Section (1916): 728–39.

36. *CSJ*, December 27, 1916.

37. Felknor, ed., *U.S. Merchant Marine at War*, 107.

38. Bauer, *Maritime History of the United States*, 298.

39. "Chapter 153, 63 Congress, Session 3, An Act: To promote the welfare of American seamen in the merchant marine of the United States; to abolish arrest and imprisonment as a penalty for desertion and to secure the abrogation of treaty provisions in relation thereto; and to promote safety at sea," U.S. Statutes at Large 38, no. Main Section (1915): 1164–85.

40. Ibid.

41. See Leo Panitch, "The Development of Corporatism in Liberal Democracies," in Philip C. Schmitter and Gerhard Lehmbruch, eds., *Trends Toward Corporatist Intermediation* (London: SAGE Publications, 1979), 121; See also James Weinstein, *The Corporate Ideal and the Liberal State, 1900–1918* (Boston: Beacon Press, 1968), particularly chapter 8: "War as Fulfillment."

42. Arthur Emil Abrecht, *The International Seamen's Union of America: A Study of its History and its Problems* (Washington, D.C.: Government Printing Office, 1923), 55.

43. Stephen Schwartz, *Brotherhood of the Sea: A History of the Sailors' Union of the Pacific, 1885–1985* (New Brunswick, N.J.: Rutgers University Press, 1986), 46.

44. *CSJ*, August 22, 1917; Goldberg, *Maritime Story*, 78.

45. *CSJ*, September 19, 1917; The Department of Commerce and Labor was split into two separate departments in 1913.

46. *CSJ*, September 19, 1917.

47. Ibid.

48. Ibid.

49. Goldberg, *Maritime Story*, 83.

50. *CSJ*, February 27, 1918.

51. Ibid.

52. *The Seamen's Journal*, October 9, 1918. After September 1918, the *Coast Seamen's Journal* changed its name to the *Seamen's Journal*.

53. Ibid.

54. Fink, *Sweatshops of the Sea*, 139.

55. Goldberg, *Maritime Story*, 79.

56. Fink, *Sweatshops of the Sea*, 139.

57. Stafford, *Wilsonian Wartime Diplomacy*, 111.

58. Of course, the last time the British arrested American sailors suspected of deserting British ships, it led to the impressment crisis that helped precipitate the War of 1812.

59. *The Seamen's Journal*, January 8, 1919.

60. See Fink, *Sweatshops at Sea*, 139.

61. Schwartz, *Brotherhood of the Sea*, 46.

62. Weintraub, *Andrew Furuseth*, 150.

63. Ibid.

64. Goldberg, *Maritime Story,* 94.

65. *CSJ,* September 19, 1917.

66. Schwartz, *Brotherhood of the Sea,* 41. *CSJ,* February 20, 1918.

67. *CSJ,* September 19, 1917.

68. Ibid.

69. *CSJ,* February 27, 1918.

70. For how war centralizes the shipping industry, see Marcus Rediker, *Between the Devil and the Deep Blue Sea: Merchants, Seamen, Pirates, and the Anglo-American Maritime World, 1700–1750* (Cambridge, U.K.: Cambridge University Press, 1987), 35; This wartime consolidation was on a vastly larger scale than anything from the eighteenth century Rediker was referencing.

71. Roland et al., *The Way of the Ship, America's Maritime History Reenvisioned, 1600–2000,* Hoboken, N.J.: John Wiley and Sons, 2008, 280.

72. *CSJ,* December 19, 1917.

73. Leo Panitch, "The Development of Corporatism in Liberal Democracies," 120 and 140; see also, Leo Panitch, "Trade Unions and the Capitalist State," in Leo Panitch, *Working Class Politics in Crisis: Essays on Labour and the State* (London: Verso, 1986), 187–214.

74. Schwartz, *Brotherhood of the Sea,* 46.

75. *CSJ,* September 19, 1917.

76. Goldberg, *Maritime Story,* 58.

77. Stafford, *Wilsonian Maritime Diplomacy,* 128.

78. Ibid.

79. *CSJ,* August 5, 1908.

80. Weintraub, *Andrew Furuseth,* 98; *CSJ,* August 12, 1908.

81. *CSJ,* September 2, 1908.

82. Weintraub, *Andrew Furuseth,* 99.

83. Goldberg, *Maritime Story,* 79.

84. J. Havelock Wilson, "Opening Address to the International Seafarers Conference," 1919 *International Seafarers Conference Minutes of Proceedings February 22nd to March 3rd, 1919* (London: International Seafarers Federation, 1919), p. 5.

85. Ibid.

86. Ibid.

87. "Resolution on the American Seamen's Act, 1915," 1919 *International Seafarers Conference Minutes of Proceedings February 22nd to March 3rd, 1919* (London: International Seafarers Federation, 1919), p. 53.

88. Ibid.

89. Arnold W. Knauth, "Alien Seamen's Rights and the War," *American Journal of International Law* 37 (January 1943): 78; see also, Fink, *Sweatshops at Sea,* 113.

90. Weintraub, *Andrew Furuseth,* 153.

91. Andrew Furuseth quoted in Weintraub, *Andrew Furuseth,* 153; Schwartz, *Brotherhood of the Sea,* 53.

92. *The Seamen's Journal,* April 30, 1919.

93. Ibid.

94. *Scharrenberg v. Dollar Steamship Co.,* 245 U.S. 122 (1917).

Chapter 5. They Always Choose Exclusion

1. "Chapter 153, 63 Congress, Session 3, An Act: To promote the welfare of American seamen in the merchant marine of the United States; to abolish arrest and imprisonment as a penalty for desertion and to secure the abrogation of treaty provisions in relation thereto; and to promote safety at sea," U.S. Statutes at Large 38, no. Main Section (1915): 1164–85.

2. *CSJ*, January 5, 1916; *CSJ*, January 12, 1916; *CSJ*, February 2, 1916.

3. *CSJ*, February 2, 1916.

4. Ibid.

5. *CSJ*, July 27, 1892; Charles Earl Commerce Department Solicitor to Commerce Secretary Oscar Strauss, June 10, 1907, quoted in *CSJ*, July 17, 1907.

6. *CSJ*, July 27, 1892.

7. "Chapter 153, 63 Congress, Session 3, An Act: To promote the welfare of American seamen in the merchant marine of the United States; to abolish arrest and imprisonment as a penalty for desertion and to secure the abrogation of treaty provisions in relation thereto; and to promote safety at sea," U.S. Statutes at Large 38, no. Main Section (1915): 1164–85.

8. Walter Macarthur, Harbor Commissioner for San Francisco to Collector of Customs for San Francisco, January 16, 1914. Walter Macarthur Papers, Carton 1, Bancroft Library, University of California, Berkeley.

9. U.S. Shipping Commissioner E. T. Chamberlain to Shipping Commissioner for San Francisco Walter Macarthur, March 20, 1914. Walter Macarthur Papers, Carton 1, Bancroft Library, University of California, Berkeley.

10. Ibid.

11. *CSJ*, November 14, 1917; *Scharrenberg v. Dollar Steamship Co.*, 245 U.S. 122 (1917).

12. These two decisions were discussed in chapters 1 and 2, respectively.

13. *CSJ*, August 3, 1892; "Chapter 322, 42 Congress, Session 2, An Act: To authorize the appointment of shipping commissioners by the several circuit courts of the United States, to superintend the shipping and discharge of seamen engaged in merchant ships belonging to the United States, and for the further protection of seamen," U.S. Statutes at Large 17, no. Main Section (1872): 262–80.

14. *CSJ*, August 3, 1892.

15. Charles Earl Commerce Department Solicitor to Commerce Secretary Oscar Strauss, June 10, 1907, quoted in *CSJ*, July 17, 1907.

16. *Scharrenberg v. Dollar Steamship Co.*, 245 U.S. 122 (1917).

17. *CSJ*, November 7, 1917; *Scharrenberg v. Dollar Steamship Co.*, 245 U.S. 122 (1917).

18. *CSJ*, November 21, 1917; *Scharrenberg v. Dollar Steamship Co.*, 245 U.S. 122 (1917).

19. See chapter 2.

20. Gill and Markholt, "The Sailor's Union of the Pacific, *1885–1929" (*Seattle: n.p., 1942), 529.

21. Dispatches from the Atlantic Unions, published in *The Seamen's Journal*, July 14, 1920. After September 1918, the *Coast Seamen's Journal* changed its name to *The Seamen's Journal.*

22. Ibid.

23. Ibid.

24. Ibid.

25. Dispatches from the Atlantic Unions, published in *The Seamen's Journal,* July 14, 1920.

26. Ibid.

27. Ibid.

28. Ibid.

29. Ibid.

30. Ibid.

31. Ibid.

32. Ibid.

33. *San Francisco Call,* February 8, 1922.

34. Ibid.

35. Ibid.; Scharrenberg is referring to a major maritime strike by Chinese sailors in Hong Kong that took place in the winter of 1922.

36. *San Francisco Call,* February 8, 1922.

37. Paul Scharrenberg, "Paul Scharrenberg: Reminiscences." Interview by Corinne Gilb in 1954, Oral History Center, Bancroft Library, University of California, Berkeley, 1954, p. 64.

38. Ibid., 63.

39. Ibid.

40. Andrew Furuseth, *American Sea Power and the Seamen's Act,* S. Doc., 228, 65th Cong., 2nd Sess. (1918).

41. For Furuseth on the general inefficacy of "Oriental" sailors and their opium use, see *Seamen's Act: Hearings on S.136, Day 10, Before the H. Comm. On the Merchant Marine and Fisheries* 63rd Cong. 233 (1914) (Statement of Andrew Furuseth, President of International Seamen's Union of America).

42. *The Chinese Exclusion Act of 1902: Hearings on S. Bill 2960, Day 5, Before the S. Comm. On Immigration,* 57th Cong. 248 (1902) (Statement of Andrew Furuseth, President of the International Seamen's Union of America).

43. *CSJ,* November 21, 1917.

44. See chapter 2 of this volume.

45. *The Immigration Act of 1924: Hearings on H.R. 101, Day 3, Before the H. Comm. On Immigration and Naturalization,* 68th Cong. 158 (1923) (Statement of Andrew Furuseth, Representative of the International Seamen's Union of America).

46. For how the 1924 Immigration dramatically expanded the modern category of "illegal alien," see Mae Ngai, *Impossible Subjects: Illegal Aliens and the Making of Modern America* (Princeton, N.J.: Princeton University Press, 2004).

47. *The Immigration Act of 1924: Hearings on H.R. 101, Day 3, Before the H. Comm. On Immigration and Naturalization,* 68th Cong. 154 (1923) (Statement of Andrew Furuseth, Representative of the International Seamen's Union of America).

48. Ibid.

49. Andrew Furuseth to President Calvin Coolidge, January 25, 1924, in Paul Scharrenberg Papers, Box 2, Letters by Andrew Furuseth, 1923–1929, Folder 2 of 5, Bancroft Library, University of California, Berkeley.

50. *The Immigration Act of 1924: Hearings on H.R. 101, Day 3, Before the H. Comm. On Immigration and Naturalization,* 68th Cong. 154 (1923) (Statement of Andrew Furuseth, Representative of the International Seamen's Union of America).

51. Letter from Andrew Furuseth to James Raker, Congressman from California and member of the House Committee for Immigration and Naturalization, December 29th, 1923, quoted in *The Immigration Act of 1924: Hearings on H.R. 101, Day 3, Before the H. Comm. On Immigration and Naturalization,* 68th Cong. 176 (1923) (Statement of Andrew Furuseth, Representative of the International Seamen's Union of America).

52. Ibid.

53. "Chapter 190, 68 Congress, Session 1, An Act: To limit the immigration of aliens into the United States, and for other purposes," U.S. Statutes at Large 43, no. Main Section (1924): 153–70.

54. Ibid.

55. *Scharrenberg v. Dollar Steamship Co.,* 245 U.S. 122 (1917).

56. "Chapter 190, 68 Congress, Session 1, An Act: To limit the immigration of aliens into the United States, and for other purposes," U.S. Statutes at Large 43, no. Main Section (1924): 153–70.

57. Ibid.

58. "Chapter 29, 64 Congress, Session 2, An Act: To regulate the immigration of aliens to, and the residence of aliens in, the United States," U.S. Statutes at Large 39, no. Main Section (1917): 874–98; expanding the barred zone to the Philippines (part of the U.S. empire) reinforces the fact that leaving out the Philippines as part of the definition was deliberate. It was always intended for deannexation at some future date.

59. Historian Mae Ngai argued that the 1924 law and its expansion of the barred zone to include the Philippines and Japan created the very concept of "Asian" as a racial category in America. She also demonstrated how the act created a "*global* racial and national hierarchy." See Ngai, *Impossible Subjects.*

60. Scharrenberg, "Paul Scharrenberg: Reminiscences," p. 23.

61. *The Seamen's Journal,* July 23, 1919.

62. Roland et al., *Way of the Ship,* 286.

63. *The Seamen's Journal,* June 9, 1920.

64. Ibid.

65. Schwartz, *Brotherhood of the Sea,* 46.

66. U.S. Shipping Board, *Minutes of Proceedings,* June 4, 1919 (S.B. Archives), quoted in Goldberg, *Maritime Story,* 87.

67. *The Seamen's Journal,* July 23, 1919.

68. *A Bill To Promote the Welfare of American Seamen: Hearings on H.R. 8069, Day 1, Before the H. Comm. On Merchant Marine and Fisheries,* 66th Cong. 39 (1919) (Statement of Captain I.N. Hibbard, Recruiting Service, United States Shipping Board). Edwin H. Duff gave these remarks during the testimony of Captain Hibbard, which is why it is cited as Captain Hibbard's statement.

69. Ibid. Note that Andrew Furuseth gave these remarks during the testimony of Captain Hibbard, which is why it is cited as Captain Hibbard's statement.

70. *A Bill To Promote the Welfare of American Seamen: Hearings on H.R. 8069, Day 1, Before the H. Comm. On Merchant Marine and Fisheries* 66th Cong., 40 (1919) (Statement of Captain I.N. Hibbard, Recruiting Service, United States Shipping Board). Note that Edwin H. Duff gave these remarks during the testimony of Captain Hibbard, which is why it is cited as Captain Hibbard's statement.

71. *The Seamen's Journal,* August 3, 1919.
72. Ibid.
73. Ibid.
74. Goldberg, *Maritime Story,* 88.
75. Ibid., 89.
76. Ibid.
77. *The Seamen's Journal,* March 29, 1922.
78. Ibid.
79. Gill and Markholt, "Sailor's Union of the Pacific," 529.
80. *The Seamen's Journal,* February 23, 1921.
81. Ibid.
82. Ibid.
83. Ibid.
84. Gill and Markholt, "Sailor's Union of the Pacific," 580; for more on J. Vance Thompson, see Bruce Nelson, "J. Vance Thompson, the Industrial Workers of the World, and the Mood of Syndicalism, 1914–1921," *Labor's Heritage* 2, no. 4 (1990): 44–65.
85. Ibid., 581.
86. *The Seamen's Journal,* July 29, 1921.
87. Ibid. See also Nelson, "J. Vance Thompson," 60; see also Bruce Nelson, *Workers on the Waterfront: Seamen, Longshoremen, and Unionism in the 1930s* (Urbana and Chicago: University of Illinois Press, 1988).
88. Weintraub, *Andrew Furuseth,* 79.
89. Ibid.
90. Ibid.
91. Scharrenberg, "Paul Scharrenberg: Reminiscences," p. 21.
92. Weintraub, *Andrew Furuseth,* 156.
93. Gill and Markholt, "Sailor's Union of the Pacific," 556.
94. Ibid.; Bruce Nelson, *Workers on the Waterfront: Seamen, Longshoremen, and Unionism in the 1930s* (Urbana: University of Illinois Press, 1988), 54.
95. Ibid.
96. Goldberg, *Maritime Story,* 101.
97. Weintraub, *Andrew Furuseth,* 161 and 158.
98. Gill Markholt, "Sailor's Union of the Pacific," 578.
99. Ibid., 579.
100. Ibid.
101. Ibid.; George P. West, "Andrew Furuseth and the Radicals," *The Survey,* November 5, 1921, 207.
102. West, "Andrew Furuseth and the Radicals," 207; see also, Gill and Markholt, "Sailor's Union of the Pacific," 582.
103. Ibid., 208.
104. Weintraub, *Andrew Furuseth,* 161.
105. Ibid.
106. Gill and Markholt, "Sailor's Union of the Pacific," 580.
107. *The Seamen's Journal,* July 27, 1921.

108. *The Seamen's Journal,* August 3, 1921.
109. Ibid.
110. Ibid.
111. Ibid.
112. Ibid.
113. Weintraub, *Andrew Furuseth,* 161.
114. Andrew Furuseth, quoted in George P. West, "Andrew Furuseth Stands Pat," *The Survey,* October 15, 1923, p. 88; see also Nelson, *Workers on the Waterfront,* 57–58, and Gill and Markholt, "Sailor's Union of the Pacific," 585.
115. Andrew Furuseth, quoted in West, "Andrew Furuseth Stands Pat," 88.
116. SUP Meeting, September 26, 1921, Resolution on IWW Propaganda within *The Seamen's Journal,* quoted in Gill and Markholt, "Sailor's Union of the Pacific," 586.
117. Ibid.
118. Gill and Markholt, "Sailor's Union of the Pacific," 587.
119. Scharrenberg, "Paul Scharrenberg: Reminiscences," p. 23; the Marine Transport Workers Industrial Union No. 510, *Exposed!* (Chicago: Industrial Workers of the World, 1922).
120. Marine Transport Workers Industrial Union No. 510, *Exposed!*, 1922.
121. Ibid.
122. Gill and Markholt, "Sailor's Union of the Pacific," 588; Marine Transport Workers Industrial Union No. 510, *Exposed!*
123. Nelson, "J. Vance Thompson," 52.
124. Marine Transport Workers Industrial Union No. 510, *Exposed!*
125. Nelson, "J. Vance Thompson," 60.
126. West, "Andrew Furuseth and the Radicals," 209.
127. Gill and Markholt, "Sailor's Union of the Pacific," 593.
128. Scharrenberg, "Paul Scharrenberg: Reminiscences," p. 21.
129. West, "Andrew Furuseth and the Radicals," 209.
130. Gill and Markholt, "Sailors Union of the Pacific," 581.
131. West, "Andrew Furuseth Stands Pat," 86.
132. *The Seamen's Journal,* February 1, 1922.
133. Ibid.
134. Gill and Markholt, "Sailor's Union of the Pacific," 595.

Conclusion

1. On the tension between exclusionists and imperialists, see Beth Lew-Williams, *"The Chinese Must Go": The Chinese Must Go: Violence, Exclusion, and the Making of the Alien in America* (Cambridge, Mass.: Harvard University Press, 2018).
2. For the latest on Asians "in and from Asia" as U.S. imperial subjects rather than aspiring U.S. immigrants, see Moon-Ho Jung, *Menace to Empire: Anti-Colonial Solidarities and the Transpacific Origins of the U.S. National Security State* (Oakland: University of California Press, 2022).
3. "Chapter 190, 68 Congress, Session 1, An Act: To limit the immigration of aliens into the United States, and for other purposes," U.S. Statutes at Large 43, no. Main Section (1924): 153–70.

4. See chapter 1.

5. Though Hawai'i was technically included in this definition, the Commerce Department's ruling of 1907 (that provided shipping companies with a legal loophole around the Exclusion Act) meant that, from the sailors' point of view, Honolulu was essentially a foreign port.

6. Judith Stein, *Pivotal Decade: How the United States Traded Factories for Finance in the Seventies* (New Haven, Conn.: Yale University Press, 2010), 11.

7. See Jefferson Cowie, *Capital Moves: RCA's Seventy Search for Cheap Labor* (Ithaca, N.Y. and London: Cornell University Press, 1999); even foreign firms have taken advantage of the uneven geographies of the American labor market, with many Japanese and European auto manufactures relocating their base of operations to the American Sunbelt, complete with cheap labor markets, weak regulation, and antiunion legislation.

8. Committee on Foreign Affairs, the Chinese Exclusion Act of 1902, H.R. Rep. No. 57–1231, Views of the Majority (1902), p. 2.

9. *Testimony Taken Before the Committee on Immigration on Bill 2960 and Certain other Bills before the Committee Providing for the Exclusion of Chinese Laborers, United States Senate,* 57th Cong., 1st session (January 21, 1902) (Statement of Maxwell Evarts, Director of Pacific Mail Steamship Line), p. 26.

10. Nathan Lillie, *A Global Union for Global Workers: Collective Bargaining and Regulatory Politics in Maritime Shipping* (New York and London: Routledge, 2006), 33.

11. Dispatched from the Atlantic Unions published in the *Seamen's Journal,* July 14, 1920.

12. Marcus Rediker, *Between the Devil and the Deep Blue Sea: Merchant Seamen, Pirates, and the Anglo-American Maritime World, 1700–1750* (Cambridge, U.K.: Cambridge University Press, 1987), 8; David Montgomery noted that the highest concentration of wage earners in late eighteenth-century America was in the merchant marine. See David Montgomery, *Citizen Worker: The Experience of Workers in the United States with Democracy and the Free Market during the Nineteenth Century* (New York: Cambridge University Press, 1993), 13.

13. Cowie, *Capital Moves,* 9. Judith Stein's *Pivotal Decade: How the United States Traded Factories for Finance in the Seventies* (New Haven, Conn. and London: Yale University Press, 2010) is more about the financialization of the U.S. economy since the 1970s. Stein demonstrates how this process helped usher in the era of operationally mobile transnational manufacturing capital. For literature on deindustrialization, see Kim Moody, *Workers in a Lean World: Unions in the International Economy* (New York: Verso, 1997); Gijsbert Van Liemt, ed., *Industry on the Move: Causes and Consequences of International Relocation in Manufacturing Industry* (Geneva: ILO, 1992); Saskia Sassen, *The Mobility of Labor and Capital: A Study in International Investment and Labor Flow* (New York: Cambridge University Press, 1988); and in the twenty-first century, many U.S. companies have moved their operations overseas, especially in the tech and textile sector. U.S. clothing manufactures such as Guess, Nike, and others have taken advantage of the cheaper labor markets of India and Bangladesh. Similarly, tech companies like Apple design their products in the United States but have them manufactured and assembled in China and Taiwan.

14. For the most recent scholarship on how transnational cooperation between labor unions, particularly between the developed and developing world, has led to key victories for workers' rights around the globe, see Andrew Herod, "Chapter Seven: Workers Fight back," in Andrew Herod, *Labor* (Cambridge and Medford, U.K.: Polity Press, 2018), 170–97; see also Michael P. Hanagan, "Labor Internationalism: An Introduction," *Social Science History* 27, no. 4 (2003): 485–99; Andrew Herod, "Geographies of Labor Internationalism," *Social Science History* 27, no. 4 (2003): 501–23; Aviva Chomsky, *Linked Labor Histories: New England, Colombia, and the Making of the Global Working Class* (Durham, N.C.: Duke University Press, 2008).

Bibliography

Primary Sources

Abrecht, Arthur Emil. *The International Seamen's Union of America: A Study of its History and its Problems.* Washington, D.C.: Government Printing Office, 1923.

Axtell, Silas, ed. *A Symposium on Andrew Furuseth.* New Bedford, Mass.: Darwin Press, 1948.

Annual Reports of the Secretary of Commerce and Labor, 1900–1907.

Asiatic Exclusion League Records, larc.ms.0145. Labor Archives and Research Center, San Francisco State University.

Commons, John R. *Race and Immigrants in America.* New York: Augustus M. Kelley Publishing, 1907.

Congressional Record.

Congressional Serial Set.

Downes v. Bidwell, 182 U.S. 244 (1901).

Foreign Relations of the United States (FRUS), 1902, Washington D.C.: Government Printing Office, 1903.

Foreign Relations of the United States (FRUS), 1915 Supplement, the World at War, ed. Joseph V. Fuller, Washington, D.C.: Government Printing Office, 1928.

Furuseth, Andrew. *American Sea Power and the Seamen's Act.* Washington, D.C.: Government Printing Office, 1918.

———. *A Message to Seamen: A Call to the Sea and to Seamanship.* Chicago: International Seamen's Union of America, 1901.

———. *Second Message to Seamen: His Relationship to the Harbor Workers and the Shipowners.* Chicago: Issued by International Seamen's Union of America, 1919.

——. *Watch-and-Watch at Sea: A Protest from the International Seamen's Union and a Warning to Shipowners.* Washington, D.C.: Government Printing Office, 1917.

Gill, Peter B. and Ottilie Markholt. "The Sailor's Union of the Pacific: 1885–1929." Unpublished manuscript, 1942. University of Washington Libraries, digital collection.

Haskell Family Papers, Bancroft Library, University of California, Berkeley.

Ira Cross Papers, Bancroft Library, University of California, Berkeley.

Jenks, Jeremiah. *Report on Certain Economic Questions in the English and Dutch Colonies in the Orient.* Washington, D.C.: Government Printing Office, 1902.

Mahan, Alfred Thayer. *The Interest of American Sea Power, Present and Future.* Boston: Little, Brown, 1917.

——. *The Influence of Sea Power on History, 1660–1782,* 12th ed. Boston: Little, Brown, 1918.

The Marine Transport Workers Industrial Union No. 510. *Exposed!* Chicago: Industrial Workers of the World, 1922.

Minutes of the International Seafarers Conference: Together with Minutes of an Open Seafarers Conference From February 22nd to March 3rd, 1919. London: International Seafarers Federation, 1919.

Pacific Mail Steamship Company Records, Huntington Library, Los Angeles, California.

Paul Sharrenberg Papers, Bancroft Library, University of California, Berkeley.

The People v. Hall, 4 Cal. 499 (1854).

Proceedings of the Asiatic Exclusion League, 1907–1913. New York: Arno Press, 1977.

Proceedings of the International Seamen's Union of America Annual Conventions, 1892–1925, Martin P. Catherwood Library of the New York State School of Industrial Relations at Cornell University.

Records of the House Committee on the Merchant Marine and Fisheries, 1894–1919.

Records of the House Committee on Foreign Affairs, 1898–1912.

Records of the House Committee on Immigration and Naturalization, 1923.

Records of the Senate Committee on Immigration, 1902–1924.

Records of the Senate Committee on Commerce, 1912–1919.

Records of the Senate Committee on Foreign Relations, 1902–1924.

Robert Dollar Papers, Bancroft Library, University of California, Berkeley.

Robertson v. Baldwin, 165 U.S. 275 (1897).

Roney, Frank. *Frank Roney: Irish Rebel and California Labor Leader: An Autobiography*. Ira Cross, ed. Berkeley and Los Angeles: University of California Press, 1931.

Sailors Union of the Pacific Minutes of Meetings 1909–1916, San Francisco Maritime Archives, San Francisco, California.

San Francisco Labor Council Records, Bancroft Library, University of California, Berkeley.

Scharrenberg v. Dollar Steamship Co., 245 U.S. 122 (1917).

Scharrenberg, Paul. "Paul Scharrenberg: Reminiscences." Interview by Corinne Gilb in 1954. Oral History Center, Bancroft Library, University of California, Berkeley, 1954.

Sinclair, Upton. *I, Candidate for Governor: And How I Got Licked.* Berkeley and Los Angeles: University of California Press, 1994 reprint.

United States, *The Statutes at Large,* Washington, D.C., Government Printing Office, 1790–1924.

Walter Macarthur Papers, Bancroft Library, University of California, Berkeley.

PERIODICALS

American Federationist

Coast Seamen's Journal

La Follette's Magazine

New York Times

San Francisco Call

Seamen's Journal

Survey

Secondary Sources

BOOKS

Alejandrino, Clark L. *The History of the 1902 Chinese Exclusion Act: American Colonial Transmission and Deterioration of Filipino-Chinese Relations.* Manila: Kaisa Para Sa Kaunlaran, 2003.

Almaguer, Tomas. *Racial Fault Lines: The Historical Origins of White Supremacy in California.* Berkeley and Los Angeles: University of California Press, 1994.

Arnesen, Eric. *Waterfront Workers of New Orleans: Race, Class, and Politics, 1863–1923.* New York and Oxford, U.K.: Oxford University Press, 1991.

Azuma, Eiichiro. *Between Two Empires: Race, History, and Transnationalism in Japanese.* New York: Oxford University Press, 2005.

Ballantyne, Tony. *Orientalism and Race: Aryanism in the British Empire.* Basingstoke, U.K.: Palgrave Press, 2002.

Bauer, K. Jack. *A Maritime History of the United States: The Role of America's Seas and Waterways.* Columbia: University of South Carolina Press, 1988.

Beard, Charles, and Mary Beard. *The Rise of American Civilization.* New York: Macmillan, 1927.

Bemis, Samuel. *A Diplomatic History of the United States.* New York: H. Holt, 1936.

Bender, Daniel E., and Jana K. Lipman, eds. *Making the Empire Work: Labor and United States Imperialism.* New York: New York University Press, 2015.

Benson, Lee. *The Concept of Jacksonian Democracy; New York, a Test Case.* Princeton, N.J.: Princeton University Press, 1961.

Benton-Cohen, Katherine. *Borderland Americans: Racial Division and Labor War in the Arizona Borderlands.* Cambridge, Mass.: Harvard University Press, 2009.

Brattain, Michelle. *The Politics of Whiteness: Race, Workers, and Culture in the Modern South.* Princeton, N.J.: Princeton University Press, 2001.

Braverman, Harry. *The Degradation of Work in the Twentieth Century.* New York: Monthly Review Press, 1974.

Burnett, Christina Duffy, and Burke Marshall. *Foreign in a Domestic Sense: Puerto Rico, American Expansion, and the Constitution.* Durham, N.C.: Duke University Press, 2001.

Campbell, James T. et al., eds. *Race, Nation, and Empire in American History.* Chapel Hill: University of North Carolina Press, 2007.

Cassel, Par Kristoffer. *Grounds of Judgment: Extraterritoriality and Imperial Power in Nineteenth-Century China and Japan.* Oxford, U.K.: Oxford University Press, 2012.

Chanderl, Alfred D. *The Visible Hand: The Managerial Revolution in American Business.* Cambridge, Mass.: Belknap Press, 1977.

Chang, Kornel. *Pacific Connections: The Making of the U.S.–Canadian Borderlands.* Berkeley and Los Angeles: University of California Press, 2012.

Chilton, Lisa. *Agents of Empire: British Female Migration to Canada and Australia, 1860s-1930.* Toronto: University of Toronto Press, 2007.

Chirot, Daniel, and Anthony Reid, eds. *Essential Outsiders: Chinese and Jews in the Modern Transformation of Southeast Asia and Central Europe.* Seattle: University of Washington Press, 1997.

Chomsky, Aviva. *West Indian Workers and the United Fruit Company in Costa Rica.* Baton Rouge: Louisiana State University Press, 1996.

Cohen, William. *At Freedom's Edge: Black Mobility and the Southern Quest for Racial Control, 1861–1915.* Baton Rouge: Louisiana State University Press, 1991.

Colby, Jason. *The Business of Empire: United Fruit, Race, and U.S. Expansion in Central America.* Ithaca, N.Y.: Cornell University Press, 2011.

Cole, Peter, David Struthers, and Kenyon Zimmer, eds. *Wobblies of the World: A Global History of the IWW.* London: Pluto Press, 2017.

Cowie, Jefferson. *Capital Moves: RCA's Seventy-Year Quest for Cheap Labor.* Ithaca, N.Y.: Cornell University Press, 1999.

Cronon, William. *Nature's Metropolis: Chicago and the Great West.* New York: W.W. Norton, 1991.

Cross, Ira B. *A History of the Labor Movement in California.* Berkeley and Los Angeles: University of California Press, 1935.

Daniels, Roger. *The Politics of Prejudice: The Anti-Japanese Movement in California and the Struggle for Japanese Exclusion.* New York: Antheneum, 1972.

De La Pedraja, Rene. *The Rise and Decline of the American Merchant Shipping in the Twentieth Century.* New York: Twayne Publishers, 1992.

Deutsch, Sarah. *No Separate Refuge: Culture, Class, and Gender on an Anglo-Hispanic Frontier in the American Southwest, 1880–1940.* New York: Oxford University Press, 1987.

Dirlik, Arif, ed. *What is in a Rim? Critical Perspectives on the Pacific Region Idea.* Lanham, Md.: Rowman & Littlefield Publishers, 1998.

Dubofsky, Melvyn. *We Shall Be All: A History of the Industrial Workers of the World.* Chicago: Quadrangle Books, 1969.

Du Bois, W. E. B. *Black Reconstruction: An Essay Toward a History of the Part which Black Folk Played in the Attempt to Reconstruct Democracy in America, 1860–1880.* Philadelphia: Albert Saifeer, 1934.

Felknor, Bruce L., ed. *The U.S. Merchant Marine at War, 1775–1945.* Annapolis, Md.: Naval Institute Press, 1998.

Fink, Leon. *Sweatshops of the Sea: Merchant Seamen in the World's First Globalized Industry, From 1812 to the Present.* Chapel Hill: University of North Carolina Press, 2011.

Fink, Leon, with Eileen Boris, John French, Julie Greene, Joan Sangster, and Sheldon Stromquest, assoc. eds. *Workers Across the Americas: The Transnational Turn in Labor History*. New York: Oxford University Press, 2011.

Foley, Neil. *The White Scourge: Mexicans and Poor Whites in Texas Cotton Culture.* Berkeley: University of California Press, 1997.

Foner, Eric. *Free Soil, Free Labor, Free Men: The Ideology of the Republican Party Before the Civil War.* London and New York: Oxford University Press, 1970.

——. *The Politics and Ideology of the American Civil War.* New York: Oxford University Press, 1980.

Gabaccia, Donna. *Foreign Relations: American Immigration in a Global Perspective.* Princeton, N.J.: Princeton University Press, 2012.

Glenn, Evelyn Nakano. *Unequal Freedom: How Race and Gender Shaped American Citizenship and Labor.* Cambridge, Mass.: Harvard University Press, 2002.

Goldberg, Joseph P. *The Maritime Story: A Study in Labor-Management Relations.* Cambridge, Mass.: Harvard University Press, 1958.

Gordon, Linda. *The Great Arizona Orphan Abduction.* Cambridge, Mass.: Harvard University Press, 1999.

Grandin, Greg. *Fordlandia: The Rise and Fall of Henry Ford's Forgotten Jungle City.* New York: Picador, 2010.

Greene, Julie. *The Canal Builders: Making America's Empire at the Panama Canal.* New York: Penguin Press, 2009.

——. *Pure and Simple Politics: The American Federation of Labor and Political Action, 1881–1917.* Cambridge, U.K.: Cambridge University Press, 1998.

Guglielmo, Thomas A. *White on Arrival: Italians, Race, Color and Power in Chicago, 1890–1945.* New York: Oxford University Press, 2003.

Halpern, Rick. *Down on the Killing Floor: Black and White Workers in Chicago's Packinghouses, 1904–1954.* Urbana and Chicago: University of Illinois Press, 1997.

Hannigan, Robert F. *The New World Power: American Foreign Policy, 1898–1917.* Philadelphia: University of Pennsylvania Press, 2002.

Harvey, David. *The Enigma of Capital and the Crisis of Capitalism.* Oxford, U.K.: Oxford University Press, 2011.

Herod, Andrew. *Labor.* Cambridge and Medford, U.K.: Polity Press, 2018.

Hobsbawm, Eric. *Labouring Men: Studies in the History of Labour.* London: Weidenfeld and Nicolson, 1964.

Hoganson, Kristin. *Fighting for American Manhood: How Gender Politics Provoked the Spanish-American and Philippine-American Wars.* New Haven, Conn. and London: Yale University Press, 1998.

Horne, Gerald. *The White Pacific: U.S. Imperialism and Black Slavery in the South Seas After the Civil War.* Honolulu: University of Hawai'i Press, 2007.

Huttenback, Robert A. *Empire and Racism. White Settlers and Colored Immigrants in the British Self-governing Colonies, 1830–1910.* Ithaca, N.Y.: Cornell University Press, 1976.

Ignatiev, Noel. *How the Irish Became White.* New York: Routledge, 1995.

Jacobson, Matthew Fry. *Barbarian Virtues: The United States Encounter with Foreign People at Home and Abroad, 1876–1917.* New York: Hill and Wang, 2000.

——. *Whiteness of a Different Color: European Immigrants and the Alchemy of Race.* Cambridge, Mass.: Harvard University Press, 1998.

Jung, Moon-Ho. *Coolies and Cane: Race, Labor, and Sugar in the Age of Emancipation.* Baltimore: Johns Hopkins University Press, 2008.

——. *Menace to Empire: Anticolonial Solidarities and the Transpacific Origins of the U.S. Security State.* Oakland: University of California Press, 2022.

Kantrowitz, Stephen. *Ben Tillman and the Reconstruction of White Supremacy.* Chapel Hill: University of North Carolina Press, 2000.

Kaplan, Amy. *The Anarchy of Empire in the Making of U.S. Culture.* Cambridge, Mass.: Harvard University Press, 2002.

Katznelson, Ira, and Aristide R. Zolberg. *Working Class Formation: Nineteenth-Century Patterns in Western Europe and the United States.* Princeton, N.J.: Princeton University Press, 1986.

Kaufman, Stuart Bruce. *Samuel Gompers and the Origins of the American Federation of Labor, 1848–1896.* London: Greenwood Press, 1973.

Kazin, Michael. *Barons of Labor: The San Francisco Building Trades and Union Power in the Progressive Era.* Urbana: University of Illinois Press, 1987.

Kennan, George F. *American Diplomacy, 1900–1950.* Chicago: University of Chicago Press, 1951.

Kerr, James E. *The Insular Cases: The Role of the Judiciary in American Expansionism.* Port Washington, N.Y.: Kennikat Press, 1982.

Kousser, J. Morgan, and James M. McPherson, eds. *Region, Race, and Reconstruction: Essays in Honor of C. Vann Woodward.* New York: Oxford University Press, 1982.

Kramer, Paul A. *The Blood of Government: Race, Empire, the United States, and the Philippines.* Chapel Hill: University of North Carolina Press, 2006.

Kwonk-Chu, Wong. *The Chinese in the Philippine Economy, 1898–1941.* Manila: Ateneo de Manila University Press, 1999.

LaFeber, Walter. *The New Empire: An Interpretation of American Expansion.* Ithaca, N.Y.: Cornell University Press, 1963.

Lake, Marilyn, and Henry Reynolds. *Drawing the Global Colour Line: White Men's Countries and the International Challenge of Racial Equality.* Cambridge, U.K.: Cambridge University Press, 2008.

Laurie, Bruce. *Artisans into Workers: Labor in Nineteenth-Century America.* New York: Noonday Press, 1989.

Lee, Erika. *At America's Gates: Chinese Immigration During the Exclusion Era, 1882–1943.* Chapel Hill: University of North Carolina Press, 2003.

Levine, Bruce. *Half Slave Half Free: The Roots of the Civil War.* New York: Hill and Wang, 1992.

Lew-Williams, Beth. *"The Chinese Must Go": Violence, Exclusion, and the Making of the Alien in America.* Cambridge, Mass.: Harvard University Press, 2018.

Lichtenstein, Alex. *Twice the Work of Free Labor: The Political Economy of Convict Labor in the New South.* New York: Verso, 1996.

Liemt, Gijsbert Van, ed. *Industry on the Move: Causes and Consequences of International Relocation in Manufacturing Industry.* Geneva: ILO, 1992.

Lillie, Nathan. *Global Union for Global Workers: Collective Bargaining and Regulatory Politics in Maritime Shipping.* New York: Routledge, 2006.

Limerick, Patricia Nelson. *The Legacy of Conquest: The Unbroken Past of the American West.* New York: Norton, 1987.

Linden, Marcel van der, and Jan Lucassen et al., eds. *Racism and the Labour Market.* Berne: Peter Lang, 1995.

Linebaugh, Peter, and Marcus Rediker. *The Many-Headed Hydra: Sailors, Slaves, Commoners, and the Hidden History of the Revolutionary Atlantic.* Boston: Beacon Press, 2000.

Lipman, Jana K. *Guantanamo: A Working-Class History Between Empire and Revolution.* Berkeley and Los Angeles: University of California Press, 2008.

Love, Eric T. *Racism Over Empire: Racism and U.S. Imperialism, 1865–1900.* Chapel Hill: University of North Carolina Press, 2004.

Lowe, Lisa. *Immigrant Acts: On Asian Cultural Politics.* Durham, N.C.: Duke University Press, 1996.

May, Ernest. *Imperial Democracy: The Emergence of America as Great Power.* Chicago: Imprint Publications, 1961.

Maier, Charles. *One Within Borders: Territories of Power, Wealth, and Belonging Since 1500.* Cambridge, Mass.: Harvard University Press, 2016.

McCartin, Joseph A. *Labor's War: The Struggle for Industrial Democracy and the Origins of Modern American Labor Relations, 1912–1921.* Chapel Hill: University of North Carolina Press, 1997.

McColy, Alfred, and Francisco A. Scarano. *Colonial Crucible: Empire in the Making of the Modern American State.* Madison: University of Wisconsin Press, 2009.

McGuinness, Aims. *The Path of Empire: Panama and the California Gold Rush.* Ithaca, N.Y. and London: Cornell University Press, 2008.

McKweon, Adam. *Melancholy Order: Asian Immigration and the Globalization of Borders*, New York: Columbia University Press, 2008.

McKormick, Thomas. *The China Market: America's Quest for Informal Empire, 1893–1901.* Chicago: Quadrangle Books, 1967.

Merleaux, April. *Sugar and Civilization: American Empire and the Cultural Politics of Sweetness.* Chapel Hill: University of North Carolina Press, 2015.

Memea Kruse, Line-Noue. *The Pacific Insular Case of American Samoa: Land Rights and Law in Unincorporated U.S. Territories.* New York: Palgrave, 2018.

Montgomery, David. *Citizen Worker: The Experience of Workers in the United States with Democracy and the Free Market during the Nineteenth Century.* New Haven, Conn.: Yale University Press, 1993.

———. *The Fall of the House of Labor: The Workplace, The State, and American Labor Activism.* Cambridge, U.K.: Cambridge University Press, 1987.

——. *Workers Control in America: Studies in History of Work, Technologies, and Labor Struggles.* New York: Cambridge University Press, 1979.

Moore, Gregory. *Defining and Defending the Open Door Policy: Theodore Roosevelt and China, 1901–1909*. New York: Lexington Books, 2015.

Moody, Kim. *Workers in a Lean World: Unions in the International Economy.* New York: Verso, 1997.

Ngai, Mae. *Impossible Subjects: Illegal Aliens and the Making of Modern America.* Princeton, N.J.: Princeton University Press, 2004.

Nelson, Bruce. *Workers on the Waterfront: Seamen, Longshoremen, and Unionism in the 1930s.* Urbana: University of Illinois Press, 1988.

Neptune, Harvey. *Caliban and the Yanks: Trinidad and the United States Occupation.* Chapel Hill: University of North Carolina Press, 2007.

Newman, Gerald L., and Tomiko Brown-Nargin, eds. *Reconsidering the Insular Cases: The Present and Future of American Empire.* Cambridge, Mass.: Harvard University Press, 2015.

Panitch, Leo, and Sam Gindin. *The Making of Global Capitalism: The Political Economy of the American Empire.* London and Brooklyn, N.Y.: Verso, 2012.

Panitch, Leo. *Working Class Politics in Crisis: Essays on Labour and the State.* London: Verso, 1986.

Phelan, Craig. *William Green: Biography of a Labor Leader.* Albany, N.Y.: State University of New York Press, 1989.

Potter, David M. *The Impending Crisis, 1848–1861.* New York: Harper & Row, 1976.

Ramos, Efren Rivera. *The Legal Construction of Identity: The Judicial and Social Legacy of American Colonialism in Puerto Rico.* Washington, D.C.: American Psychological Association, 2001.

Rediker, Marcus. *Between the Devil and the Deep Blue Sea: Merchant Seamen, Pirates, and the Anglo-American Maritime World, 1700–1750.* Cambridge, Mass.: Cambridge University Press, 1987.

Roediger, David. *The Wages of Whiteness: Race and the Making of the American Working Class.* New York: Verso, 1991.

——. *Working Toward Whiteness: How America's Immigrants Became White.* New York: Basic Books, 2005.

Roland, Alex, et al. *The Way of the Ship: America's Maritime History Reenvisioned, 1600–2000.* Hoboken, N.J.: John Wiley and Sons, 2008.

Rouleau, Brian. *White Sails Whitening Every Sea: Mariners and the Making of An American Maritime Empire.* Ithaca, N.Y.: Cornell University Press, 2014.

Russ, William Adam. *The Hawaiian Revolution (1893–94).* Selinsgrove, Pa.: Susquehanna University Press, 1959.

Sassen, Saskia. *The Mobility of Labor and Capital: A Study in International Investment and Labor Flow.* New York: Cambridge University Press, 1988.

Saxton, Alexander. *The Indispensable Enemy: Labor and the Anti-Chinese Movement in California.* Berkeley and Los Angeles: University of California Press, 1971.

——. *The Rise and Fall of the White Republic: Class Politics and Mass Culture in Nineteenth-Century America.* London and New York: Verso Press, 1990.

Schlesinger, Arthur M. *The Age of Jackson.* Boston: Little, Brown, 1945.

Schmitter, Philip C., and Gerhard Lehmbruch, eds. *Trends Toward Corporatist Intermediation.* London: SAGE Publications, 1979.

Schwartz, Stephen. *Brotherhood of the Sea: A History of the Sailors' Union of the Pacific, 1885–1985.* New Brunswick, N.J.: Rutgers University Press, 1986.

Shumsky, Neil M. *The Evolution of Political Protest and the Workingmen's Party of California.* Columbus: Ohio State University Press, 1991.

Sellers, Charles. *The Market Revolution: Jacksonian America, 1815–1946.* New York: Oxford University Press, 1991.

Smith, Neil. *American Empire: Roosevelt's Geographer and the Prelude to Globalization.* Berkeley and Los Angeles: University of California Press, 2003.

Stafford, Jeffry J. *Wilsonian Maritime Diplomacy, 1913–1921.* New Brunswick, N.J.: Rutgers University Press, 1978.

Stein, Judith. *Pivotal Decade: How the United States Traded Factories for Finance in the Seventies.* New Haven, Conn.: Yale University Press, 2010.

Steinfeld, Robert J. *Coercion, Contract, and Free Labor in the Nineteenth Century.* New York: Cambridge University Press, 2001.

———. *The Invention of Free Labor: The Employment Relation in English and American Law and Culture, 1350–1870.* Chapel Hill: University of North Carolina Press, 1991.

Sparrow, Bartholomew H. *The Insular Cases and the Emergence of the American Empire.* Lawrence: University of Kansas Press, 2006.

Stoler, Ann Laura, and Frederick Cooper, eds. *Tensions of Empire: Colonial Cultures in a Bourgeois World.* Berkeley and Los Angeles: University of California Press, 1997.

Stoler, Ann Laura, Carole McGranahan, and Peter Perdue, eds. *Imperial Formations.* Santa Fe, N.M.: School for Advanced Research Press, 2007.

Takaki, Ronald. *Iron Cages: Race and Culture in 19th-Century America.* New York: Oxford University Press, 2000.

———. *Pan Hana: Plantation Life and Labor in Hawaii, 1835–1920.* Honolulu: University of Hawaii Press, 1983.

Taylor, Paul S. *The Sailors' Union of the Pacific.* New York: Arno Press, 1971.

Tyrell, Ian. *Transnational Nation: United States History in Global Perspective Since 1789.* Basingstoke, U.K.: Palgrave Macmillan, 2007.

Vickers, Daniel. *Young Men and the Sea: Yankee Seafarers in the Age of Sail.* New Haven, Conn.: Yale University Press, 2005.

Weinstein, James. *The Corporate Ideal and the Liberal State, 1900–1918.* Boston: Beacon Press, 1968.

Weintraub, Hyman Andrew. *Furuseth: Emancipator of the Seamen.* Berkeley and Los Angeles: University of California Press, 1959.

White, Richard. *It's Your Misfortune and None of My Own: A History of The American West.* Norman: University of Oklahoma Press, 1991.

Whitehurst, Clinton H., Jr., ed. *The U.S. Merchant Marine: In Search of an Enduring Policy.* Annapolis, Md.: Naval Institute Press, 1984.

Wickberg, Edgar. *The Chinese in Philippine Life, 1850–1898.* London: Yale University Press, 1965.

Williams, William Appleman. *The Contours of American History*. Cleveland: World Publishing, 1961.

———. *The Tragedy of American Diplomacy*. New York and Cleveland: World Publishing, 1959.

Winichakul, Thongchai. *Siam Mapped: A History of the Geo-Body of a Nation*. Honolulu: University of Hawai'i Press, 1994.

Wolfe, Eric. *Europe and the People without History*. Berkeley: University of California Press, 1982.

Woodward, C. Vann. *Origins of the New South*. Baton Rouge: Louisiana State University Press, 1951.

Wright, Gavin. *Old South, New South: Revolutions in the Southern Economy Since the Civil War*. Baton Rouge: Louisiana State University Press, 1997.

Young, Elliott. *Alien Nation: Chinese Migration in the Americas from the Coolie Era Through World War II*. Chapel Hill: University of North Carolina Press, 2014.

Zolberg, Aristide R. *A Nation by Design: Immigration Policy in the Fashioning of America*. New York: Russel Sage Foundation, 2006.

ARTICLES

Ahuja, Ravi. "Mobility and Containment: The Voyage of South Asian Seamen, c. 1900–1960." *International Review of Social History* 51, no. S14 (2006): 11–141.

Appel, John C. "American Labor and the Annexation of Hawaii: A Study in Logic and Economic Interest." *Pacific Historical Review* 23, no. 1 (February 1954): 1–18.

Arnesen, Eric. "Whiteness of and the Historians' Imagination." *International Labor and Working-Class History* 60 (Fall 2001): 3–32.

Aurbach, Jerold S. "Progressives at Sea: The La Follette Seamen's Act of 1915." *Labor History* 2, no. 3 (1961): 344–60.

Balachandran, Goplan. "Conflicts in the International Maritime Labour Market: British and Indian Seamen, Employers, and the State, 1890–1939." *Indian Economic and Social History Review* 39, no. 1 (2002): 71–100.

Bemis, Samuel. "American Foreign Policy and the Blessings of Liberty." 1961 American Historical Association Presidential Address, http://www.historians.org/info/aha_history/sfbemis.htm.

Burnett, Christina Duffy. "American Expansion and Territorial Deannexation." *Chicago Law Review* 72, no. 3 (Summer 2005): 797–879.

Chang, Kornel. "Enforcing Transnational White Solidarity: Asian Migration and the Formation of the U.S.–Canadian Boundary." *American Quarterly* 60., no. 3 (September 2008): 671–96.

Chin, Gabriel J. "A Chinaman's Chance in Court: Asia Pacific Americans and Racial Rules of Evidence." *University of California Irvine Law Review* 3, no. 4 (December 2013): 966–90.

Fisher, Michael H. "Working Across the Seas: Indian Maritime Labourers in India, Britain, and in Between." *International Review of Social History* 51, no. 14 (2006): 21–45.

Greene, Julie. "GAPE Presidential Address: Movable Empire: Labor, Migration, and U.S Global Power During the Gilded Age and Progressive Era." *Journal of Gilded Age and Progressive Era* vol., 15, no. 1 (2016): 4–20.

Hanagan, Michael P. "Labor Internationalism: An Introduction." *Social Science History* 27, no. 4 (2003): 485–99.

Herod, Andrew. "Geographies of Labor Internationalism." *Social Science History* 27, no. 4 (2003): 501–23.

Hyslop, Jonathan. "The Imperial Working Class Makes Itself 'White': White Labourism in Britain, Australia, and South Africa Before the First World War." *Journal of Historical Sociology* 12, no. 4 (December 1999): 398–421.

———. "Steamship Empire: Asian, African, and British Sailors in the Merchant Marine, c. 1880–1945." *Journal of Asian and African Studies* 44, no. 1 (2009): 69–95.

Jackson, Justin. "The Right Kind of Man: Flexible Capacity, Chinese Exclusion, and the Imperial Origins of Maritime Labor Reform in the United States, 1898–1905." *Labor: Studies in Working-Class History of the Americas* 10, no. 4 (Winter 2013): 39–60.

Knauth, Arnold W. "Alien Seamen's Rights and the War." *American Journal of International Law* 37, no. 1 (1943): 74–80.

Kramer, Paul A. "Embedding Capital: Political-Economic History, the United States, and the World." *Journal of the Gilded Age and Progressive Era* 15, no. 3 (2016): 332–62.

———. "Imperial Openings: Civilization, Exemption, and the Geopolitics of Mobility in the History of Chinese Exclusion, 1868–1910." *Journal of the Gilded Age and Progressive Era* 14, no. 3 (2015): 317–47.

———. "Power and Connection: Imperial Histories of the United States in the World." *American Historical Review* 116, no. 5 (2011): 1348–91.

Lillie, Nathan. "Global Collective Bargaining on the Flag of Convenience Shipping." *British Journal of Industrial Relations* 42 (March 2004): 153–79.

Lorence, James. "Organized Business and the Myth of the China Market: The American Asiatic Association, 1898–1937." *Transactions in the American Philosophical Society* 71, no. 4 (1981): 1–112.

McInnis, Verity G. "Indirect Agents of Empire: Army Officers' Wives in British India and the American West, 1830–1875." *Pacific Historical Review* 83, no. 3 (August 2014): 378–409.

Montgomery, David. "SHGAPE Distinguished Historian Address: Workers Movements in the United States Confront Imperialism: The Progressive Era Experience." *Journal of the Gilded Age and Progressive Era* 7, no. 1 (January 2008): 7–42.

Morgan, William Michael. "The Anti-Japanese Origins of the Hawaiian Annexation Treaty of 1897." *Diplomatic History* 6, no. 4 (1982): 23–44.

Nelson, Bruce. "J. Vance Thompson, the Industrial Workers of the World, and the Mood of Syndicalism, 1914–1921." *Labor's Heritage* 2, no. 4 (1990): 44–65.

Ngai, Mai. "Trouble with the Rand: The Chinese Question in South Africa and the Apogee of White Settlerism." *International Labor and Working-Class History* 91, no. 1 (Spring 2017): 59–78.

Norris, Martin J. "The Seamen as Wards of the Admiralty." *Michigan Law Review* 52 (February 1954): 479–504.

Rossum, Matthias van. "The 'Yellow Danger'? Global Forces and Global Fears in the North Sea and Beyond (1600–1950)." *International Journal of Maritime History* 27 no. 4 (2015): 743–54.

Scully, Eileen P. "Taking the Low Road to Sino-American Relations: Open Door Expansionists and the Two China Markets." *Journal of American History* 82, no. 1 (June 1995): 62–83.

Sumida, Jon. "Alfred Thayer Mahan, Geopolitician." *Journal of Strategic Studies* 2–3, no. 22 (June 1999): 39–62.

Index

WILLIAM D. RIDDELL is an assistant professor of history at the University of Toronto.

THE WORKING CLASS IN AMERICAN HISTORY

Worker City, Company Town: Iron and Cotton-Worker Protest in Troy and Cohoes, New York, 1855–84 *Daniel J. Walkowitz*

Life, Work, and Rebellion in the Coal Fields: The Southern West Virginia Miners, 1880–1922 *David Alan Corbin*

Women and American Socialism, 1870–1920 *Mari Jo Buhle*

Lives of Their Own: Blacks, Italians, and Poles in Pittsburgh, 1900–1960 *John Bodnar, Roger Simon, and Michael P. Weber*

Working-Class America: Essays on Labor, Community, and American Society *Edited by Michael H. Frisch and Daniel J. Walkowitz*

Eugene V. Debs: Citizen and Socialist *Nick Salvatore*

American Labor and Immigration History, 1877–1920s: Recent European Research *Edited by Dirk Hoerder*

Workingmen's Democracy: The Knights of Labor and American Politics *Leon Fink*

The Electrical Workers: A History of Labor at General Electric and Westinghouse, 1923–60 *Ronald W. Schatz*

The Mechanics of Baltimore: Workers and Politics in the Age of Revolution, 1763–1812 *Charles G. Steffen*

The Practice of Solidarity: American Hat Finishers in the Nineteenth Century *David Bensman*

The Labor History Reader *Edited by Daniel J. Leab*

Solidarity and Fragmentation: Working People and Class Consciousness in Detroit, 1875–1900 *Richard Oestreicher*

Counter Cultures: Saleswomen, Managers, and Customers in American Department Stores, 1890–1940 *Susan Porter Benson*

The New England Working Class and the New Labor History *Edited by Herbert G. Gutman and Donald H. Bell*

Labor Leaders in America *Edited by Melvyn Dubofsky and Warren Van Tine*

Barons of Labor: The San Francisco Building Trades and Union Power in the Progressive Era *Michael Kazin*

Gender at Work: The Dynamics of Job Segregation by Sex during World War II *Ruth Milkman*

Once a Cigar Maker: Men, Women, and Work Culture in American Cigar Factories, 1900–1919 *Patricia A. Cooper*

A Generation of Boomers: The Pattern of Railroad Labor Conflict in Nineteenth-Century America *Shelton Stromquist*

Work and Community in the Jungle: Chicago's Packinghouse Workers, 1894–1922 *James R. Barrett*

Workers, Managers, and Welfare Capitalism: The Shoeworkers and Tanners of Endicott Johnson, 1890–1950 *Gerald Zahavi*

Men, Women, and Work: Class, Gender, and Protest in the New England Shoe Industry, 1780–1910 *Mary Blewett*

Workers on the Waterfront: Seamen, Longshoremen, and Unionism in the 1930s *Bruce Nelson*

German Workers in Chicago: A Documentary History of Working-Class Culture from 1850 to World War I *Edited by Hartmut Keil and John B. Jentz*

On the Line: Essays in the History of Auto Work *Edited by Nelson Lichtenstein and Stephen Meyer III*

Labor's Flaming Youth: Telephone Operators and Worker Militancy, 1878–1923 *Stephen H. Norwood*

Another Civil War: Labor, Capital, and the State in the Anthracite Regions of Pennsylvania, 1840–68 *Grace Palladino*

Coal, Class, and Color: Blacks in Southern West Virginia, 1915–32 *Joe William Trotter Jr.*

For Democracy, Workers, and God: Labor Song-Poems and Labor Protest, 1865–95 *Clark D. Halker*

Dishing It Out: Waitresses and Their Unions in the Twentieth Century *Dorothy Sue Cobble*

The Spirit of 1848: German Immigrants, Labor Conflict, and the Coming of the Civil War *Bruce Levine*

Working Women of Collar City: Gender, Class, and Community in Troy, New York, 1864–86 *Carole Turbin*

Southern Labor and Black Civil Rights: Organizing Memphis Workers *Michael K. Honey*

Radicals of the Worst Sort: Laboring Women in Lawrence, Massachusetts, 1860–1912 *Ardis Cameron*

Producers, Proletarians, and Politicians: Workers and Party Politics in Evansville and New Albany, Indiana, 1850–87 *Lawrence M. Lipin*

The New Left and Labor in the 1960s *Peter B. Levy*

The Making of Western Labor Radicalism: Denver's Organized Workers, 1878–1905 *David Brundage*

In Search of the Working Class: Essays in American Labor History and Political Culture *Leon Fink*

Lawyers against Labor: From Individual Rights to Corporate Liberalism *Daniel R. Ernst*

"We Are All Leaders": The Alternative Unionism of the Early 1930s *Edited by Staughton Lynd*

The Female Economy: The Millinery and Dressmaking Trades, 1860–1930 *Wendy Gamber*

"Negro and White, Unite and Fight!": A Social History of Industrial Unionism in Meatpacking, 1930–90 *Roger Horowitz*

Power at Odds: The 1922 National Railroad Shopmen's Strike *Colin J. Davis*

The Common Ground of Womanhood: Class, Gender, and Working Girls' Clubs, 1884–1928 *Priscilla Murolo*

Marching Together: Women of the Brotherhood of Sleeping Car Porters *Melinda Chateauvert*

Down on the Killing Floor: Black and White Workers in Chicago's Packinghouses, 1904–54 *Rick Halpern*

Labor and Urban Politics: Class Conflict and the Origins of Modern Liberalism in Chicago, 1864–97 *Richard Schneirov*

All That Glitters: Class, Conflict, and Community in Cripple Creek *Elizabeth Jameson*

Waterfront Workers: New Perspectives on Race and Class *Edited by Calvin Winslow*
Labor Histories: Class, Politics, and the Working-Class Experience
Edited by Eric Arnesen, Julie Greene, and Bruce Laurie
The Pullman Strike and the Crisis of the 1890s: Essays on Labor and Politics
Edited by Richard Schneirov, Shelton Stromquist, and Nick Salvatore
AlabamaNorth: African-American Migrants, Community, and Working-Class Activism in Cleveland, 1914–45 *Kimberley L. Phillips*
Imagining Internationalism in American and British Labor, 1939–49 *Victor Silverman*
William Z. Foster and the Tragedy of American Radicalism *James R. Barrett*
Colliers across the Sea: A Comparative Study of Class Formation in Scotland and the American Midwest, 1830–1924 *John H. M. Laslett*
"Rights, Not Roses": Unions and the Rise of Working-Class Feminism, 1945–80
Dennis A. Deslippe
Testing the New Deal: The General Textile Strike of 1934 in the American South
Janet Irons
Hard Work: The Making of Labor History *Melvyn Dubofsky*
Southern Workers and the Search for Community: Spartanburg County, South Carolina *G. C. Waldrep III*
We Shall Be All: A History of the Industrial Workers of the World (abridged edition)
Melvyn Dubofsky, ed. Joseph A. McCartin
Race, Class, and Power in the Alabama Coalfields, 1908–21 *Brian Kelly*
Duquesne and the Rise of Steel Unionism *James D. Rose*
Anaconda: Labor, Community, and Culture in Montana's Smelter City *Laurie Mercier*
Bridgeport's Socialist New Deal, 1915–36 *Cecelia Bucki*
Indispensable Outcasts: Hobo Workers and Community in the American Midwest, 1880–1930 *Frank Tobias Higbie*
After the Strike: A Century of Labor Struggle at Pullman *Susan Eleanor Hirsch*
Corruption and Reform in the Teamsters Union *David Witwer*
Waterfront Revolts: New York and London Dockworkers, 1946–61 *Colin J. Davis*
Black Workers' Struggle for Equality in Birmingham
Horace Huntley and David Montgomery
The Tribe of Black Ulysses: African American Men in the Industrial South
William P. Jones
City of Clerks: Office and Sales Workers in Philadelphia, 1870–1920 *Jerome P. Bjelopera*
Reinventing "The People": The Progressive Movement, the Class Problem, and the Origins of Modern Liberalism *Shelton Stromquist*
Radical Unionism in the Midwest, 1900–1950 *Rosemary Feurer*
Gendering Labor History *Alice Kessler-Harris*
James P. Cannon and the Origins of the American Revolutionary Left, 1890–1928
Bryan D. Palmer
Glass Towns: Industry, Labor, and Political Economy in Appalachia, 1890–1930s
Ken Fones-Wolf
Workers and the Wild: Conservation, Consumerism, and Labor in Oregon, 1910–30
Lawrence M. Lipin

Wobblies on the Waterfront: Interracial Unionism in Progressive-Era Philadelphia *Peter Cole*
Red Chicago: American Communism at Its Grassroots, 1928–35 *Randi Storch*
Labor's Cold War: Local Politics in a Global Context *Edited by Shelton Stromquist*
Bessie Abramowitz Hillman and the Making of the Amalgamated Clothing Workers of America *Karen Pastorello*
The Great Strikes of 1877 *Edited by David O. Stowell*
Union-Free America: Workers and Antiunion Culture *Lawrence Richards*
Race against Liberalism: Black Workers and the UAW in Detroit *David M. Lewis-Colman*
Teachers and Reform: Chicago Public Education, 1929–70 *John F. Lyons*
Upheaval in the Quiet Zone: 1199/SEIU and the Politics of Healthcare Unionism *Leon Fink and Brian Greenberg*
Shadow of the Racketeer: Scandal in Organized Labor *David Witwer*
Sweet Tyranny: Migrant Labor, Industrial Agriculture, and Imperial Politics *Kathleen Mapes*
Staley: The Fight for a New American Labor Movement *Steven K. Ashby and C. J. Hawking*
On the Ground: Labor Struggles in the American Airline Industry *Liesl Miller Orenic*
NAFTA and Labor in North America *Norman Caulfield*
Making Capitalism Safe: Work Safety and Health Regulation in America, 1880–1940 *Donald W. Rogers*
Good, Reliable, White Men: Railroad Brotherhoods, 1877–1917 *Paul Michel Taillon*
Spirit of Rebellion: Labor and Religion in the New Cotton South *Jarod Roll*
The Labor Question in America: Economic Democracy in the Gilded Age *Rosanne Currarino*
Banded Together: Economic Democratization in the Brass Valley *Jeremy Brecher*
The Gospel of the Working Class: Labor's Southern Prophets in New Deal America *Erik Gellman and Jarod Roll*
Guest Workers and Resistance to U.S. Corporate Despotism *Immanuel Ness*
Gleanings of Freedom: Free and Slave Labor along the Mason-Dixon Line, 1790–1860 *Max Grivno*
Chicago in the Age of Capital: Class, Politics, and Democracy during the Civil War and Reconstruction *John B. Jentz and Richard Schneirov*
Child Care in Black and White: Working Parents and the History of Orphanages *Jessie B. Ramey*
The Haymarket Conspiracy: Transatlantic Anarchist Networks *Timothy Messer-Kruse*
Detroit's Cold War: The Origins of Postwar Conservatism *Colleen Doody*
A Renegade Union: Interracial Organizing and Labor Radicalism *Lisa Phillips*
Palomino: Clinton Jencks and Mexican-American Unionism in the American Southwest *James J. Lorence*
Latin American Migrations to the U.S. Heartland: Changing Cultural Landscapes in Middle America *Edited by Linda Allegro and Andrew Grant Wood*
Man of Fire: Selected Writings *Ernesto Galarza, ed. Armando Ibarra and Rodolfo D. Torres*
A Contest of Ideas: Capital, Politics, and Labor *Nelson Lichtenstein*

Making the World Safe for Workers: Labor, the Left, and Wilsonian Internationalism *Elizabeth McKillen*

The Rise of the Chicago Police Department: Class and Conflict, 1850–1894 *Sam Mitrani*

Workers in Hard Times: A Long View of Economic Crises *Edited by Leon Fink, Joseph A. McCartin, and Joan Sangster*

Redeeming Time: Protestantism and Chicago's Eight-Hour Movement, 1866–1912 *William A. Mirola*

Struggle for the Soul of the Postwar South: White Evangelical Protestants and Operation Dixie *Elizabeth Fones-Wolf and Ken Fones-Wolf*

Free Labor: The Civil War and the Making of an American Working Class *Mark A. Lause*

Death and Dying in the Working Class, 1865–1920 *Michael K. Rosenow*

Immigrants against the State: Yiddish and Italian Anarchism in America *Kenyon Zimmer*

Fighting for Total Person Unionism: Harold Gibbons, Ernest Calloway, and Working-Class Citizenship *Robert Bussel*

Smokestacks in the Hills: Rural-Industrial Workers in West Virginia *Louis Martin*

Disaster Citizenship: Survivors, Solidarity, and Power in the Progressive Era *Jacob A. C. Remes*

The Pew and the Picket Line: Christianity and the American Working Class *Edited by Christopher D. Cantwell, Heath W. Carter, and Janine Giordano Drake*

Conservative Counterrevolution: Challenging Liberalism in 1950s Milwaukee *Tula A. Connell*

Manhood on the Line: Working-Class Masculinities in the American Heartland *Steve Meyer*

On Gender, Labor, and Inequality *Ruth Milkman*

The Making of Working-Class Religion *Matthew Pehl*

Civic Labors: Scholar Activism and Working-Class Studies *Edited by Dennis Deslippe, Eric Fure-Slocum, and John W. McKerley*

Victor Arnautoff and the Politics of Art *Robert W. Cherny*

Against Labor: How U.S. Employers Organized to Defeat Union Activism *Edited by Rosemary Feurer and Chad Pearson*

Teacher Strike! Public Education and the Making of a New American Political Order *Jon Shelton*

Hillbilly Hellraisers: Federal Power and Populist Defiance in the Ozarks *J. Blake Perkins*

Sewing the Fabric of Statehood: Garment Unions, American Labor, and the Establishment of the State of Israel *Adam Howard*

Labor and Justice across the America *Edited by Leon Fink and Juan Manuel Palacio*

Frontiers of Labor: Comparative Histories of the United States and Australia *Edited by Greg Patmore and Shelton Stromquist*

Women Have Always Worked: A Concise History, Second Edition *Alice Kessler-Harris*

Remembering Lattimer: Labor, Migration, and Race in Pennsylvania Anthracite Country *Paul A. Shackel*

Disruption in Detroit: Autoworkers and the Elusive Postwar Boom *Daniel J. Clark*
To Live Here, You Have to Fight: How Women Led Appalachian Movements for Social Justice *Jessica Wilkerson*
Dockworker Power: Race and Activism in Durban and the San Francisco Bay Area *Peter Cole*
Labor's Mind: A History of Working-Class Intellectual Life *Tobias Higbie*
The World in a City: Multiethnic Radicalism in Early Twentieth-Century Los Angeles *David M. Struthers*
Death to Fascism: Louis Adamic's Fight for Democracy *John P. Enyeart*
Upon the Altar of Work: Child Labor and the Rise of a New American Sectionalism *Betsy Wood*
Workers against the City: The Fight for Free Speech in *Hague v. CIO* *Donald W. Rogers*
Union Renegades: Miners, Capitalism, and Organizing in the Gilded Age *Dana M. Caldemeyer*
The Labor Board Crew: Remaking Worker-Employer Relations from Pearl Harbor to the Reagan Era *Ronald W. Schatz*
Grand Army of Labor: Workers, Veterans, and the Meaning of the Civil War *Matthew E. Stanley*
A Matter of Moral Justice: Black Women Laundry Workers and the Fight for Justice *Jenny Carson*
Labor's End: How the Promise of Automation Degraded Work *Jason Resnikoff*
Toward a Cooperative Commonwealth: The Transplanted Roots of Farmer-Labor Radicalism in Texas *Thomas Alter II*
Working in the Magic City: Moral Economy in Early Twentieth-Century Miami *Thomas A. Castillo*
Where Are the Workers? Labor's Stories at Museums and Historic Sites *Edited by Robert Forrant and Mary Anne Trasciatti*
Labor's Outcasts: Migrant Farmworkers and Unions in North America, 1934–1966 *Andrew J. Hazelton*
Fraying Fabric: How Trade Policy and Industrial Decline Transformed America *James C. Benton*
Harry Bridges: Labor Radical, Labor Legend *Robert W. Cherny*
Strong Winds and Widow Makers: Workers, Nature, and Environmental Conflict in Pacific Northwest Timber Country *Steven C. Beda*
Purple Power: The History and Global Impact of the SEIU *Edited by Luís LM Aguiar and Joseph A. McCartin*
The Bosses' Union: How Employers Organized to Fight Labor before the New Deal *Vilja Hulden*
Workers of All Colors Unite: Race and the Origins of American Socialism *Lorenzo Costaguta*
The Ruined Anthracite: Historical Trauma in Extractive Labor Communities *Paul A. Shackel*
On the Waves of Empire: U.S. Imperialism and Merchant Sailors, 1872–1924 *William D. Riddell*

The University of Illinois Press
is a founding member of the
Association of University Presses.

University of Illinois Press
1325 South Oak Street
Champaign, IL 61820-6903
www.press.uillinois.edu